Tolley's Practical Tax Guide

First Edition

by

Arnold Homer

Rita Burrows

Tolley Publishing Company Ltd
AN EXTEL GROUP PUBLICATION

First Edition December 1983

Published by
Tolley Publishing Co Ltd
Tolley House
17 Scarbrook Road
Croydon Surrey CR0 1SQ
England

Text and cover design by Jonathan Newdick

Printed in Great Britain at The Pitman Press, Bath

About this book

This is the first edition of Tolley's Practical Tax Guide. In future it will be published every year shortly after the appearance of the main Finance Act, and joins the range of Tolley annuals on all aspects of taxation.

Tolley's Practical Tax Guide is a clear and concise ready reference guide to all the areas of taxation which the businessman, practitioner or professional adviser may come across from day to day. It deals not only with income tax, corporation tax and capital gains tax, but also with the fundamental principles of capital transfer tax, development land tax, value added tax and stamp duties. There are useful chapters on national insurance contributions and statutory sick pay.

The aim of the book is to enable those who are not tax specialists to work out their, or their company's or client's, tax liabilities, and to know when they should seek further guidance. As well as numerous worked examples, a particularly helpful feature is the addition of a number of 'tax points' at the end of most chapters. These draw on the authors' wealth of practical experience to highlight the tax planning opportunities arising out of the subject matter of each chapter.

This first edition gives the position for the tax year 1983/84 by reference to all legislation, statements of practice and other relevant sources of information up to 30 September 1983. Where appropriate, the position for earlier years is also explained.

The authors wish to thank their professional colleagues, and in particular Alan Robertson and other partners and staff of Clement Keys & Co, for their assistance.

Any comments on this new publication will as always be welcomed by the publishers.

TOLLEY PUBLISHING COMPANY LIMITED

Contents

CONTENTS

CONTENTS

CONTENTS

Abbreviations

ACT	=	Advance Corporation Tax
Board	=	Board of Inland Revenue
CAA 1968	=	Capital Allowances Act 1968
CGT	=	Capital Gains Tax
CGTA 1979	=	Capital Gains Tax Act 1979
CTT	=	Capital Transfer Tax
DHSS	=	Department of Health and Social Security
DLT	=	Development Land Tax
DLTA 1976	=	Development Land Tax Act 1976
EEC	=	European Economic Community
FA	=	Finance Act
MIRAS	=	Mortgage Interest Relief At Source
NI	=	National Insurance
PAYE	=	Pay As You Earn
reg	=	regulation
s	=	section
SA 1891	=	Stamp Act 1981
SAYE	=	Save As You Earn
Sch	=	Schedule
SI	=	Statutory Instrument
SP	=	Inland Revenue Statement of Practice
SSA 1975	=	Social Security Act 1975
SSP	=	Statutory Sick Pay
TA 1970	=	Income and Corporation Taxes Act 1970
TMA 1970	=	Taxes Management Act 1970
VAT	=	Value Added Tax
VATA 1983	=	Value Added Tax Act 1983

Table of rates and allowances

Income and corporation tax

Personal allowances (see chapter 3 for full description)

	1982/83 £	1983/84 £
Single person's allowance	1,565	1,785
Married man's allowance	2,445	2,795
Wife's earned income relief (earnings up to)	1,565	1,785
Age allowance—single	2,070	2,360
—married	3,295	3,755
—income limit for full allowance	6,700	7,600
Additional personal allowance for children	880	1,010
Widow's bereavement allowance	880	1,010
Dependent relative allowance		
—certain women claimants	145	145
—other claimants	100	100
—income limit for full allowance	1,600	1,731
Housekeeper allowance	100	100
Services of son or daughter	55	55
Blind person's allowance	360	360

Income tax rates on taxable income (see chapter 3)

1982/83	Rate	1983/84
First £12,800	30%	First £14,600
Next £2,300	40%	Next £2,600
Next £4,000	45%	Next £4,600
Next £6,200	50%	Next £7,100
Next £6,200	55%	Next £7,100
Over £31,500	60%	Over £36,000

Investment income surcharge—15% on investment income in excess of £7,100 (1983/84), £6,250 (1982/83).

Car and fuel benefit scale rates (see chapter 11)

1982/83 car scale benefits (no fuel scale benefits)

	Age of car at end of year	
Original market value up to £11,500	Under 4 years	4 years or more
(a) with cylinder capacity of:	£	£
up to 1,300 cc	270	180
1,301 cc to 1,800 cc	360	240
1,801 cc or more	540	360
(b) without a cylinder capacity but of original market value:		
up to £3,599	270	180
£3,600 to £5,099	360	240
£5,100 to £11,500	540	360
Original market value over £11,500		
£11,501 to £17,300	780	528
£17,301 or more	1,260	840

1983/84

	Car benefit Age of car at end of year		Fuel benefit
Original market value up to £14,000	Under 4 years	4 years or more	
(a) with cylinder capacity of:	£	£	£
up to 1,300 cc	325	225	325
1,301 cc to 1,800 cc	425	300	425
1,801 cc or more	650	450	650
(b) without a cylinder capacity but of original market value:			
up to £4,299	325	225	325
£4,300 to £6,099	425	300	425
£6,100 to £14,000	650	450	650
Original market value over £14,000			
£14,001 to £21,000	950	650 ⎫	650
£21,001 or more	1,500	1,000 ⎭	

1984/85

	Car benefit Age of car at end of year		Fuel benefit
Original market value up to £16,000	Under 4 years	4 years or more	
(a) with a cylinder capacity of:	£	£	£
up to 1,300 cc	375	250	375
1,301 cc to 1,800 cc	480	320	480
1,801 cc or more	750	500	750
(b) without a cylinder capacity but of original market value:			
up to £4,949	375	250	375
£4,950 to £6,999	480	320	480
£7,000 to £16,000	750	500	750
Original market value over £16,000			
£16,001 to £24,000	1,100	740 ⎫	750
£24,001 or more	1,725	1,150 ⎭	

Corporation tax rates (see chapter 4)

Year beginning	Full rate	Small companies			
		rate	upper profit limit	marginal	relief
				upper profit limit	relief fraction
1 April 1980	52%	40%	£80,000	£200,000	2/25
1 April 1981	52%	40%	£90,000	£225,000	2/25
1 April 1982	52%	38%	£100,000	£500,000	7/200

Capital gains are charged at 52% on 15/26 ths of the gain, giving an effective rate on chargeable gains of 30%

All stocks index

	1979	1980	1981	1982	1983
January	156.4	185.6	198.6	217.0	229.1
February	158.0	188.4	199.8	218.6	230.5
March	160.6	189.9	201.7	218.9	231.4
April	163.4	190.4	204.0	219.7	233.4
May	165.0	190.9	205.5	220.6	234.4
June	167.1	192.1	206.4	220.5	235.2
July	169.5	193.9	206.5	221.1	235.5
August	171.3	194.1	208.6	221.7	
September	173.2	194.8	209.9	223.0	
October	175.9	195.6	211.8	224.3	
November	177.5	196.2	213.1	225.3	
December	179.5	196.5	214.5	227.1	

	Increase on previous year			
	1980 over 1979	1981 over 1980	1982 over 1981	1983 over 1982
January	18.68%	7.01%	9.27%	5.58%
February	19.25%	6.06%	9.41%	5.45%
March	18.25%	6.22%	8.53%	5.72%
April	16.53%	7.15%	7.70%	6.24%
May	15.70%	7.65%	7.35%	6.26%
June	14.97%	7.45%	6.84%	6.67%
July	14.40%	6.50%	7.08%	6.52%
August	13.31%	7.48%	6.28%	
September	12.48%	7.76%	6.25%	
October	11.20%	8.29%	5.91%	
November	10.54%	8.62%	5.73%	
December	9.48%	9.17%	5.88%	

Provisional values have also been published as follows

		Increase on previous year
August 1983	236.6	6.73%
September 1983	238.6	7.00%

National insurance contribution rates

Employers and employees (see chapter 14)

Contribution rates for 1983/84 on earnings up to £235 per week

	Employee	Employer	
		to 31/7/83	from 1/8/83
Not contracted out:			
standard rate	9%	11.95%	11.45%
reduced rate	3.85%	as for standard rate	
Contracted out:			
standard rate			
on first £32.50 p.w.	9%	11.95%	11.45%
between £32.50 and £235 p.w.	6.85%	7.85%	7.35%
reduced rate	3.85%	as for standard rate	

Self-employed (see chapter 25)

	1982/83	1983/84
Class 2 contributions per week	£3.75	£4.40
Class 4 contributions		
rate	6.0%	6.3%
on profits between	£3,450 and £11,000	£3,800 and £12,000

Statutory sick pay from 6 April 1983 (see chapter 15)

Average weekly earnings	£65 and over	£48.50–£64.99	£32.50–£48.49
SSP weekly rate	£40.25	£33.75	£27.20
Annual maximum	£322.00	£270.00	£217.60

Value added tax (see chapter 9)

Standard rate (from 18/6/79) 15%	
Registration threshold (from 16/3/83)	
—taxable supplies in last quarter	£6,000 or more
—taxable supplies in last four quarters	£18,000 or more
—taxable supplies in any future year	£18,000 or more
Deregistration limits (from 1/6/83)	
—taxable supplies in each of last two years	£18,000 or less
—taxable supplies in next year	£17,000 or less

Capital gains tax (see chapter 5)

Rate   30%
Annual exemption   1983/84   £5,300
                 1982/83   £5,000

Development land tax (see chapter 6)

Rate (from 11/6/79)   60%
Annual exemption (from 11/6/79)   £50,000

Capital transfer tax (see chapter 7)

Rates from 9 March 1982 to 14 March 1983

Gross chargeable transfers	Gross cumulative total	Tax payable			
		lifetime transfers		on death	
		rate	cumulative total tax	rate	cumulative total tax
£	£	%	£	%	£
First 55,000	55,000	Nil	Nil	Nil	Nil
Next 20,000	75,000	15	3,000	30	6,000
25,000	100,000	17½	7,375	35	14,750
30,000	130,000	20	13,375	40	26,750
35,000	165,000	22½	21,250	45	42,500
35,000	200,000	25	30,000	50	60,000
50,000	250,000	30	45,000	55	87,500
400,000	650,000	35	185,000	60	327,500
600,000	1,250,000	40	425,000	65	717,500
1,250,000	2,500,000	45	987,500	70	1,592,500
above 2,500,000		50		75	

Rates after 14 March 1983

Gross chargeable transfers	Gross cumulative total	Tax payable			
		lifetime transfers		on death	
		rate	cumulative total tax	rate	cumulative total tax
£	£	%	£	%	£
First 60,000	60,000	Nil	Nil	Nil	Nil
Next 20,000	80,000	15	3,000	30	6,000
30,000	110,000	17½	8,250	35	16,500
30,000	140,000	20	14,250	40	28,500
35,000	175,000	22½	22,125	45	44,250
45,000	220,000	25	33,375	50	66,750
50,000	270,000	30	48,375	55	94,250
430,000	700,000	35	198,875	60	352,250
625,000	1,325,000	40	448,875	65	758,500
1,325,000	2,650,000	45	1,045,125	70	1,686,000
above 2,650,000		50		75	

Stamp duty on conveyances or transfers on sale (certified transactions) (see chapter 8)

From 22 March 1982

Consideration (£)	Rate per £50 or part
0–25,000	Nil
25,001–30,000	25p
30,001–35,000	50p
35,001–40,000	75p
over 40,000	£1

1
Introduction

A trader thinks very carefully before taking in a partner. He would certainly not entertain such a notion at all if the newcomer was going to take a large slice of the profits without making any contribution towards earning them. Yet it is a fact that the taxman is a senior partner in many businesses. He takes up to 60% of the profits above a certain level, and not only does nothing in return, but adds insult to injury by requiring the proprietor to act as an unpaid tax collector, gathering in and handing over income tax and national insurance contributions on employees' wages, and value added tax on sales. For companies, again the unwanted shareholder takes the lion's share of the profits, and requires the company additionally to account for tax in respect of all its dividends and other distributions.

Clearly, there is no way that this enforced association can be dissolved, nor the Revenue's claim on the funds of a company or individual resisted, so it is in the best interests of traders, company directors and individual taxpayers to be aware of exactly where they stand, in law and in practice, and of the full range of tax saving and planning opportunities open to them.

The tax rules change constantly and are embodied in the annual Finance Acts. From time to time these Acts are consolidated, so that they appear, unaltered, in just one Statute. The latest consolidation of the law relating to income tax and corporation tax is the Income and Corporation Taxes Act 1970, although another is planned to be introduced in 1987/88. For capital gains tax, it is the Capital Gains Tax Act 1979.

Although the legislation is comprehensive and detailed, there are bound to be situations where the taxpayer and the local inspector of taxes disagree, and are unable to resolve the matter by negotiation. An appeal against an assessment made by the inspector is then the only way in which a taxpayer can seek to have his view upheld. Appeals are heard by the Appeal Commissioners. These are the General Commissioners, who are usually local businessmen acting in a voluntary unpaid capacity, and the Special Commissioners, who are full-time civil servants employed to hear tax appeals, having their base in London and travelling on circuit to the different parts of the country. The General Commissioners hear the majority of appeals, although certain appeals on specialised matters have to go to the Special Commissioners. As the law presently stands, a taxpayer can elect for most appeals to be heard by the Special Commissioners, but this is not likely to remain the case for very much longer as it is anticipated that Special

Commissioners hearings will in the near future be reserved for the more difficult cases.

A taxpayer's appeal against an assessment may be on a question of fact or on a question of law, or it may be a mixture of both. For instance, a taxpayer may be late in submitting his business accounts. If the inspector raises an estimated assessment showing profits of £6,000, whereas the accounts when produced show a profit of £5,000, then this is a matter of fact. On the other hand, suppose that the taxpayer is a sub-contracting bricklayer who uses his home as his workbase, and who claims to deduct the cost of travelling from home to the various sites at which he works. Both the taxpayer and the inspector are in agreement as to what travelling expenses have in fact been incurred, but the inspector considers that the expenses are not, as the tax law requires, 'wholly and exclusively for the purposes of the trade', because he feels that the trade does not commence until the bricklayer reaches the site. This dispute is on a matter of law, and is taken from the actual case of Horton v Young, in which the bricklayer, Mr. Horton, was successful in establishing his right to deduct the travelling expenses.

The distinction between fact and law is an important one, because what the Appeal Commissioners decide about disputes on matters of fact is generally binding on both the taxpayer and the Revenue. If a dispute concerns a point of law, however, further appeal is possible to the High Court and then to the Court of Appeal, or to the equivalent Scottish or Irish Courts. A final appeal then lies to the House of Lords.

Taxpayers may well be forgiven for wondering how disputes about points of law can arise at all. The wording of an Act of Parliament ought to leave no room for doubt as to how it is to be interpreted. This ideal, is, however, almost impossible to achieve, because different people read different meanings into the same words. The office manager, for instance, when asked for details of his staff 'broken down by age and sex', replied: 'They all are!'. Likewise, the judge who remarked in 1966, when required to give his ruling on what a particular section of the legislation meant: 'I reach my decision without confidence. Were I a betting man I should lay the odds on its being right at six to four on'.

Where there is disagreement about how a particular provision ought to be interpreted, only the Courts can give the final decision, and whatever they decide is then in effect a part of the law whenever the same provision is called into question again. It can only be overruled by a later decision in a higher Court or by amending legislation.

The tax law in this country is regarded by many as being a jungle through which only the most experienced explorers can hope to pass unscathed. Whatever the truth of this, there are many opportunities open to a taxpayer to plan his affairs in such a way as to minimise his tax liability and to stop the Revenue putting, as one judge said in 1929, 'the largest possible shovel into his stores'.

Provided that these tax saving opportunities are within the requirements of the law then full advantage may be taken of them, because if Parliament does not intend them to exist then the remedy is in Parliament's own hands.

It is obviously important, however, to draw a distinction between tax planning and avoidance, in the sense of taking advantage of tax saving opportunities that exist within the law, and tax evasion, which, being outside the law, carries heavy monetary penalties and sometimes even a gaol sentence.

The chapters of this book explain in detail how tax liabilities are calculated and highlight some of the ways in which they may be minimised.

2
Main tax changes

The tax changes for 1983/84 have been relatively few because of the election. The Finance Act 1983 was passed before the election took place, and the Finance (No 2) Act 1983 became law on 26 July 1983. Changes in line with inflation in the capital gains exempt threshold and in value added tax have been made by statutory instrument (see below). The increased income tax personal allowances and tax rate bands and thresholds are shown in the table at the front of this book. Other main changes are as follows.

Income Tax

Wife's earnings election

An election for separate taxation of wife's earnings will not normally be beneficial unless joint income is £22,067 or more, with wife's earnings at least £5,682. See chapter 37.

Widow's bereavement allowance

The widow's bereavement allowance is now available in the year following that in which the husband dies as well as in the year of death, unless the widow remarries before the end of the year of death. If the widow has remarried in a year when the allowance is available and she has insufficient income of her own to utilise the allowance, she cannot transfer any unused allowance to her new husband.

Mortgage interest relief

The limit of house purchase loans qualifying for relief is increased from £25,000 to £30,000. Those with existing loans between £25,000 and £30,000 will not get the benefit of tax deduction at source under the MIRAS scheme until 1984/85, so they will continue to get the relief through a coding adjustment or adjustment in an assessment for 1983/84. New borrowers under the MIRAS scheme will get relief straight away on loans up to £30,000. See also chapter 30.

Anti-avoidance provisions re mortgage loans

The ability to double the available mortgage interest relief limit by obtaining an interest-free loan from one's employer and then a further loan from an outside lender has now been stopped by provisions which treat the 'employer's loan' as being made last, so that any excess of the combined loans over £30,000 will incur a tax charge on interest at the beneficial loan interest rate on the interest-free loan.

Investment in employee-controlled companies

Relief is now available for interest paid on a loan to an employee or his spouse to buy shares in an unquoted employee-controlled trading company. A company is employee-controlled if at least 75% of the issued ordinary share capital and at least 75% of the voting power is beneficially owned by full-time employees or their spouses. Any holding by an employee and spouse in excess of 5% does not count towards the 75% requirement.

Life assurance policies — secondhand bonds

Provisions have been introduced from 26 June 1982 to counter avoidance of income tax by the purchase of second-hand single premium insurance bonds and guaranteed growth bonds.

Scholarships

The decision of the House of Lords in Wicks v Firth in relation to scholarships for the children of directors and higher paid employees has been nullified from 15 March 1983, so that such scholarships now attract a tax charge on the director or employee, unless they are made under a trust fund or scheme from which not more than 25% of the total funds would be so chargeable in the year in question. An exception is made for scholarships awarded before 15 March 1983 where the first payment is before 6 April 1984, so long as the child remains at the same educational establishment.

Living accommodation

Where an employee is provided with free or subsidised living accommodation, then from 1984/85 there will be a charge in addition to that on the annual value of the property, if the property cost more than £75,000. The excess of the cost over £75,000 will be charged to tax at the beneficial loan interest rate (currently 12%). If the employee is paying rent in excess of the annual value, the excess will be deducted from the additional charge. See also chapter 11.

PAYE for directors

If PAYE is accounted for to the Revenue but is not deducted from a director's remuneration, the amount that should have been deducted is treated as an emolument under Schedule E. This does not apply where the director owns not more than 5% of the ordinary share capital and either works full-time for the company or is employed by a non-profit-making body.

Covenanted payments to charities

The annual limit of covenanted payments to charities qualifying for relief at all rates of tax is increased from £3,000 to £5,000.

Profit sharing schemes

The limit of shares that may be allocated to an employee tax-free under a profit sharing scheme is now the greater of £1,250 (the existing limit) or 10% of the employee's earnings in either the current or previous year, with an overall maximum of £5,000. See chapter 12.

Business expansion scheme

The business start-up scheme has been replaced from 6 April 1983 with the business expansion scheme, which is less restrictive and applies to existing as well as new companies. The annual limit on which tax relief is given is increased to £40,000 per person and the 50% limit on the shares in any company which may qualify for relief is removed. The scheme will run until 5 April 1987. The detailed provisions are in chapter 29.

Capital allowances

Industrial buildings allowances are given in full despite part of the building not coming within the industrial buildings definition, provided that the expenditure on the non-qualifying part does not exceed a stipulated fraction. For expenditure after 15 March 1983 the fraction is increased from one-tenth to one quarter. The 100% allowance on very small workshops is now available in respect of expenditure to convert existing buildings into industrial units not exceeding 1,250 square feet on average, but this does not apply where a building has remained wholly or partly unused prior to such conversion. See chapter 32.

The transitional provisions continuing capital allowances (as plant) on British films are extended for a further three years to 31 March 1987, and those in relation to rented teletext receivers and adaptors for a further one year, so that first-year allowances on both viewdata and teletext sets will be given at 100% to 31 May 1984, then 75% to 31 May 1985 and 50% to 31 May 1986. See chapter 22.

Corporation Tax

Small companies rate

For the year to 31 March 1983, the small companies rate has been reduced from 40% to 38% for income up to £100,000, and marginal relief extended to £500,000, with a tapering fraction of 7/200ths. This gives an effective marginal rate of corporation tax of $55\frac{1}{2}$% within the marginal relief tranche. See chapter 4.

Company employees seconded to charities
From 1 April 1983, expenditure by a company on an employee temporarily seconded to a charity is a deductible expense as if the employee's services continued to be available to the company.

Capital Gains Tax

Threshold

The capital gains tax exempt threshold has been increased to £5,300. See chapter 5.

Parallel pooling

Following the immense complexities of handling large share portfolios because of the introduction of the indexation allowance, provisions have been introduced to allow companies (not individuals) to adopt a system of 'parallel pooling' once shares have been held for twelve months. Broadly, this enables them to operate two pools for each shareholding, one indexed and the other unindexed, and to calculate the indexation allowance on a disposal by taking a proportionate part of the value of each pool, the indexation allowance being the difference between the two. As always, the indexation allowance cannot create or increase a loss. The provisions are dealt with in chapter 35.

Capital Transfer Tax

Rates

The lifetime and death scales have been revised as shown on page xxvi and the exempt threshold is increased to £60,000. See chapter 7.

Gifts to charities

The restriction of £250,000 on exempt gifts to charities made on death or within twelve months before death has now been removed, so that all lifetime and death gifts to charities are now exempt. See chapter 7.

Business property relief and agricultural property relief

For transfers on or after 15 March 1983, the percentage reduction of transfers out of minority shareholdings, and also of the value of tenanted agricultural property, is increased from 20% to 30%, so that there are now only two rates of relief, 50% and 30%. See chapter 7.

Payment of tax by instalments

For transfers on or after 15 March 1983, payment of tax by instalments will be by ten yearly instalments instead of eight yearly or sixteen half yearly instalments. The minimum value of a minority unquoted holding in order to qualify for the instalment option is increased from £5,000 to £20,000. See chapter 7.

Domicile

For transfers on or after 15 March 1983, persons becoming domiciled in the Channel Islands or Isle of Man (either before or after that date) are no longer deemed to remain UK domiciled.

Burden of tax

For deaths on or after 26 July 1983, where the personal representatives are liable to pay tax on unsettled UK property, the tax is to be borne by the residue of the estate unless the will provides otherwise. Land etc. no longer bears its own tax unless this is specifically provided in the will.

Value Added Tax

Threshold

The turnover limit for registration is increased from £17,000 to £18,000 as from 16 March 1983. The quarterly limit of £6,000 remains unchanged. See chapter 9.

De-registration

From 1 June 1983 liability to be registered ceases if either the turnover has not exceeded £18,000 in the previous two years and is not expected to exceed £18,000 in the following year, or the turnover is not expected to exceed £17,000 in the following year. See chapter 9.

Partial exemption

From 1 April 1983 the monetary limits below which input tax need not be restricted are increased as follows:

(a) Less than £200 per month on average; or
(b) Less than £8,000 per month on average and less than 50% of the value of all supplies; or
(c) Less than £16,000 per month on average and less than 25% of the value of all supplies; or
(d) Less than 5% of the value of all supplies.

National Insurance

The national insurance surcharge is reduced from $1\frac{1}{2}$% to 1% for earnings paid on or after 1 August 1983.

Development Land Tax and Stamp Duty

No major changes have occurred.

3
Income tax: general principles

Basis of charge

Income tax is charged on what the law defines as income. This comprises not only items which would normally be regarded as income, but also items included by the various taxing statutes, and by legal interpretation through tax cases, which might otherwise be regarded as capital items subject to capital gains tax and/or development land tax, or perhaps not chargeable to tax at all. For example, a capital profit on the disposal of patent rights is specifically chargeable as income by statute.

The distinction is important as income tax rates rise progressively up to 60% on chargeable income in excess of £36,000, plus an extra 15% on investment income in excess of £7,100, whereas the rate of capital gains tax is a constant 30% after an exemption for the first £5,300 of chargeable gains (see chapter 5).

Exempt income

Certain types of income are specifically exempt from tax, including the following, which are dealt with in the chapter indicated:

	Chapter
The first £70 interest from national savings bank ordinary accounts.	34
Increase in value of national savings certificates.	41
Premium bond prizes.	41
Bonuses and profits on life assurance policies (subject to detailed anti-avoidance rules).	43
Certain social security benefits.	11

Persons chargeable

Individuals are chargeable in respect of their own income, and personal representatives and trustees in respect of estate and trust income. Income tax is charged broadly on the world income of UK residents, subject to certain deductions for earnings abroad and for individuals who are not ordinarily resident or not domiciled in the UK. Non-residents are liable to income tax only on income that arises in the UK. Double tax relief is available where income is taxed both in the UK and abroad. For detailed provisions on the overseas aspect see chapter 44.

Calculation of taxable income

Income is measured according to the rules for the source from which it arises, the sources being classified into 'Schedules' and sometimes subdivided into 'Cases'. The schedules are mutually exclusive and income assessable under one schedule cannot be charged under another.

Deductions are allowed for charges on income, such as mortgage interest, and for personal reliefs. The balance is taxable at the following rates:

The first £14,600	Basic rate of 30%
The next £2,600	40%
The next £4,600	45%
The next £7,100	50%
The next £7,100	55%
Remainder over £36,000	60%

There is in addition a 15% investment income surcharge on net unearned income in excess of £7,100. Earned income broadly comprises:

Income from employment and self-employment.
State pensions and pensions from former employers and under self-employed pension schemes.
Income from woodlands chargeable under Schedule B (see chapter 31).

The tax due is accounted for in various ways, some by deduction at source when the income is received, some collected by employers through the PAYE system and some by direct assessment.

The income tax year runs from 6 April in one year to 5 April in the next, but the assessment of income is not always based on the amount arising during that period, the statutes setting out different bases of assessment for each class of income. The total assessable income is known as 'statutory total income'.

The detailed rules for calculating income from the various sources are dealt with in the appropriate chapters, but are summarised in the following table.

Schedule and Case	Type of income	Basis of assessment	Normal due date of payment
Schedule A	Rents from UK	Rent due in the year of assessment, whether received or not, less allowable expenses	1 January in year of assessment

Schedule B	Occupation of commercially managed woodlands	One third of the gross annual value. Taxpayer may elect to be taxed as a trader under Schedule D, Case I instead	1 January in year of assessment
Schedule C	Income from Government Stocks, UK and foreign, paid through UK paying agent such as a bank	Gross income received in the tax year	Basic rate tax deducted at source by payer. Excess over basic rate due 1 December following tax year
Schedule D			
Case I	Profits of trade	Normally profits of accounting year ended in previous tax year, with special rules for opening and closing years and on change of accounting date	Equal instalments on 1 January in year of assessment and 1 July following
Case II	Profits of profession or vocation		
Case III	Interest, annuities or other annual payments	Gross income received in tax year where tax is deducted at source. Where tax is not deducted at source, normally the amount received or credited in the previous tax year, with special rules for opening and closing years. There is no relief for expenses	As for Schedule C if tax is deducted at source, otherwise 1 January in year of assessment
Case IV	Income from foreign securities	Normally the amount arising in previous tax year with special rules for opening and closing years, subject to percentage deductions where the	Normally 1 January in year of assessment but as for Case I for foreign businesses
Case V	Income from foreign possessions		

		income is from earnings or pension. Remittances basis if taxpayer resident but not ordinarily resident and/or not domiciled in UK	
Case VI	Income not assessable under any other Schedule or Case	Actual profits or gains of the tax year	1 January in year of assessment
Schedule E			
Case I	Earnings of employee resident and ordinarily resident in UK, other than 'foreign emoluments' earned wholly abroad	All earnings for the tax year whether duties are performed in the UK or abroad, but subject to a deduction for duties performed abroad and for 'foreign emoluments' earned wholly or partly in UK. (Foreign emoluments are earnings of non-UK-domiciled employee from non-UK-resident employer)	PAYE system
Case II	Earnings of employee not resident or resident but not ordinarily resident in UK	Earnings for UK duties, subject to a deduction for 'foreign emoluments'	PAYE system if possible, otherwise collected directly, usually by 4 instalments
Case III	'Foreign emoluments' earned wholly abroad by person UK resident and ordinarily resident	Remittances in tax year. No charge if not remitted	Tax is normally collected after end of tax-year

	Earnings abroad of person resident but not ordinarily resident in UK		
Schedule F	Dividends and distributions of UK-resident company	Dividends and distributions in the tax year plus accompanying tax credits (the tax credits being equivalent to basic rate tax on the grossed up equivalent of the dividend or distribution)	Tax credit covers basic rate tax. Excess over basic rate due 1 December following tax-year

Where assessments are issued late, the due date of payment of tax is thirty days after the issue of the assessment.

Interest on local authority loans, company debentures and most government stocks is paid after deduction of tax. The main items of interest received gross are bank interest and interest on $3\frac{1}{2}\%$ War Loan.

Interest received from building societies is subject to a special arrangement between the building societies and the Revenue and is deemed to be a net amount after basic rate tax. It is included in statutory total income at its gross equivalent. Building societies do not, however, account to the Revenue for basic rate tax on the interest, except for certain limited company and trust accounts. Instead they account to the Revenue at an agreed composite rate. The consequence is that although interest is grossed up at the basic rate for inclusion in statutory total income (and thus attracts higher rates and surcharge where appropriate) the notional tax cannot be repaid, making a personal building society investment inappropriate for those with unused personal reliefs.

Charges on income

The main charges deductible in computing taxable income comprise:

Allowable interest payments (see below).
Alimony and maintenance payments.
Payments under deed of covenant.

Relief is available at all rates of tax on allowable interest, alimony and maintenance payments, but usually only at the basic rate on covenanted payments, the main exception being covenanted payments to charity of up to £5,000 per tax-year.

Relief at the basic rate is obtained by deduction and retention of tax at source when you pay:

> Interest under the MIRAS scheme (mortgage interest relief at source).
>
> Covenanted payments.
>
> Alimony and maintenance, other than court order payments below certain limits—called small maintenance payments—which are paid gross (see chapter 37).

This tax retention at source covers the total relief due on most non-charitable covenants, for example those to dependent relatives or student children. If relief is due at all rates and your income is high enough to attract tax at rates above the basic rate, the additional relief is given in charging the tax on your income by extending the band of income chargeable at the basic rate and increasing the investment income surcharge exempt threshold. This is effected either by a coding adjustment or in charging tax by direct assessment.

Other charges, such as interest outside the MIRAS scheme and small maintenance payments, are paid gross and relief at all rates is given either by a coding adjustment or in an assessment.

See example 1.

Basic rate tax deducted under the MIRAS scheme may be retained whether you are a taxpayer or not. Non-taxpayers cannot retain tax deducted from other charges and must account for it to the Revenue (who will issue an assessment under TA 1970, s 53 for this purpose).

Allowable interest (FA 1972, s 75 and Schs 9, 10; FA 1974, Sch 1)

Not all interest payments are deductible from statutory total income in calculating taxable income. Most allowable interest payments are dealt with in context in the appropriate chapters, but they can be summarised as follows:

(a) On up to £30,000 of borrowing for purchase or improvement of only or main residence, or of a home for future occupation if you live in job-related accommodation (see chapter 30).

(b) Within the £30,000 umbrella figure in (a), borrowing for purchase or improvement of a dwelling for occupation by a divorced or separated spouse and/or a dwelling occupied rent free and without other consideration by a dependent relative (see chapters 30 and 37).

(c) Bridging loans for change of only or main residence on up to £30,000 of borrowing, in addition to (a) and (b) above, for a statutory period of one year, generally extended by Revenue concession to two years (see chapter 30).

(d) On borrowing for purchase or improvement of property let for 26 weeks

Example 1	£4,000 charges paid gross		£4,000 charges paid less tax	
Earned income		13,000		13,000
Unearned income	12,000		12,000	
Less charges	4,000	8,000		
		21,000		25,000
Personal reliefs, say		4,600		4,600
Taxable income		16,400		20,400
Tax payable				
At basic rate	14,600 @ 30%	4,380	14,600	
Extension re charges			4,000	
			18,600 @ 30%	5,580
Balance of	1,800 @ 40%	720	1,800 @ 40%	720
	16,400		20,400	
Investment income surcharge				
Exempt threshold	7,100	—	7,100	
Increase re charges			4,000	
			11,100	—
Balance of	900 @ 15%	135	900 @ 15%	135
	8,000		12,000	
		5,235		6,435
Less retained when paying charges, £4,000 @ 30%		—		1,200
Net tax borne		£5,235		£5,235

out of 52 and, when not so let, available for letting or not available because of repairs or improvements or owner occupation as qualifying main residence. (Allowed as a deduction from rent and not as a charge on general income.)

(e) On a loan for the purchase of a partnership share, for introducing capital to a partnership or for lending money to it, provided that you are a working partner.

(f) On a loan for the purchase of shares in or lending money to a close trading company so long as you work full-time in the management of the company or own more than 5% of the issued ordinary share capital.

(g) On a loan for the purchase of plant or machinery (for example a car) for use in your partnership or employment. Relief is available for interest paid in the tax year of purchase and the next three tax years. Where there is part private use relief is restricted accordingly.

(h) On a loan to personal representatives of a deceased person to pay capital transfer tax (see chapter 39).

(i) Where husband or wife is over 65 years of age, on a loan secured on their dwelling to purchase a life annuity.

(j) On a loan to acquire shares in an employee-controlled trading company.

(k) On a loan to acquire a share or shares in a co-operative.

Interest is allowable on loans which replace other qualifying loans. Relief is only available as the interest is paid. It is not spread over the period of accrual and will not be allowed if it is never paid.

Bank overdraft interest is never deductible from statutory total income. Relief is only available where the overdraft is part of the funding of a trade and therefore allowable as an expense in arriving at trading profits.

Personal reliefs

In addition to relief for charges, you may claim personal reliefs, which do not, however, reduce your income liable to investment income surcharge. The following reliefs are currently available:

Personal allowance

| Single person | £1,785 |
| Married man | £2,795 |

The married man's allowance is available to a man whose wife lives with him or is *wholly* maintained by him (by voluntary rather than by enforceable payments).

The allowance for a married man commences in the year of marriage, but in that year it is reduced by one-twelfth of the difference between single and married allowances (£84.17 for 1983/84) for each complete tax month (ending on the 5th) before the wedding date. The allowance is given in full in the year of divorce, separation or death of either spouse.

Age allowance

In the tax year in which you attain age 65 (or, if you are a married man, either you or your wife attain age 65) and in subsequent years you may claim personal allowance at an increased rate as follows:

Single person	£2,360
Married man	£3,755

For both single and married people, the age allowance is reduced by two thirds of the excess of the net total income (after deducting charges) over £7,600. In the case of a married couple it is their joint income that is taken into account in this calculation. If the restriction would reduce the allowance to below the normal personal allowance level, the normal personal allowance is given instead.

Wife's earned income relief

Where a wife has earned income, a relief is given of £1,785, or of the amount the wife earns if less.

Additional personal allowance for single parents etc.

Relief of £1,010 is available to a single person who has one or more qualifying children resident with him or her for all or part of the year. A qualifying child is one who is under 16 or in full-time education (or undergoing a minimum two year full-time training for a trade, profession or vocation), and is either a child of the claimant or is both under 18 at the beginning of the year and maintained for all or part of the year by the claimant. A child of the claimant includes a stepchild, an illegitimate child if the parents have subsequently married and an adopted child if the child was under 18 when adopted. The relief is apportioned where there are two or more claimants in respect of the same child, but if, say, separated parents each claim for a different child the full relief is available to each if the conditions are satisfied.

A man entitled to the married man's allowance can claim the relief only if his wife has throughout the year been totally incapacitated by physical or mental infirmity.

Widow's bereavement allowance

In the tax year in which her husband dies and in the following tax year (unless she marries before the beginning of it) a widow is entitled to a bereavement allowance of £1,010.

Dependent relative relief

Dependent relative relief is available at two levels:

If the claimant is a woman not living with her husband, if any	£145
Other claimants	£100

The relief is given if you maintain at your own expense a dependent relative, defined as:

(a) Your mother or your spouse's mother who is widowed, divorced or separated.

(b) Any other relative of either of you who is incapacitated by old age or infirmity.

The allowance is reduced by the amount if any by which the relative's income exceeds the basic retirement pension.

The maintenance must be unenforceable, which excludes covenanted payments. If two or more people claim relief for the same relative it is apportioned according to their respective contributions.

In the unlikely event that your contribution to the relative's support is less than the relief available, the relief is restricted accordingly.

Housekeeper relief

A relief of £100 is available to a widow or widower with a resident housekeeper. This relief cannot be claimed in addition to the additional personal allowance for single parents.

Relief for services of son or daughter

If you are compelled by your own or your wife's old age or infirmity to depend on the services of a son or daughter living with you and maintained by you, you can claim a relief of £55. Widows or widowers would usually be able to claim the housekeeper relief instead (but you cannot claim both).

Blind person's relief

Relief of £360 is available to a blind person, or £720 if a married couple are both blind. A claim for son's or daughter's services relief cannot be made as well.

Life assurance relief

Life assurance relief is available at the rate of 15% of qualifying premiums, subject to a limit on allowable premiums of either one-sixth of total income or £1,500, whichever is greater.

Relief is obtained by deduction at source when the premium is paid, and, as with interest relief under the MIRAS scheme, the relief may be retained whether you are a taxpayer or not.

There are many restrictions on what policies qualify for relief, and anti-avoidance rules to claw back excess relief. The provisions are dealt with in detail in chapter 43. The main points are that the policy must be on the life of the payer or his spouse and must normally be for a minimum ten-year term.

Aggregation of income

The income of a married woman living with her husband is deemed for tax purposes to be his income and not hers. This may increase the amounts chargeable at higher rates and to investment income surcharge. If the wife is employed tax is collected from her through the PAYE scheme, but otherwise tax on her income is normally assessed on her husband. It is possible to be separately assessed or in some cases to save tax by having the wife's earnings charged separately (see chapter 37).

Children are assessable individuals in their own right and the personal allowance is available against any income they have however young they are. The income of infant unmarried children is, however, aggregated with that of the parents if it derives from the parents, either directly from a covenanted payment or indirectly from a capital sum provided by the parent. (It is possible to establish an effective settlement of capital on children in some circumstances—see chapter 48.) So a parent who provides a capital sum for, say, a building society or bank deposit account in the child's name does not avoid income tax on the income arising. Once a child reaches age 18 or marries before that age, parents can effectively transfer income to the child, for example by covenant to a student, and the child's personal allowance would be available against it.

Postponement applications and interest on overdue tax (TMA 1970 ss 55, 86, 88)

Tax is due for payment either on the normal due date indicated in the table of statutory income shown above or 30 days after the issue of the assessment if later. The due date of payment may be affected by an application for postponement of the tax charged, made when making an appeal against an assessment. If postponement is not applied for, tax is due on the normal due date despite the appeal.

If tax is to be postponed a separate postponement application must be made within thirty days after the date of the assessment. Late applications may be made if changed circumstances result in your having grounds for believing that you have been overcharged.

It is not sufficient in a postponement application to say that the tax may be excessive. The application must state by how much you believe you have been overcharged and your reasons for that belief. This is almost the same as advancing your arguments on the appeal itself and care is therefore required in making postponement applications.

Following an agreement between you and your tax inspector as to how much tax may be postponed, or following a decision of the appeal commissioners if you do not agree, the inspector will issue a notice of determination of how much tax is payable immediately, the tax being due within thirty days after issue of that notice or on the normal due date if later. If the outcome of the appeal is that all or part of the tax postponed is payable, it is due for payment thirty days after the appeal is settled (or the normal due date, if later).

Interest arises when tax is not paid on the due date, but if it amounts to £30 or less it is ignored. The rate is prescribed by treasury order and is currently 8% p.a.. The interest is not deductible for tax purposes.

Interest is charged from the 'reckonable date', which normally means the date when the tax is actually due for payment. Where any of the tax has been postponed, however, the reckonable date is either the date that the tax is due for payment or, if earlier:

For Schedules A and D	1 July after the tax year (e.g. 1 July 1984 for 1983/84).
For higher rates and surcharge on taxed income	1 June in next but one tax year (e.g. 1 June 1985 for 1983/84).

Interest will run from the normal due date where the taxpayer is culpable. (See chapter 10.)

Certificates of tax deposit

Certificates of tax deposit may be purchased by individuals, partnerships, personal representatives, trustees or companies, subject to an initial deposit of £2,000, with minimum additions of £500. The certificates may be used to pay any tax except PAYE, VAT and tax deducted from payments to sub-contractors. Interest accrues daily for a maximum of six years, and provision is made for varying interest rates during the term of the deposit. A lower rate of interest applies if the deposit is withdrawn for cash rather than used to settle tax liabilities. Tax deposit certificates are a way of ensuring that liquid resources are earmarked for the payment of tax when due.

Repayment claims

Repayment claims will arise consistently where the taxpayer's income is wholly or mainly subject to deduction at source so that it has not been possible to allow the personal reliefs. This is particularly likely to apply in the case of old people entitled to age allowance and to students with covenanted income from their parents. See example 2.

Repayment claims will also arise in other circumstances, for example when relief is claimed for trading losses of new businesses by carry back against the income of the previous three years.

Repayment supplement (F (No 2) A 1975, s 47)

A tax free repayment supplement is paid to individuals receiving a repayment of at least £25 more than one year after the end of the tax year to which it relates. The supplement runs from the end of the tax year following the year for which the repayment is made (or from the end of the tax year in which the tax was paid if later).

Responsibility to provide information to the Revenue

Apart from returns made by employers in respect of emoluments of their

Example 2

Income of widow aged 67 in 1983/84 is £1,800 widow's pension and £700 dividends received.

A repayment claim arises as follows:

			Tax paid
Pension		1,800	
Dividends	700		
Tax credit thereon	300	1,000	300
	───	─────	
		2,800	
Age allowance		2,360	
		─────	
Taxable income		440	
		─────	
Tax thereon @ 30%			132
			───
Repayment due			£168
			───

employees, there are various reporting requirements, such as by banks and building societies as to interest paid, payers of commissions and royalties, and recipients of profits and income belonging to other people (for example interest or rent collected by solicitors or other agents).

4
Corporation tax: general principles

Basis of charge (TA 1970, s 238)

Corporation tax is charged on the profits of companies and of unincorporated bodies other than partnerships (for example members' clubs). The term profits includes all sources of income (other than dividends from UK companies) and also capital gains, but the amount included in respect of gains is only a fraction of the full gain in order to reduce the effective rate of corporation tax on gains to the 30% rate paid by an individual.

Corporation tax is charged on the world profits of UK-resident companies. Non-resident companies carrying on a trade in the UK through a branch or agency are charged on the income arising from the branch or agency and on capital gains on the disposal of assets in the UK used for the purposes of the trade or otherwise for the branch or agency. The overseas aspect is dealt with in chapter 44.

Calculation of profits (TA 1970, ss 250, 265, 343; FA 1972, s 93)

A company's income is computed using income tax Schedules and Cases, but always on the basis of the current accounting period (see below). The preceding year basis never applies. Where income, such as interest on government stocks, is subject to deduction of income tax at source, the gross amount is nonetheless included in the company's profits for corporation tax. The income tax suffered is recovered either by set-off against the company's liability to account for income tax it has deducted from its own payments, or by set-off against its corporation tax liability, or, if that is insufficient, by repayment. Building Society interest is included at its gross equivalent (by multiplying by 10/7ths, for example building society interest of £70 is included as income of £100), the notional tax being deducted in arriving at the corporation tax payable or being repaid if it exceeds the corporation tax liability. (This differs from the position for income tax, where the building society credit is never recoverable, see p 13.) The only source of income that escapes corporation tax is dividends or other distributions from UK-resident companies. Such dividends, with their related tax credits, are called franked investment income and their tax treatment is dealt with below.

In computing the company's trading profits, capital allowances and stock relief are deducted as trading expenses, and balancing charges treated as trading receipts. Pre-trading expenditure of a revenue nature incurred not more than three years before commencement of trading is treated as incurred on the day the trade commences.

A company's capital gains are computed using capital gains tax principles (see chapter 5). The amount of the gains is then reduced by 11/26ths, leaving only 15/26ths to be included in the profits chargeable to corporation tax. With corporation tax at 52% this gives an effective rate of 30%, e.g.:

Gain	£520 × 15/26ths = £300 @ 52%	£156
Gain	£520 @ 30%	£156

Companies are not, however, entitled to any annual exemption, and furthermore there is an effective double tax charge because the gain will ultimately be reflected in the price a shareholder gets for his shares or the amount he receives on a liquidation.

Charges on income (TA 1970, ss 53, 54, 248; FA 1972, s 104 and Sch 20)

Having arrived at the company's total profits (both income and capital), charges on income are deducted to arrive at the profits chargeable to corporation tax. Charges usually comprise the payments from which the company has deducted income tax at source, e.g. interest payments (other than bank interest), patent royalties and covenanted payments to charity. On rare occasions, bank interest may be treated as a charge where not allowed as a business expense.

The gross amount of the charges paid is deducted from profits, and the company has to account to the Revenue for the income tax it has deducted (subject to a set-off for any income tax suffered on its income). The income tax is accounted for on a quarterly basis to 31 March, 30 June, 30 September and 31 December, the tax being due within fourteen days after the quarter ends. Where a company's accounting year does not end on one of the four calendar quarter days the company has five return periods, the first running from the first day of the account to the next calendar quarter day and the last ending at the end of the accounting period.

If the charges exceed profits, they may be carried forward as a trading loss provided that they are wholly and exclusively for the purposes of the trade (which usually means all charges except charitable covenants). This aspect is dealt with in chapter 26 on company losses.

Periods of account and chargeable accounting periods (TA 1970, s 247)

A company's profits are computed for a chargeable accounting period, which normally means the period for which the company's accounts are made up, no matter how short it is. If, however, a company makes up an account for a period greater than 12 months, it is split into chargeable accounting periods of 12 months each and of the balance of the account.

In arriving at the split of profits for an account exceeding twelve months, the trading profit is usually split on a time basis. Stock relief is calculated for the whole period and is thus split in the same way as the trading profit. Capital allowances, on the other hand, are calculated for each chargeable accounting period, so that if for example an account was made up for the fifteen months from 1 January 1983 to 31 March 1984 and plant was bought in February 1984, the first-year allowance would be given against the profit of the three months to 31 March 1984.

Other sources of income, such as rents and bank interest, are allocated to the chargeable accounting period in which they arise (with no apportionment over the period during which they accrue). Chargeable gains are allocated to the chargeable accounting period in which the disposal occurs, and charges on income to the chargeable accounting period in which they are paid.

If a company ceases to trade, the date of cessation marks the end of a chargeable accounting period even if the period of account continues to the normal accounting date.

Losses (TA 1970, ss 177–179)

When a company makes a trading loss, it may set the loss against any other profits of the same accounting period, both income and capital, and then, if it wishes, carry any balance back against the total profits of the previous accounting period(s) for a length of time equal to the loss period. If the loss includes first-year allowances on plant, the carry-back period is a full three years. Any balance of loss remaining (or the whole loss if the company does not wish to claim the current set-off and carry-back) is carried forward to set against later profits of the same trade. The detailed provisions are in chapter 26, which also deals with terminal losses arising on cessation of trade and transfer of trading losses within groups.

If a company sustains losses on other sources of income, for example on rented property, the income tax rules for set-off apply, with the set-off being confined to the same source of income (and in the case of rented property, depending on the type of lease—see chapter 33).

Capital losses can only be set against capital gains of the same chargeable accounting period, any excess being carried forward to set against future gains. The 11/26ths reduction (see above) is made from the net gains after deducting losses.

Rate of tax (TA 1970, s 243)

Corporation tax rates are fixed annually in arrear for financial years ending 31 March. Financial years are identified by the calendar year in which they commence, so the financial year 1983 is the year to 31 March 1984. The full corporation tax rate has been 52% since 1973. A lower small companies rate applies to the income of companies with profits below a stipulated threshold (see below).

Where the tax rate changes during a company's chargeable accounting period the profits are apportioned on a time basis and charged at the respective rates, and the tax is aggregated to give the total tax payable.

Small companies rate (FA 1972, s 95)

Where a company's profits (as defined) are below a stipulated amount, a lower rate of tax is charged on the company's income. The rate for the year to 31 March 1983 is 38%. Where the profits lie between the stipulated amount and an upper maximum, marginal relief is available. The lower and upper limits for the year to 31 March 1983 are £100,000 and £500,000.

The definition of profits for small companies rate purposes is:

(a) Income chargeable to corporation tax; plus
(b) 15/26ths of chargeable gains; plus
(c) Franked investment income (i.e. UK dividends plus related tax credits).

Although these three items are included in the calculation, the small companies rate only applies to the first of them. It never applies to chargeable gains, which are always taxed at 52%, having already been reduced by the 11/26ths fraction to give an effective 30% rate. Franked investment income is not chargeable to corporation tax at all.

Where profits exceed the lower limit, marginal relief is given by calculating tax on income at the 52% rate and reducing it by an amount arrived at by the following formula:

$$(M - P) \times \frac{I}{P} \times \frac{7}{200}$$

where M = Upper maximum of £500,000
P = Profits as defined for small companies rate purposes (see above)
I = Income chargeable to corporation tax

The marginal relief ensures that the corporation tax rate on the profits is gradually increased to the full 52% level, but the effect is that the income in the marginal tranche suffers a tax rate in excess of 52%. With the current lower and upper limits this marginal rate is $55\frac{1}{2}\%$ where there are no chargeable gains or franked investment income. (Where there are gains and franked investment income the marginal rate is less.) See example 1.

To the extent that a company is able to reduce its profits within the marginal tranche, it can thus save approximately $55\frac{1}{2}\%$ tax.

The lower and upper limits are annual limits and they are scaled down proportionately if an accounting period is less than 12 months. They are also scaled down where for any part of a chargeable accounting period a company has associated companies. Associated companies include both companies associated through being members of the same group and companies controlled by the same persons. If, for example, the same

Example 1

Profits (all income) chargeable to corporation tax:		£
(i) £100,000 @ 38%		38,000
(ii) £110,000 @ 52%	57,200	

Marginal relief $(500,000 - 110,000) \times \dfrac{110,000}{110,000} \times \dfrac{7}{200}$ 13,650 43,550

Additional corporation tax on extra £10,000 profits $(55\frac{1}{2}\%)$ £ 5,550

persons control four companies, the limits for each are £25,000 and £125,000. If three have profits of £30,000 and one £10,000 the small companies rate will only apply to the last one, and the others will have profits subject to the marginal rate. On the other hand if, say, there were two associated companies and one's profits were £500,000 and the other's £50,000, the company with £50,000 profits would qualify for small companies rate even though the group profits exceeded the upper maximum.

Date of payment of tax (TA 1970, ss 243, 244)

Corporation tax is payable nine months after the end of the chargeable accounting period unless the company was established before April 1965, when corporation tax commenced. Pre-April 1965 companies preserve the same time interval as they used to have for income tax. Income tax was payable by companies on 1 January in the next income tax year following their accounting year end, so if a company made up accounts to 31 December 1964, tax was due on 1 January 1966 and the time interval was one year plus one day. If that company now makes up a fifteen-month account from 1 January 1983 to 31 March 1984, corporation tax will be due as follows.

On profits of chargeable accounting period:	Due date
From 1 January 1983 to 31 December 1983	1 January 1985
From 1 January 1984 to 31 March 1984	1 April 1985

If the company makes up future accounts annually to 31 March, the annual payment date will be 1 April. Old established companies that have not changed their accounting date will still be paying tax annually on 1 January.

Assessments are not always issued on time, and in no case is tax due earlier than thirty days after the date of issue of the assessment.

Interest on overdue tax and repayment supplement (TMA 1970, s 86; F(No 2) A 1975, s 48)

Interest is charged on overdue corporation tax, currently at 8% p.a., and the interest is not tax deductible. The interest runs from the due date of payment unless an application has been made for postponement of tax pending an appeal, in which case any of the postponed tax that remains chargeable after settlement of the appeal attracts interest either from the actual due date of payment or, if earlier, from six months after the normal due date. Interest will always run from the normal due date in cases of neglect, fraud or wilful default. See chapter 10.

Where a company has overpaid tax and a repayment of not less than £100 is made more than twelve months after the due date of payment, it attracts a tax-free repayment supplement, currently at the rate of 8% p.a. The supplement is given for each complete tax month in the period commencing one year after the due date of payment and ending at the end of the tax month in which the repayment is made, but a year's supplement is lost for each full year the tax was paid after the due date.

Franked investment income (FA 1972, s 88)

Dividends and other distributions of company profits are not allowable deductions in calculating the profits chargeable to corporation tax. Where dividends from UK-resident companies are received by a company, they do not have to be included in that company's profits chargeable to corporation tax because they have already been 'franked' by the payment of corporation tax by the paying company. In the hands of the receiving company the dividends plus their related tax credits are termed 'franked investment income'. Such income may be passed on to the company's shareholders without tax consequences and the shareholders then get the benefit of the tax credit.

Dividend payments and other distributions (FA 1972, ss 84–89 and Sch 14)

When a company pays dividends or makes other qualifying distributions (see below), such as distributions in kind instead of cash, it has to pay over in advance some of the corporation tax on the profits of the period in which the dividend is paid, except to the extent that the dividend payment is made out of franked investment income as indicated above. The advance payment of corporation tax (ACT) is at the rate of 3/7ths of the dividend, and thus represents 30% of the sum of the dividend plus the ACT. Although this payment reduces the company's liability to corporation tax on its income, it is 'imputed' to the shareholder in the form of a tax credit to satisfy the shareholder's liability to income tax at the basic rate. If the shareholder is not liable to tax the credit is repaid to him.

Within fourteen days after the end of each calendar quarter ended 31 March, 30 June, 30 September and 31 December the company has to account to the Revenue for the ACT on dividends paid during the quarter. If the company's accounting period does not end on one of those dates there are five return periods, the fifth ending at the end of the accounting period, with the ACT due within fourteen days thereafter.

In order to compute the amount of ACT payable, franked payments (that is, dividends paid plus related tax credits) are compared with franked investment income (that is, dividends received plus related tax credits) and the company is liable to pay ACT at the rate of 30% on the excess payments (if any).

Where there is a change in the rate during an accounting period, the parts before and after the change are treated as separate accounting periods for ACT purposes.

If a company's franked investment income exceeds its franked payments, the excess, known as surplus franked investment income, may be carried forward to frank a later dividend payment. It may alternatively be used to obtain a repayment where a company has made a trading loss. This is dealt with in chapter 26.

As the name indicates, advance corporation tax is an advance payment of the company's liability to pay corporation tax, and, subject to a maximum set-off limit, it reduces the corporation tax on the profits of the accounting period in which the dividend is paid. The set-off limit is an amount equal to basic rate income tax on the company's income chargeable to corporation tax. In no circumstances may ACT be set against that part of the corporation tax that relates to capital gains.

Surplus ACT (FA 1972, s 85)

If the amount of ACT paid exceeds the permitted set-off, the excess—called surplus ACT—may be carried back and set against the corporation tax liability of accounting periods commencing in the previous two years, latest first, but again subject to the maximum relief limit for those years. The carry-back claim must be made within two years of the end of the accounting period in which the surplus ACT arises. Any balance of ACT remaining unrelieved may be carried forward without time limit.

Where ACT is carried back, the tax for the earlier period will usually already have been paid, so that a tax repayment will result. In calculating any repayment supplement arising the ACT cannot be treated as having been paid in the earlier period and the supplement will run only from one year after the due date for corporation tax in respect of the accounting period in which the surplus ACT arose.

The balance of corporation tax payable after the set-off of ACT is popularly called mainstream corporation tax, although this is not a statutory term.

See example 2.

Qualifying and non-qualifying distributions (FA 1972, ss 84, 105 and Sch 21)

The legislation distinguishes between 'qualifying distributions' and 'non-qualifying distributions'. Qualifying distributions attract an ACT liability as indicated above. Non-qualifying distributions are broadly those that confer a future rather than a current claim on the company's assets, such as a

Example 2

	Year to 31 March		
	1982	1983	1984
	£	£	£
Profits chargeable to corporation tax:			
Income	20,000	70,000	80,000
15/26ths chargeable gains	5,000	10,000	20,000
	25,000	80,000	100,000
ACT rate constant at 3/7ths.			
Maximum ACT set-off (30% of income)	6,000	21,000	24,000
Corporation tax payable:			
At small companies rate on income			
(1982 40%, 38% thereafter)	8,000	26,600	30,400
At 52% on gains	2,600	5,200	10,400
	10,600	31,800	40,800
Less ACT paid	(5,000)	(15,000)	(34,000)
Surplus ACT carried back	(1,000)	(6,000)	7,000
Surplus ACT carried forward			3,000
Mainstream corporation tax payable	£4,600	£10,800	£16,800
Comprised of: Tax on gains (52%)	2,600	5,200	10,400
Tax on income			
(1982 10%, then 8%)	2,000	5,600	6,400

bonus issue of redeemable shares. The company has no tax liability on such a distribution, but the shareholder is liable where appropriate to the excess of higher rates and surcharge over basic rate tax. The company is required to notify the Revenue within fourteen days after the end of the quarter in which the non-qualifying distribution is made.

When the shares are redeemed the redemption is a qualifying distribution liable to ACT, but the tax paid by the shareholder on the non-qualifying distribution may be set against that due on the later qualifying distribution.

Company liquidations (TA 1970, s 247)

When a company goes into liquidation this is usually preceded by a cessation of trade. The cessation of trade denotes the end of a chargeable accounting period, and a chargeable accounting period also ends at the commencement of winding-up.

Problems can arise when a company that has been making trading losses realises chargeable gains on the sale of its assets, because if the gains are realised after the trade ceases there will be no current trading losses to offset them, but it is not possible to part with the assets until the trade has ceased. This problem can be avoided if the contract for sale of the assets takes place before ceasing to trade, with completion taking place subsequently. The contract date is the relevant disposal date for capital gains tax purposes, and any losses occurring in the accounting period in which the trade ceases will then be available to reduce the gains.

Close companies (TA 1970, ss 282–287A, 302, 303; FA 1972, s 94 and Sch 16)

A close company is a company under the control of five or fewer participators (which broadly means shareholders, although it is defined more widely), or under the control of its directors. In considering what rights an individual has in a company, the rights of his 'associates' are included, which covers close family, partners and the trustees of any family settlements.

As well as being subject to the normal corporation tax rules, close companies are subject to additional requirements.

Benefits in kind to participators are treated as distributions (except where already treated as earnings under the Schedule E benefits rules, see chapter 11) and loans to participators attract a tax liability. These provisions are dealt with in chapter 13.

A close company used to be required to distribute a certain proportion of all its income, and the shareholders suffered adverse tax consequences if it did not. This requirement has now been considerably relaxed for trading companies, who are no longer subject to any required level of distribution of trading income, but they still have a requirement to distribute part of their estate and investment income, including their franked investment income. This prevents the shareholders using a company as an investment vehicle in order to avoid higher rates of income tax and surcharge on the investment income.

The required level of distribution of investment income is called 'relevant income'. The legislation prescribes a maximum, but this may be reduced if its distribution would be prejudicial to the requirements of the company's business. The maximum level is 50% of the after-tax estate income (which is usually net rents, although income from woodlands under Schedule B would be included), plus any other investment income after tax. In arriving at the estate income an abatement is given by reference to the ratio of after-tax estate income to after-tax estate and trading income (the 'appropriate fraction'). If the after-tax estate income is less than the appropriate fraction of £75,000, it is reduced by one-half of the difference; if it is less than the appropriate fraction of £25,000, it is ignored altogether. Other investment income is abated by the smaller of 10% of the after-tax estate and trading income and £3,000.

(The abatement limits are scaled down where there are associated companies and for accounts less than 12 months, except that the £3,000 abatement is given to each associated company.)

The 'relevant income' is compared with the distributions made by the company in respect of the accounting period, either within it or within a reasonable time afterwards, and if the relevant income exceeds the distributions the excess is apportioned among the participators and treated as a notional dividend received by them on the last day of the accounting period. A tax credit is deemed to be attached, so that the participator would only be liable to the extent of the excess of higher rates and surcharge over basic-rate tax. The notional credit is not available for repayment if it exceeds a participator's tax liability.

There are two de minimis provisions. There is no apportionment for a trading company if the excess is £1,000 or less, and there is no apportionment to an individual shareholder if the amount apportioned to him, with its related tax credit, is less than £200 and also less than 5% of the total apportionment.

See example 3 overleaf generally.

A close company is also subject to apportionment in respect of any annual charges that have been deducted in arriving at relevant income that would not have been allowable to the participators personally in calculating their own liability at excess rates. This principally concerns charitable covenants and will not be relevant unless an amount apportioned to an individual takes his total charitable covenants above £5,000 for any tax year.

Now that trading income does not have to be apportioned, apportionment is not usually a problem except for close investment companies.

Close company liquidations (FA 1972, Sch 16)

Where a close trading company ceases to trade and goes into liquidation, all its estate income of the period in which it ceases to trade, and not just 50%, is liable to apportionment, and the requirements of the company's business are not taken into account. The abatement of investment income of the smaller of £3,000 and 10% of the estate and trading income will still apply in that period. In subsequent accounting periods when the company is no longer a trading company, all its income will be liable to apportionment, with no abatement available at all. But once the winding-up has commenced, that income can only reach the shareholders as a capital payment by way of a larger distribution in the course of winding-up. The shareholders will thus be subject to income tax on the apportionment and to capital gains tax on the distribution in the winding-up. By concession, any capital gains tax that can be shown to relate to the accumulation of income for a period after the commencement of winding-up can be deducted from any liability to income tax at excess rates on that income as a result of apportionment.

Groups of companies (TA 1970, ss 256–264, 272–279; FA 1972, s 93)

The Taxes Acts do not treat a group of companies as a taxable entity. The

Example 3

Company's after-tax profits for the year to 31 March 1983 are:

	£
Schedule D, Case I trading income	24,800
Schedule A rents	12,400
Total estate and trading income (estate income being 1/3)	37,200
Schedule D Case III interest	6,200
Franked investment income (net of tax credits)	7,000
Total investment income	13,200
Chargeable gains (which are not liable to apportionment)	7,000

Calculation of relevant income	Estate income	Investment income	
	12,400	13,200	
Abatement of estate income $\frac{1}{2}((75,000 \times 1/3) - 12,400)$	6,300		
Abatement of investment income Smaller of £3,000 and 10% of £37,200		3,000	
	6,100	10,200	
Prescribed distribution level	50%	100%	
Relevant income	3,050	+ 10,200 =	13,250
Dividends paid for period were			10,000
Excess of relevant income liable to apportionment			£3,250
Minimum additional dividend required to avoid apportionment (which would leave a de minimis £1,000 excess)			£2,250

corporation tax position of each company in the group is computed independently (small companies rate and various other limits being scaled down according to the number of associated companies). There are, however, various provisions that recognise the group structure and give special treatment in the appropriate circumstances.

Holding company and its 51% subsidiaries

(a) ACT paid by the holding company on dividends (not other distributions) may be surrendered to one or more subsidiaries for use against
the subsidiary's corporation tax liability for the corresponding or future
accounting periods. It cannot be carried back by a subsidiary.

(b) A subsidiary cannot surrender ACT to its holding company, but it can
avoid paying ACT in the first place, because an election may be made
for a subsidiary to pay a dividend to its holding company (or to a fellow
subsidiary) without accounting for ACT. Such a dividend is termed
'group income'. The receiving company will thus have no tax credit
passed to it and will pay ACT in the normal way as and when it passes
the dividend on to its own shareholders. These provisions also apply to
dividends paid by a trading company to a consortium of UK resident
companies who own 75% or more of its issued ordinary share capital.

(c) Charges on income may be paid gross by any group company to
another.

Holding company and its 75% subsidiaries

(a) Trading losses (and trade charges in excess of other profits) can be
surrendered to other group members for use against total profits
(including 15/26ths of chargeable gains) of the corresponding accounting period. These provisions—called group relief—are dealt with in
chapter 26.

(b) Chargeable assets for capital gains purposes can be transferred to
another group company without a chargeable gain arising, the transferee company assuming the base cost and acquisition date of the
transferor company. In this way assets to be sold outside the group can
first be centralised in one company for setting off losses against profits.
Otherwise there is no facility for chargeable gains of one group
company to be relieved by capital losses of another.

(c) A chargeable gain made by one group company on a business asset
qualifying for roll-over relief may be rolled over or held over against an
acquisition by another group company. Roll-over relief is dealt with in
chapter 5.

Recent developments

Over the past few years the Government has introduced various measures
to enable companies to operate in a tax-efficient manner and to stimulate
investment in new and expanding ventures:

> Business start-up scheme, now extended and renamed the busi-
> ness expansion scheme.
> Purchase of own shares by company.
> Demergers.

These are dealt with separately in chapter 29.

5
Capital gains tax: general principles

Basis of charge (CGTA 1979, ss 1, 4, 5)

Capital gains tax was introduced with effect from 6 April 1965 to charge tax on gains arising on the disposal of chargeable assets. Gains and losses are calculated on each asset and then aggregated to give the net chargeable gains or allowable losses for the year. The first £5,300 is exempt and the balance is charged at 30%. If losses exceed gains the excess is carried forward to set against later chargeable gains.

Persons liable (CGTA 1979, ss 2, 12, 14)

Those who are resident or ordinarily resident in the UK are liable on all gains wherever they arise, if UK domiciled, and on gains arising in, or remitted to, the UK if domiciled elsewhere. Non-residents carrying on a trade in the UK are liable on gains arising on the disposal of business assets in the UK. The overseas aspect is dealt with in chapter 44.

Husband and wife (CGTA 1979, ss 4, 44, 45)

Gains of husband and wife are calculated separately but are then aggregated and assessed on the husband, unless one of them applies for separate assessment. One spouse may, however, elect for his or her losses to be carried forward instead of being set against the other's gains. Disposals between husband and wife in a tax-year when they are living together are not chargeable. The acquiring spouse adopts the base value and acquisition date of the other spouse for the purposes of calculating a gain or loss on a future disposal. For the effect of indexation allowance on transfers between spouses, see p 44 below under 'No gain/no loss disposals'.

Companies (TA 1970, ss 238, 265; FA 1972, s 93)

Gains are computed on capital gains tax principles but are charged to corporation tax and not capital gains tax. The annual exemption is not available. The chargeable gains are first reduced by 11/26th and then included in profits chargeable to corporation tax at 52%, giving an effective rate of 30%, which is the same as the rate for individuals.

Chargeable assets and exempt assets (CGTA 1979, ss 19–21, 134)

All forms of property are chargeable unless specifically exempt. A charge may also arise when a capital sum is realised without any disposal taking place (for example if compensation is received for damage to an asset

---

Exempt assets

	CGTA 1979 reference	See chapter
An individual's only or main residence	101, 102	30
One other residence occupied rent free and without other consideration by a dependent relative	105	30
Chattels which are wasting assets, unless used in a business	127	42
Non-wasting and business chattels where disposal proceeds do not exceed £3,000	128	42
Government securities owned for more than 12 months	67	34
SAYE contracts, savings certificates and premium bonds	71	41
Prizes and bettings winnings	19	
Private motor cars, including veteran and vintage cars	130	
Sterling currency, and foreign currency for an individual's own spending and maintenance of assets abroad	19, 133	42
Decorations for valour if disposed of by the original holder or legatees but not by a purchaser	131	
Compensation or damages for personal or professional wrong or injury	19	
Life insurance policies but only in the hands of the original owner or beneficiaries	143	43
Small gifts with a total value of £100 or less in any year	6	
Gifts of assets of national, historic or scientific interest where they are exempt or conditionally exempt from capital transfer tax (see p 58), but breach of the CTT exemption will nullify the CGT exemption	147	
Gifts to charities	146	46

---

although if the compensation is used to restore the asset no gain arises).

Where a loss arises on money lent, the loss is not normally allowable unless the debt is a 'debt on a security', which usually means secured or unsecured loan stock. Special provisions apply, however, to losses on certain loans (see p 43).

Where an asset is exempt no chargeable gain or allowable loss can arise. See the table above for exempt assets and the chapter in this book which deals with them.

Computation of gains and losses (CGTA 1979, ss 28–35, 107, Schs 3 and 5; FA 1982, ss 86, 87 and Sch 13)

Gains and losses are computed by deducting from the sale proceeds or, in some instances, market value (see p 42):

Original cost and incidental costs of acquisition
Enhancement expenditure
Incidental costs of disposal

and then, if the resulting figure is a gain (called the 'gross gain') deducting the indexation allowance (see p 37 below). See example 1 below.

Example 1

Mr A sells for £18,000 a painting which he acquired six years ago for £8,000. The indexation allowance due (see below) is £1,000.

	£
Sale proceeds	18,000
Cost of painting	8,000
Gross gain	10,000
Indexation allowance	1,000
Chargeable gain	£9,000

Assets held on 6 April 1965

There are special provisions which ensure that gains and losses relating to the period before 6 April 1965 are left out of account, with separate rules for land with development value, for quoted securities and for all other assets.

The gain or loss on land with development value is calculated by comparing the proceeds either with the original cost or with the value at 6 April 1965 whichever shows the lower gain or loss. If one method shows a gain and the other a loss there is neither gain nor loss. The same rules apply to quoted securities, except that it is possible to elect for quoted securities to be deemed to have been acquired on 6 April 1965 at their value on that date. The detailed provisions are in chapter 35.

Where an asset other than quoted securities or land with development value was acquired before 6 April 1965, only the time proportion of the gain falling after 6 April 1965 is chargeable, although the earliest date that can be used in a time apportionment calculation is 6 April 1945. You may elect to have the gain computed using the 6 April 1965 value as the cost instead of using time apportionment, but once made this election is irrevocable, even if it results in more tax being payable. Where the allowable expenditure is incurred on different dates, the overall gain is first apportioned in proportion to the respective blocks of expenditure. The time apportionment formula is then applied to those gains where the expenditure was incurred before 6 April 1965, gains where the expenditure was incurred after that date being wholly chargeable. See example 2 below.

Indexation allowance

No allowance was made for the effects of inflation until the introduction of an indexation allowance in FA 1982. The indexation allowance applies to disposals on or after 6 April 1982 (1 April 1982 for companies) provided that the asset has been held for at least twelve months. It is arrived at by applying the fraction $(RD - RI)/RI$ to each item of allowable expenditure and aggregating the results, where RD is the retail prices index for the month of disposal and RI is the retail prices index for March 1982 or for the twelfth month after that in which the expenditure is incurred if later. The fraction is expressed as a decimal and is rounded to three decimal places.

No allowance is given on any item of expenditure incurred less than thirteen months before the month of disposal. In addition, if RD is less than RI for any item of expenditure, the indexed rise on that item is nil.

Where a gain is subject to time apportionment because the asset was acquired before 6 April 1965 (see above) the indexation allowance is deducted before applying time apportionment (see example 2 below).

The indexation allowance is not available to increase losses, and if it exceeds the gain that would otherwise arise it produces a no gain/no loss result rather than turning the gain into a loss.

Part disposals

Where part only of an asset is disposed of, the cost of the part disposed of is the proportion of the overall cost that the sale proceeds bear to the sum of the sale proceeds plus the market value of what remains unsold. The indexation allowance is calculated on the apportioned part of the cost and not on the total.

Where the proceeds of a part disposal of land are £10,000 (£20,000 after 5 April 1983 if proposed legislation is enacted) or less, and they represent not more than 5% of the value of the land, the taxpayer may claim to have the proceeds deducted from the base cost of the land rather than being treated

Example 2

Mr B sells a freehold investment property, the relevant particulars being:

	£
Sale proceeds less expenses, 1 December 1984	13,000
Cost, 1 December 1955	5,500
Cost of extension, 1 December 1982	2,000
Market value at 6 April 1965	7,900

The retail prices index is assumed to be as follows:
March 1982, 313.4; December 1983, 366.0; December 1984, 396.0

Time apportionment method

	£	£
Sale proceeds less expenses		13,000
Less cost		
1.12.55	5,500	
1.12.82	2,000	7,500
Gross gain		5,500
Less indexation allowance		
On 1.12.55 cost		

$$£5,500 \times \left(\frac{396.0 - 313.4}{313.4} = .264 \right) \qquad 1,452$$

On 1.12.82 cost

$$£2,000 \times \left(\frac{396.0 - 366.0}{366.0} = .082 \right) \qquad 164 \qquad 1,616$$

Gain		£3,884
Apportion gain to expenditure		
1.12.55 cost 5,500/7,500 × £3,884		2,848
1.12.82 cost 2,000/7,500 × £3,884		1,036
		£3,884

Time apportionment

$$\frac{6.4.65\text{–}1.12.84}{1.12.55\text{–}1.12.84} = \frac{19\frac{2}{3}}{29} \times £2,848 \qquad 1,931$$

Gain wholly post 6.4.65		1,036
Chargeable gain		£2,967

6 April 1965 market value election

Sale proceeds less expenses		13,000
Less 6.4.65 market value	7,900	
Post 6.4.65 expenditure	2,000	9,900
Gross gain		3,100
Less indexation allowance		
On 6.4.65 value £7,900 × .264	2,086	
On 1.12.82 cost (as before)	164	2,250
Chargeable gain		£850
The election is beneficial so the chargeable gain is		£850

as from a part disposal. This claim may not be made if other disposals of land are made in the same year with total proceeds for all disposals of land exceeding £10,000 (or £20,000). The indexation allowance on a subsequent disposal is calculated on the full cost in the usual way, then reduced to take account of the previous part disposal.

Leases

The grant of a lease at a premium gives rise to a capital gains tax liability, and also an income tax liability if the term is 50 years or less. The calculation of the income and capital elements is shown in chapter 33. Where a tenant assigns a lease at a premium to another tenant, the premium is charged to tax in the normal way if the lease has more than 50 years to run at the time of the assignment. If, however, it has 50 years or less to run, it is a wasting asset and the cost has to be depreciated over that 50 years according to a table set out in CGTA 1979, Sch 3 which ensures that the cost is depreciated more slowly during the early part of the 50-year period than during the later years.

Annual exemption (CGTA 1979, s 5 and Sch 1; FA 1982, s 80)

The annual exemption, which is £5,300 in 1983/84, is increased each year in line with increases in the retail prices index. Although gains and losses in the same year must be netted off, brought-forward losses need not be set against gains covered by the exemption. So if, say, there are net gains in the current year of £5,000 and brought forward losses of £4,000, the £4,000 losses are carried forward intact. If the gains are £6,000, only £700 of the brought-forward losses is used to reduce the gains to the exempt £5,300, leaving £3,300 to be carried forward.

Where husband and wife are living together the exempt limit of £5,300 is divided between them in the ratio of the net gains accruing to each in the year of assessment, or, where the aggregate net gains do not exceed £5,300 and allowable losses accruing to either of them in a previous year are carried forward from that year, in such proportion as they agree. Where the husband dies, or there is a separation or divorce in the tax-year, the above rules as to apportionment or loss set-off apply to the date of death etc., but the wife then gets a full exemption for the remainder of the year as if it were a separate year of assessment. A full exemption is also available to each spouse in the year of marriage.

Reliefs

Specific reliefs are available for:

(a) replacement of business assets;
(b) retirement of a sole trader, partner or family company director;
(c) gifts;
(d) transfer of a business to a company; and
(e) relief for losses on certain loans.

These are dealt with in the following paragraphs, except for (d) which is dealt with in chapter 27.

Replacement of business assets and compulsorily purchased land (CGTA 1979, ss 111A, 115–119)

Where a chargeable gain arises on the disposal of a business asset and the proceeds are reinvested in another business asset within the period commencing one year before and ending three years after the disposal, the gain may be deferred. The relief applies to land and buildings, fixed plant and machinery, ships, aircraft, hovercraft, and goodwill. The replacement asset need not be used in the same trade where one person carries on two or more trades either successively or at the same time.

If only part of the sale proceeds are reinvested in replacement assets within the roll-over period, part of the gain is chargeable immediately.

If the replacement asset has a life of more than 60 years (e.g. freehold land) the gain is rolled over and treated as reducing the cost of the replacement asset. Indexation allowance applies on the replacement asset after twelve months in the usual way and is calculated on the cost less the rolled over gain.

If the replacement is a depreciating asset with a life of less than 60 years (which in fact applies to most of the business assets qualifying for relief) the gain is deferred for a maximum of ten years. It becomes chargeable when the replacement asset is sold or ceases to be used in the business, or, at latest, ten years after acquisition of the replacement asset. The gain will not crystallise at that point, however, if in the meantime a non-depreciating asset has been acquired against which the gain may be rolled over instead.

Rollover relief is not available on investment property unless it is the subject of compulsory purchase, in which case the relief is available provided that the replacement is not a capital gains tax exempt dwelling-house (see chapter 30).

Retirement relief (CGTA 1979, s 124)

Where an individual aged 60 or over disposes of all or part of his business or partnership share, or of shares in his family company, all or part of the gains arising on the business assets are exempt up to a maximum of £50,000 (£100,000 after 5 April 1983 if proposed legislation is enacted). 'Family company' means either one in which the individual owns not less than 25% of the voting rights or one in which he and his family together own not less than 51%, with his own share being at least 5%.

The exemption applies at the rate of £10,000 (£20,000 after 5 April 1983 if proposed legislation is enacted) per annum for each year over the age of 60, with a corresponding amount for part of a year, up to the maximum £50,000 (or £100,000) at age 65. The available exemption is reduced proportionately where the business has not been owned for the whole of the previous ten years, or, in the case of family companies, where the director has not been a full-time working director for that period. The minimum period of ownership or full-time directorship to enable relief to be claimed is one year. See example 3.

Example 3

Mr C has gains of £160,000 on disposal of business assets on retirement at age 63 from a business he has owned throughout the previous seven years. (It is assumed that the proposed legislation referred to above is enacted.)

Gains exempt are 70% × £60,000 = £42,000, leaving £118,000 chargeable

i.e. 70% for seven years out of ten, and £60,000 being the appropriate proportion of £100,000 for someone aged 63.

Where the disposal is of shares in a family company, the gain on the shares is reduced in the proportion of the company's chargeable business assets to the total chargeable assets to arrive at the gain qualifying for relief. Chargeable assets are all assets on which a chargeable gain or allowable loss would arise if the company disposed of them (or which would be treated as disposed of for neither gain nor loss). Current assets are therefore excluded. Chargeable business assets are chargeable assets used in the business, including goodwill but excluding investments. Where a group of companies is concerned, the shares held in subsidiaries are investments for this purpose and thus do not attract relief. Plant or machinery is a chargeable business asset unless it is moveable plant or machinery with a cost and value of £3,000 or less (when it would be an exempt chattel). Private cars are excluded since they are exempt.

Gifts (CGTA 1979, ss 29A, 62, 63, 126; FA 1980, s 79; FA 1981, s 78; FA 1982, s 82)

For capital gains tax a gift is deemed to be a disposal at open market value, so that in the absence of special rules a chargeable gain or allowable loss would result.

Not only gifts but all transactions between connected persons, or not at arm's length, are deemed to be at open market value. Broadly, a person is connected with husband or wife, with close relatives and relatives' spouses, with business partners and their spouses and relatives (except in relation to normal commercial transactions), and, if he is the trustee of a settlement, with the settlor (if an individual) and with any person connected with the settlor. Companies under the same control are connected with each other and with the persons controlling them.

Where an asset is disposed of to a connected person and a loss arises, the loss may not be set against general gains but only against a later gain on a transaction with the same connected person.

Where a gain arises on a gift, then provided that the gift is made by an individual or trustees, and the donee is either an individual or trustees, the gain which would otherwise be chargeable may be held over and treated as reducing the base acquisition cost of the donee. It is thus possible to escape tax at the time of the gift although the lower base cost will increase future potential gains for the donee.

The gifts rollover relief is also available where assets are not given outright but are disposed of for less than their value. However the gain arising may then only be rolled over to the extent to which it exceeds the amount received.

Claims for gifts relief to apply must be made by the donor and donee jointly except where the donees are trustees, in which case only the donor need make the claim.

Where part of a gain on a gift is covered by the retirement exemption, gifts relief may be claimed on the balance. Where a gift attracts capital transfer tax, the capital transfer tax attributable to the value of the asset gifted is added to the donee's base cost for capital gains tax (but not so as to create a loss on future disposal).

Where an asset is given to a company rather than to an individual or trustees, gifts relief may only be claimed if the asset is a business asset (as defined for retirement relief above), or shares in a family company, in which case the relief is confined to the business assets proportion (again as defined for retirement relief above).

Indexation allowance will reduce the gain otherwise arising on a gift. If the donee subsequently disposes of the gifted asset at a loss, the loss is reduced by the indexation allowance arising on the gift, but not so as to create a chargeable gain. Indexation allowance in respect of the donee's ownership will commence in the usual way from twelve months after the date of the gift.

Relief for losses on loans (CGTA 1979, s 136)

Relief is available for losses on loans or guarantees where a loan is made, or a guarantee is given, after 11 April 1978 and where the borrower is a UK resident and uses the money lent wholly for the purposes of a trade carried on by him. Upon an appropriate claim, an irrecoverable loan or payment under guarantee gives rise to an allowable loss for CGT at the time, respectively, of the claim or of the guarantee payment, provided that the debt or the rights acquired by subrogation under the guarantee payment are not assigned. If allowed losses prove in whole or part to be recoverable a capital gain arises on the amount recovered (whether from the borrower or from any co-guarantor).

Relief is not available if the loss arises because of an act or omission by the lender, or guarantor, nor is it available where the claimant and borrower are husband and wife or companies in the same group.

Due date of payment and interest on overdue tax (CGTA 1979, s 7; TMA 1970, ss 86, 88)

The normal due date of payment of capital gains tax is 1 December after the end of the tax-year, or 30 days after the issue of the assessment if later. Where an appeal is made against an assessment, tax is still due on the normal due date unless a postponement application is made. If any postponed tax ultimately becomes due for payment following settlement of the appeal it is due for payment 30 days after the appeal is settled (or on the normal due date if later). Interest, currently at 8%, normally runs from the actual due date of payment, but where tax has been postponed the date from which interest runs is never later than six months after the normal due date. In cases of fraud, wilful default or neglect interest runs from the date the tax ought to have been paid (see chapter 10).

Payment by instalments (CGTA 1979, ss 8 and 40)

Capital gains tax may be paid by instalments where:
(a) the proceeds are being received by instalments over 18 months or more and paying tax in one sum would cause hardship; or
(b) the tax arises on a gift of land or buildings, unquoted securities, a controlling holding of quoted securities, or assets used wholly in a business.

The instalments run over eight years, or until the last instalment of the price is received if sooner, with relief for bad debts being available if part of the consideration due proves irrecoverable.

Quoted and unquoted securities

Special problems arise on the treatment of both quoted and unquoted securities. These are dealt with in detail in chapter 35.

No gain/no loss disposals

Special provisions apply to the following disposals:

(a) Transfers on company reconstructions (TA 1970, s 267).
(b) Transfers within a 75% group of companies (TA 1970, s 273).
(c) Husband/wife transfers (CGTA 1979, s 44).
(d) Transfers by personal representatives to legatees (CGTA 1979, s 49).

A gross gain equal to the available indexation allowance is deemed to arise, effectively giving neither gain nor loss (FA 1982, Sch 13). The acquisition cost for the transferee is thus increased by the indexation allowance. If the transferee subsequently disposes of the asset at a loss, the loss is reduced by the indexation allowance arising on the no gain/no loss transfer, but not so as to turn a loss into a gain. If the transferor had held the asset for more than twelve months the indexation allowance when the transferee disposes of the asset is calculated from the time he acquired it and not from twelve months thereafter. If the no gain/no loss transfer occurs within twelve months of the transferor's acquisition of the asset, the transferee is deemed to have acquired the asset when the transferor did, thus ensuring that only one twelve-month period is taken into account in qualifying for indexation.

Death (CGTA 1979, s 49 and Sch 1)

No capital gains tax charge arises on death. If losses arise in the year of death these may be carried back and set against gains assessable in the three previous tax years, latest first (with the set-off being made only against any gains not covered by the annual exemption in those years).

The personal representatives or legatees are deemed to acquire the assets at the market value at the date of death. When personal representatives dispose of assets at values in excess of the values at death, gains arising will be charged to tax (and exemptions the deceased could have claimed may not be available, for example on a private residence) but they may claim the annual exemption of £5,300 in the tax-year of death and in each of the following two tax-years.

Where within two years after a death the persons entitled to the estate vary the way in which it is distributed, and notify the Revenue within six months after the variation, the variation is not regarded as a disposal by those originally entitled but as having been made by the deceased at the date of death so that no CGT charge arises.

Trusts (CGTA, ss 5, 54–56 and Sch 1; FA 1980, s 79; FA 1982, s 82)

Trustees are chargeable persons for capital gains tax. They are entitled to an annual exemption of £2,650, this being divided where there are associated trusts, but with each trust getting a minimum exemption of £530. The exemption is increased each year in line with the retail prices index.

When assets are placed in trust, and when they are transferred to beneficiaries other than on the death of a life tenant, a disposal at market value is deemed to take place, but gains may be rolled over under the gifts relief provisions dealt with on p 42 above. When a life interest terminates other than on the death of a life tenant this is not a chargeable event for capital gains tax. When a life interest terminates on the death of a life tenant, or a beneficiary becomes absolutely entitled following a life tenant's death, there is a tax-free uplift in the value of the trust property.

The detailed provisions on the capital gains position of trusts are dealt with in chapter 45.

6
Development land tax: general principles

Basis of charge

Development land tax (DLT) is chargeable, with certain exceptions, on realisations of development value from the disposal or deemed disposal of interests in UK land on or after 1 August 1976. Liability may arise:

(a) on the disposal of an interest in land; or
(b) when a project of material development is begun.

The tax is levied at a flat rate of 60%.

Persons liable (Development Land Tax Act 1976, ss 1, 40)

Those liable are individuals, companies, partnerships, trustees and personal representatives. Husband and wife are separate individuals for DLT purposes, and there is no inter-spouse exemption (other than the general exemption for gifts, see below).

Non-UK-residents are liable in respect of UK land. Subject to certain exceptions, someone who purchases land from a non-resident must retain half the purchase price, and remit it to the DLT office (see below).

Exempt bodies (DLTA 1976, ss 11, 24, 26)

  (i) Local authorities and certain statutory bodies.
 (ii) Charities.
(iii) Self-build housing associations.

Disposals

Disposals include any of the following.

(a) The sale of the owner's entire interest in the whole or part of the land.
(b) Disposal of part of an owner's interest in the whole of the land, for example the grant of a lease out of a freehold interest.
(c) Compensation received for loss of development value.
(d) Sums received for forfeiture or surrender of development value.

(e) Receipt of a sum for the grant of a right to take minerals out of land.

The date of disposal is the date of an unconditional contract or, if a conditional contract is entered into, the date when the contract becomes unconditional.

Options (DLTA 1976, s 8)

The consideration received on the grant of an option is regarded as the disposal proceeds for a newly created interest in the land, and no part of the cost or value of the land itself is deductible in calculating any tax payable.

If the option is exercised, the option consideration and purchase price are aggregated, and DLT calculated, as if the grant and the exercise were a single transaction at the exercise date, any DLT paid on the grant being deducted.

In practice the DLT office do not make an assessment on the grant of an option if it appears likely to be exercised within a reasonable time.

There are special provisions concerning options on leases and various other matters.

Deemed disposals (DLTA 1976, ss 2, 7 and Sch 4; FA 1981, s 133)

All major interests in land are deemed to be disposed of at market value and immediately reacquired at that value on the date when a project of material development is begun. 'Material development' is any development other than the following.

(i) Development carried out in order to obtain planning permission under a general development order.
(ii) Enlargements of, or extensions to, buildings, provided that the cubic content is not increased by more than one-third (one-tenth before 10 March 1981).
(iii) Rebuilding where the original cubic content is not exceeded by more than one-tenth.
(iv) Use of the land for agriculture or forestry.
(v) Use of the land for display of advertisements.
(vi) Use of the land for car parking for up to six years.
(vii) The change of use of buildings or land within any one of the following use classes.

    A As a dwelling-house or for any activity not carried on for profit.
    B As an office or retail shop.
    C As an hotel, guest house, boarding house or public house.
    D Use for any activity carried on for profit, but excluding use as a dwelling-house or for agriculture or forestry, or falling within B or C above or E below.
    E Use for manufacturing or storage purposes.

See also below as regards certain exempt developments.

Ascertainment of development value (DLTA 1976, ss 5, 6 and Sch 3(8); TMA 1970, s 47A)

Development value is the amount by which the net disposal proceeds (or, in the case of a project of material development, the market value of the land on commencement of that development) exceeds the highest of three base values, A, B and C. The base values are calculated as follows.

BASE A The aggregate of:
  (i) cost of acquisition, including incidental costs;
  (ii) cost of relevant improvements, i.e. those which increase the development value and not the current use value;
  (iii) the increase in current use value between the date of acquisition, or 6 April 1965 if later, and the date of disposal;
  (iv) a special addition of 15% of the cost of acquisition for each year or part year of ownership, up to a maximum of 60%, if the land was owned prior to 13 September 1974; or 10% for each year or part year up to a maximum of 40% if the land was acquired after 12 September 1974 and before 1 May 1977; and
  (v) a further addition of a similar percentage to that allowed under (iv) above applied to the cost of relevant improvements, irrespective of when they were carried out.

BASE B The aggregate of:
  (i) 115% of the current use value at the time of disposal; and
  (ii) the cost of any relevant improvements (as defined for Base A).

BASE C The aggregate of:
  (i) 115% of the cost of acquisition including incidental costs; and
  (ii) 115% of the cost of *all* improvements.
  In the case of residential building land held as stock-in-trade, the uplift for Base C under (i) and (ii) is increased to 150% on a deemed disposal after 9 March 1981.

In those cases where an actual disposal takes place the net disposal proceeds are usually the gross receipts less sale expenses. No discount is given for any part of the sale price not receivable immediately, nor is any account taken of the risk that part of the sale proceeds may prove to be irrecoverable. If the latter proves to be the case the tax payable is adjusted subsequently. Where the disposal comprises the grant of a lease the net proceeds will be the sum of any premium receivable and the capital value of the right to receive the rents. On a deemed disposal the market value of the land for the project has, if possible, to be agreed with the Inland Revenue. In the event of dispute an appeal lies to the Lands Tribunal.

Current use value (DLTA 1976, s 7)

Current use value is the market value of the land on the assumption that planning consent would not be granted for any 'material development' (see above) except for various small items of work specified in the Town and

Country Planning Act 1971, Schedule 8 (or comparable Scottish or Northern Ireland legislation). It includes the right to complete any project which was begun before the date on which the current use value is being established.

Basic exemption (DLTA 1976, ss 9, 12, 31)

The first £50,000 of development value realised in any financial year (ending 31 March) by any person is exempt. Husband and wife are regarded as separate persons for this purpose, but a disposal by one spouse does not qualify for the exemption if it occurs within twelve months of the transfer of the land from the other spouse.

Partnerships qualify for a single £50,000 exemption on the disposal of partnership assets, but subject to this each partner is assessed individually according to his partnership share. If partners own interests in land outside the partnership, their individual exemptions are available in full on disposals of those interests.

Personal representatives are entitled to a single £50,000 exemption on their disposals (see below under Death, etc.).

Exempt land (DLTA 1976, ss 14, 15, 16)

No charge arises on a disposal of any of the following.

(i) The disposer's principal private residence, with land up to one acre (or more if appropriate). No election is allowed as to which residence qualifies if more than one is owned, and the decision depends upon the facts.
   A land owner or member of his immediate family can also build one house for occupation by a member of his family or a dependent relative, on land owned at 12 September 1974, without incurring a DLT liability. Exemption is also given on the disposal of a residence occupied rent-free and without other consideration by a dependent relative, and, unlike the position for capital gains tax on such a property, husband and wife can each claim this exemption.
(ii) Land held as stock-in-trade by a builder at 12 September 1974 and having planning consent at that date.

Exempt development (DLTA 1976, ss 17, 18; FA 1980, s 110)

The following development is exempt from DLT liability.

(a) Projects begun within three years of acquisition of the land, provided that no development value would have been realised if development had begun immediately.
(b) The working of minerals by the landowner. If the landowner disposes of the right to work minerals, 50% of the mineral value is subject to tax.
(c) Disposal or development of land within an enterprise zone for a period of ten years after its inclusion in that zone.

Death, gifts and disposals at undervalue (DLTA 1976, ss 9, 10)

A disposal does not arise on death, and the personal representatives adopt the same base values and acquisition date as the deceased. If they dispose of the land they are entitled to the £50,000 exemption (see above). If they transfer the land to a beneficiary, the transfer is treated as a gift. Gifts do not give rise to a liability, and the donee adopts the donor's base values and acquisition date, but the special and further additions to the Base A value (see above) are taken into account only to the extent that they accrued before the date of the gift. If a disposal is made at an undervalue rather than as an outright gift, the liability of the disposer and the acquisition value of the purchaser are normally based on the actual consideration.

Groups of companies (DLTA 1976, ss 12, 20)

Transfers within a group comprising a parent company and its 75% subsidiaries do not give rise to a DLT liability, and the calculation on a subsequent disposal, including the special and further additions, takes into account the whole period of group ownership. The £50,000 exemption (see above) is, however, not available on a disposal outside the group if the land has been acquired from a fellow group member either

(i) within the twelve months before the disposal, or
(ii) within the six years before the disposal, where on that acquisition, or on any earlier intra-group transfer within that six-year period, the transaction had been a part-disposal of a greater interest.

Deferment of tax (DLTA 1976, ss 19, 19A, 23)

In the following cases of material development, tax is normally deferred until the land is disposed of by the developing owner.

(a) Development by statutory undertakers (e.g. gas and electricity boards).
(b) Industrial development for use by the developer.
(c) Commercial development for use by the developer begun after 9 March 1981 and before 1 April 1984.

Losses

Development losses cannot be set against profits.

Payment of tax (DLTA 1976, Sch 8; FA 1980, s 114)

The due date of payment is normally the later of three months after the disposal or deemed disposal (the 'reckonable date') and 30 days after the issue of the assessment. Interest on overdue tax (currently at 8%, non-tax-deductible) runs from the reckonable date.

In certain cases, such as deemed disposals and grants of leases, tax may be paid by yearly or half-yearly instalments over eight or nine years (unless the development is previously sold), with interest accruing only from each instalment date. Prior to the start of a project of material development, a taxpayer may give notice electing for advance assessment of DLT based on the market value at the date of the notice. Provided that the project is started within two years of the notice and that the full facts have been disclosed, the liability on the actual commencement will be treated as met by the advance assessment.

Administration

DLT is administered by the Inland Revenue from the Development Land Tax Office, 73/75 Albert Road, Middlesbrough, Cleveland TS1 2RY. Valuations of land for DLT purposes are carried out by the District Valuer in whose area the land is situated.

Notices (DLTA 1976, Sch 8)

Notices of disposal of an interest in land must be given to the DLT Office within twelve months, unless the stamp duty office has already been notified (see chapter 8). Notification of a project of material development must be given to the DLT Office within 60 days before or 30 days after commencement.

Interrelation with other taxes (DLTA 1976, Sch 6)

Chargeable realised development value is treated as a deduction in calculating chargeable gains or trading profits if a liability arises on the same disposal. It cannot increase or create a capital loss. Where DLT is payable on commencement of a project which does not constitute a disposal for other tax purposes, the chargeable realised development value will rank as a deduction on a subsequent capital gains tax or trading disposal.

Example

An individual owns the freehold interest in a garage and car showroom from which he currently trades. Following the grant of planning permission for office development, the property has been put up for sale and an offer of £400,000 has been accepted.

The freehold interest was acquired in 1966 for £32,000 with incidental costs of £750. The front portion of the premises was converted into a showroom in 1972 at a cost of £7,500. The current use value in 1966 was £30,000 and at present it is £100,000. It was necessary to spend £5,000 in architect's and consultants' fees to obtain the planning consent and £1,000 to insure against a defective title. The costs of sale and of negotiating the DLT value are expected to be £8,000.

COMPUTATION OF POTENTIAL DLT LIABILITY ON SALE

			£
Proceeds of sale			400,000
Less expenses (including fee for negotiating DLT value)			8,000
Net sale proceeds			392,000

Base values

Base A	Purchase price	32,000	
	Incidental costs of acquisition	750	32,750
	Expenditure on relevant improvements:		
	Cost of obtaining planning consent	5,000	
	Insurance re defective title	1,000	6,000
	Increase in current use value (see note):		
	Value in 1983	100,000	
	Value in 1966	30,000	70,000
	Special addition £32,750 × 60%		19,650
	Further addition £6,000 × 60%		3,600
			132,000

Note The £7,500 conversion costs in 1972 increased the current use value and are therefore reflected in the increase of £70,000.

Base B	Current use value £100,000 × 115%		115,000
	Relevant improvements (as for Base A)		6,000
			121,000

Base C	Acquisition cost		32,750	
	Improvements			
	—showroom addition	7,500		
	—planning consent	5,000		
	—title insurance	1,000	13,500	46,250
	Add 15%			6,938
				53,188

Most favourable value is Base A		
Net sale proceeds		392,000
Less Base A value		132,000
		260,000
Less annual exemption		50,000
Chargeable realised development value		210,000
DLT payable thereon at 60%		£126,000

CAPITAL GAINS TAX COMPUTATION

Net sale proceeds		392,000
Cost in 1966	32,000	
Incidental costs of acquisition	750	
Conversion 1972	7,500	
Enhancement and protection of title	6,000	46,250
		345,750
Less chargeable to DLT		210,000
Chargeable to capital gains tax (subject to indexation allowance)		£135,750

7
Capital transfer tax: general principles

Basis of charge (FA 1975, ss 19–22, 37; FA 1982, s 91)

Capital transfer tax (CTT) was introduced to replace estate duty as a tax on wealth at death and to extend it by charging tax on lifetime gifts and on certain transfers to and from trusts. Not all lifetime gifts are liable, those which are being called chargeable transfers. There are two scales of rates, one applying to transfers on death or within the three years before death, and the other to lifetime transfers made more than three years before death.

Transfers are accumulated and tax is payable when a statutory threshold is reached, currently £60,000. The rate of tax then rises progressively through various bands. See the tables of rates at the front of the book. Transfers made more than ten years earlier are excluded from the accumulation. A final transfer is deemed to be made on death and the tax charged on the estate depends on the cumulative total of lifetime transfers in the previous ten years and the deemed transfer at death.

The threshold and the rate bands are increased annually in line with increases in the retail prices index. However these increases do not enable tax paid on earlier transfers to be recovered.

Persons liable (FA 1975, ss 24, 45, Sch 7(7)(8))

UK domiciled individuals are chargeable in respect of property anywhere in the world and non-UK domiciled individuals in respect of property in the UK. In contrast to the income tax and capital gains tax treatment (see pages 263 and 34), husband and wife are separate chargeable persons for capital transfer tax. Domicile (see page 303 for the normal interpretation of domicile) has an extended meaning for capital transfer tax, and a person is deemed to be UK domiciled if:

(a) he was UK domiciled on or after 10 December 1974 and within the three years preceding the transfer, or
(b) he was resident in the UK on or after 10 December 1974 and in at least 17 of the 20 tax years up to and including the year of transfer.

Those becoming domiciled in the Channel Islands or the Isle of Man used to be deemed to remain UK domiciled but this provision has been removed for transfers on or after 15 March 1983.

Double taxation relief is given where the transfer of assets attracts tax overseas as well as in the UK.

Essential definitions (FA 1975, ss 20, 23, 24, Sch 5 and Sch 7)

A person's estate is the aggregate of all the property to which he is beneficially entitled. As well as his own property, this includes:

(i) An interest as a joint tenant. Such an interest accrues by survivorship to the other joint tenant(s). (This differs from a share as a tenant in common, which means each person has a separate share which he may dispose of as he wishes.)
(ii) An entitlement to receive the income from a trust fund (called an interest in possession).

The inclusion of trust funds in a person's estate means that on his death or earlier cessation to the entitlement from the fund he is deemed to make a chargeable transfer of the amount comprised in the fund, although the tax is paid by the trustees. Special provisions apply in relation to discretionary trusts, where no-one is entitled as of right to the income from the fund, and the trustees merely have a discretionary power to pay it. Favourable treatment is given to discretionary trusts that are accumulation and maintenance trusts for minor children. The treatment of the various types of trust is dealt with in detail in chapter 45.

A transfer of value is any disposition made by a person (the transferor) as a result of which the value of his estate immediately after the disposition is less than it would be but for the disposition and this decrease in the value of the estate is the value transferred by the transfer.

There is a choice as to who pays the CTT which affects the amount of the transfer. If the transferor pays the CTT this decreases his estate still further and the amount of the transfer includes the CTT payable. If the person receiving the gift (the transferee) pays the CTT the tax does not decrease the transferor's estate and is not part of the transfer of value. This means that the amount of the transfer is lower (and so is the CTT) if the transferee pays the tax. It also means that a gift has to be 'grossed-up' to arrive at the tax payable if the transferor pays the tax. This is illustrated in example 1 below.

If any capital gains tax is payable as a result of the gift, it is left out of account in calculating the decrease in the estate. In addition transfers of 'excluded property' are ignored. The most common forms of excluded property are property situated overseas where the owner is not domiciled in the UK, and reversionary interests in trust funds.

Commercial transactions and other arm's length transactions are not treated as transfers of value.

A chargeable transfer is any transfer of value made after 26 March 1974 other than an exempt transfer (see below).

Effect of changes in the tax threshold and rate bands

Where there are changes in the tax threshold, rate bands and rates of tax, the new levels are used to calculate the tax on subsequent transfers, but there is no question of a repayment being made of tax paid earlier. The changes may, however, mean that part of the tax-free threshold and lower rate bands can be used again. See example 1.

Example 1

Mr A's first chargeable transfer was on 30 November 1982 when he made a gift of £72,000. He paid the CTT himself. On 30 June 1983 he made a further chargeable transfer of £35,000 but this time the recipient, Mr B, paid the tax.

	Chargeable transfers £	CTT £	'Net' transfers £
Transfer on 30 November 1982	75,000	3,000	72,000
CTT payable by Mr A is £3,000			
Change of rates on 15 March 1983			
Adjustment of previous transfers	75,000	2,250	72,750
Transfer on 30 June 1983	35,000	6,000	29,000
Cumulative transfers carried forward	£110,000	£8,250	£101,750
CTT payable by Mr B is £6,000			

The fact that transfers made more than ten years earlier drop out of account may also enable that part of the threshold and the lower rate bands to be used again.

Death within three years after a lifetime transfer

In the first instance tax on a lifetime transfer will be calculated according to the lifetime rates. However if the transferor dies within three years of the transfer, tax is recomputed on the higher death scale and any additional tax arising is payable by the donee. If the tax rates have changed between the lifetime transfer and the date of death, the additional tax due at death is calculated by deducting the tax originally paid from that shown to be due using the new scale.

Exempt transfers

A transfer of value is reduced by exemptions to arrive at the chargeable transfer. Some of these exemptions apply only to lifetime transfers. Others apply on death as well.

Transfers between husband and wife in lifetime or on death (FA 1975, Sch 6)

All such transfers are exempt, except where the transferee spouse is foreign domiciled and the transferor spouse is UK domiciled, when transfers are only exempt to a cumulative total of £55,000.

Small gifts to same person (FA 1975, Sch 6)

Any outright lifetime gifts to any one person in any one tax year are exempt if the total gifts to that person do not exceed £250 in that year.

Annual transfers not exceeding £3,000 (FA 1975, Sch 6)

The first £3,000 of lifetime transfers in any tax year are exempt. Any unused portion of the exemption may be carried forward for one year only for use in the following tax year after the exemption for that following year has been used.

Normal expenditure out of income (FA 1975, Sch 6)

To obtain exemption the gift must be:

(a) Part of the donor's normal expenditure
(b) Made out of income (taking one year with another)
(c) Such as will not reduce the donor's available net income (after all other transfers) below that required to maintain his usual standard of living. The exemption will usually apply to life assurance policy premiums paid for the benefit of another.

Gifts in consideration of marriage (FA 1975, Sch 6)

A gift of up to £5,000 by a parent of a party to a marriage, of £2,500 by a lineal ancestor, of £2,500 by one party to the marriage to the other, or of £1,000 by any other person, is exempt providing it is a lifetime gift made in consideration of the marriage. If the gift is into a marriage settlement it must be primarily for the benefit of the parties to the marriage, their children or their children's spouses. The limit applies to gifts by any one donor for any one marriage.

Gifts to charities (FA 1975, Sch 6)

Gifts to charities, either outright or to be held on trust for charitable purposes, are wholly exempt. The £250,000 limit on transfers made on or within one year of death has been removed for transfers on or after 15 March 1983.

Gifts to political parties (FA 1975, Sch 6)

If the gift is made to a political party more than twelve months before death it is wholly exempt, but if made within one year before or on death, only the first £100,000 is exempt. To qualify, a party must either have at least two MPs in the House of Commons, or one MP and at least 150,000 votes in its favour in the last general election.

Gifts for national purposes or public benefit (FA 1975, Sch 6)

All such qualifying gifts are exempt.

Conditional exemption for heritage property (FA 1976, ss 76–83)

In certain circumstances, conditional exemption will be given on the transfer of property that is designated by the Treasury as of national, scientific, historic, artistic, architectural or scenic interest (e.g. works of art and historic buildings). Various undertakings regarding the property must be given and if there is any material breach of an undertaking, capital transfer tax becomes payable.

Maintenance funds for heritage property (FA 1982, ss 93–95, 117, and Sch 16)

Transfers into a settlement established for the maintenance, repair or preservation of heritage property are exempt providing a Treasury direction is made in respect of the property.

Voidable transfers (FA 1976, s 88)

Where a transfer is set aside by enactment or rule of law (e.g. bankruptcy) the original transfer and the transfer back become exempt.

Mutual transfers (FA 1976, ss 86 and 87; FA 1980, s 87; FA 1981, s 93)

Where a person makes a chargeable transfer and within ten years the recipient makes a gift back to him, the gift back is wholly or partially exempt from CTT (depending on the amounts involved), and the original transfer is wholly or partly cancelled with a resulting repayment of tax to the original transferor. The amount cancelled depends on the amounts of the transfers and the time lapse between them.

Capital transfers for family maintenance (FA 1975, s 46)

It may sometimes be necessary to make transfers of capital for family provision, for example following the dissolution of a marriage, when the usual exemption for transfer between husband and wife has ceased to apply, or for the reasonable provision of a dependent relative. Such transfers may be made without attracting capital transfer tax.

Waivers of remuneration and dividends (FA 1976, ss 91 and 92)

A waiver or repayment of remuneration is not a transfer of value. Similarly a waiver of dividends made within twelve months before any right to the dividend has accrued is not a transfer of value.

Valuation of property (FA 1975, ss 22, 38, and Sch 10)

The value of property for capital transfer tax is the amount it might reasonably be expected to fetch if sold in the open market. The price is not, however, to be reduced on the grounds that the whole property is placed on the market at one time.

If the asset to be transferred will give rise to a capital gains tax liability, and the donee agrees to pay that tax, then the value transferred is reduced by the capital gains tax paid. However, capital gains tax will often not arise on gifts because of the gifts roll-over provisions. See page 42.

Valuation on death

Apart from life assurance policies (see below) the value of property to be included in the estate at death is that immediately prior to death. Changes in the value of the estate as a result of the death are taken into account, other than changes relating to life interests or property passing by survivorship. Allowance is made for reasonable funeral expenses. In the case of overseas property, allowance is also made for additional expenses incurred because of its situation, subject to a limit of 5% of the value of the property.

Quoted securities and land transferred on death

Where an estate on death includes quoted securities and they are sold within twelve months of death, then the aggregate sales proceeds before expenses of all such securities may be substituted for the death value. Similarly if the estate includes land which is sold within three years after death, relief is available for the reduction in value by comparing the gross sale value of all land sold within three years after death with the value at death.

Related property

In some instances, if an asset is divided up, the total value of the parts may be less than the value of the whole. There are special 'related property' provisions to counter this type of tax avoidance. Property in a person's estate is related to:

(a) Property belonging to his spouse
(b) Property which was the subject of an exempt transfer by the taxpayer to a charity, political party or national heritage body and which is still owned by that body or has been so owned at any time within the previous five years.

If it produces a higher value than its unrelated value, the value of a part of related property is taken as an appropriate portion of the total value of all the property. See example 2.

If related property is sold within three years after death to an unconnected person, a claim may be made for the tax at death to be recomputed using its unrelated value.

Example 2

The shareholders of Related Ltd, an unquoted company, are Mr R 40%, Mrs R 25%, others 35%. Shareholdings are valued as follows:

65%	£58,500
40%	£24,000
25%	£15,000

Capital transfer tax values are:

Mr R $40/65 \times$ £58,500 £36,000 (being greater than £24,000)
Mrs R $25/65 \times$ £58,500 £22,500 (being greater than £15,000)

Life assurance policies

The valuation of life assurance policies depends on whether the transfer is during the lifetime or on the death of the transferor. Policies subject to a lifetime transfer are valued at market value except that they cannot normally be valued at less than the total of the premiums paid. Sometimes it is the policy premiums, rather than the policy itself, which are transfers of value (e.g. where a policy is written in trust for another person) and in such cases each premium payment will be a chargeable transfer unless it is covered by one of the exemptions (see pages 57 to 58).

On death the maturity value of a policy taken out by a person on his own life will be included in his estate unless it has been assigned to someone else, or it has been written in trust. The premiums on assigned and trust policies will usually have been covered by exemptions.

Associated operations (FA 1975, s 44)

There are rules to enable the Revenue to treat a series of connected operations as a single transfer made at the time of the last of them.

Business property relief (FA 1976, Sch 10)

Business property relief is given on valuing transfers of business property, providing certain conditions as to the length of ownership and type of business are satisfied. The relief is given at the following rates:

A business or interest in a business (including a partnership share) and controlling shareholdings 50%
Non-controlling unquoted shareholdings and land or buildings, machinery or plant used for a business carried on by:
a company of which the transferor has control; or
a partnership in which the transferor was a partner; or
the transferor, being settled property in which he had an interest in possession 30%

The property must normally have been owned by the transferor throughout the previous two years. Business property relief is not available where the business consists of dealing in stocks and shares (except stock-jobbers and discount houses), dealing in land and buildings or holding investments (including land which is let).

The relief is applied automatically without a claim and is given after agricultural property relief (see below) but before exemptions (see pages 57 to 58 above).

Agricultural property relief (FA 1981, Sch 14)

Agricultural property relief is available on the transfer of agricultural property so long as various conditions are met. The relief, which is a percentage reduction of the transfer of value (see below), only applies to the agricultural value of the property and in arriving at that value any loan secured on the agricultural property must be deducted.

The agricultural property must at the time of the transfer have been either occupied by the transferor for agriculture throughout the two years ending with the date of transfer or owned by the transferor throughout the previous seven years and occupied for agriculture by him or another throughout that period. In certain circumstances these rules are modified if the property transferred was acquired as a replacement for other agricultural property.

Relief is available both on the transfer of agricultural property itself, and on the transfer of shares out of a controlling holding in a farming company to the extent of the underlying agricultural value.

Relief is given at the rate of 50% where the transferor had the right to vacant possession immediately before the transfer (or the right to obtain vacant possession within the next twelve months) and 30% on tenanted agricultural property. Transitional provisions enable relief to be claimed at the 50% rate on tenanted agricultural property where the transferor had been beneficially entitled to his interest in the property since before 10 March 1981 and would have been entitled to the 50% rate under the former provisions for agricultural relief which operated before that date.

Where agricultural property satisfies the conditions for business property relief, agricultural property relief is given first and business property relief is given on the non-agricultural value. As with business property relief, agricultural property relief is given without the need for a claim.

Binding contract for sale (FA 1976, Sch 10(3); FA 1981, Sch 14(14))

Property does not qualify for business or agricultural relief if it is subject to a binding contract for sale (except in cases of a conversion of an unincorporated business to a company, or a company reconstruction). A 'buy and sell' agreement made by partners or company directors to take effect on their death is considered by the Revenue to constitute such a contract, but it is understood that a double option agreement whereby the deceased's personal representatives have an option to sell and the surviving partners or directors an option to buy would not be so treated.

Growing timber (FA 1975, Sch 9)

Where an estate on death includes growing timber, an election may be made to leave the timber (but not the land on which it stands) out of account in valuing the estate at death. The relief is dealt with in chapter 31.

Quick succession relief (FA 1981, s 101)

Where a person dies shortly after receiving a chargeable transfer, the transfer has increased his estate at death and therefore attracts tax in his estate as well as having been taxed at the time of the earlier transfer. Relief is given where the death occurs within five years of the earlier transfer. There is no requirement to retain the actual asset obtained by that transfer.

The total tax on the chargeable estate is calculated in the normal way and reduced by the quick succession relief. The relief is the following percentage of the tax paid on the previous transfer, reduced in the proportion of net value received by the deceased over the gross chargeable transfer:

Period between transfer and death	Percentage relief
Less than 1 year	100%
1–2 years	80%
2–3 years	60%
3–4 years	40%
4–5 years	20%

Quick succession relief is also available where there are successive charges within five years on trust property in which there subsists an interest in possession. The rates of relief are the same as those quoted above, with the percentage relief depending on the period between the successive charges.

Survivorship clauses (FA 1975, Sch 5(22A))

Although the tax on successive transfers is mitigated by quick succession relief where death occurs within five years, this is not so beneficial as the value not being included at all. It is possible to include a survivorship clause in a will stipulating that assets do not pass to the intended beneficiary unless he/she survives the deceased by a prescribed period, limited to a maximum of six months. This avoids the double charge to tax.

Deeds of family arrangement (FA 1978, s 68)

The way in which a deceased's estate is distributed, either under a will or on intestacy, may be varied by those entitled to it, and legacies may be disclaimed wholly or in part. Where this happens within two years of the death the variation or disclaimer is not a separate transfer of value provided that written notice is given to the Revenue within six months of the date of the instrument of variation or disclaimer. This must be signed by those making it and by the personal representatives if it results in additional tax being paid by them. Capital transfer tax will then be payable as if the revised distribution had operated at death.

Interest free loans

Where a loan is made free of interest there is no transfer of capital and it is usually possible to regard the interest foregone as being normal expenditure out of income and thus exempt. If, however, a loan is made for a fixed period, or is not repayable on demand, it may be treated as a transfer of value equal to the difference between the amount lent and the present value of the future right to repayment.

Date of payment and interest on overdue tax (FA 1975, Sch 4; F (No 2)A 1983, s 11)

The normal due dates of payment and interest provisions are as follows:

	Due date	Interest per annum
Lifetime transfers between 6 April and 30 September	30 April in following year	8% from due date of payment
Lifetime transfers between 1 October and 5 April	6 months after end of month in which transfer was made	8% from due date of payment
Death—additional tax on lifetime transfers or tax on gifts to political parties	6 months after end of month in which death occurs	6% from due date of payment
Death—other assets	On delivery of the account by personal representatives.	6% from six months after end of month in which death occurred.

Interest on overdue tax is not tax deductible and interest on overpaid tax is tax free. Overpayments carry interest from the date of payment at the same rate as that charged on overdue tax.

Where tax has not been paid because a transfer was conditionally exempt the due date is six months after the end of the month in which the event by reason of which it is chargeable occurs.

Payment by instalments

Tax may be paid by equal yearly instalments over ten years (previously eight yearly or sixteen half yearly instalments prior to 15 March 1983) on certain assets transferred on death, and also on lifetime transfers if the *donee* pays the tax. The first instalment is due on death transfers six months from the end of the month in which the death occurred, and on lifetime transfers on the normal due date.

The instalment option applies to land wherever situated, to a business or interest in a business, to timber when it becomes chargeable after being left out of account on a previous death, to controlling shareholdings, and to unquoted shares if certain conditions are met.

Interest normally runs only from the date the instalment falls due and not on the full amount of the deferred tax. This does not apply in the case of land, other than business or agricultural land, nor in the case of shares in an investment company. Interest in those two cases is charged on the total amount remaining unpaid after the normal due date, the interest being added to each instalment as it falls due.

If the property is sold the outstanding tax becomes payable immediately.

Liability for tax (FA 1975, ss 25, 26 and 28)

On lifetime transfers of unsettled property, primary liability for payment rests with the donor (except in the case of transfers within three years prior to death where the liability for any extra tax payable is that of the donee). The donor and donee may, however, agree between them who is to pay, the transfer having to be grossed up if the donor pays.

In the case of lifetime transfers of settled property, the primary liability is that of the trustees.

On transfers made on death, the personal representatives are liable to pay the tax on unsettled property and on settled UK land that devolves on them; for other settled property the liability rests with the trustees.

In addition to the persons mentioned, certain other people may be liable to pay capital transfer tax, but usually only where tax remains unpaid after the due date. Where tax is unpaid there is normally an Inland Revenue charge on the property concerned.

Where a gift to a political party is chargeable on the excess over £100,000 because it is made within one year before death, only the political party is liable for the tax.

The person who is liable to pay capital transfer tax is not necessarily the person who ultimately bears the tax. The trustees of a settlement are liable to pay the tax arising on the transfer of trust funds, but the next person to enjoy the income or to receive the capital bears the tax because the trust funds are correspondingly lower. Personal representatives are liable to pay the tax on the free estate at death, but the residuary legatees will suffer the tax by a reduction in the amount available for them, the other legatees receiving their legacies in full unless the will specifies that any particular legacy should bear its own tax.

8
Stamp and capital duties

Background

Stamp duty is a fixed or ad valorem charge on legal instruments. It has been charged since the seventeenth century, and present legislation is based on the Stamp Act 1981 as amended by numerous subsequent Finance and other Acts.

Capital duty was introduced in the Finance Act 1973. It is an ad valorem duty on chargeable transactions (which need not, though invariably will, involve the use of instruments), payable only by capital companies.

Both duties are administered by the Commissioners of Inland Revenue through the Office of the Controller of Stamps.

Stamp duty

'Heads' and basis of charge (mainly in SA 1891, Sch 1)

Stamp duty is charged on instruments executed in the UK or relating to UK property or transactions. No duty arises on transactions which are carried out orally.

Generally instruments should be stamped before execution although in practice the Commissioners permit stamping within thirty days without charging any penalty.

Duty is either fixed or ad valorem depending upon the head of charge under which the transaction falls. Some of the main heads of charge and rates of duty (some of which are on a sliding scale) are given in the table below.

Head of charge	Rate of duty
Bearer instruments	
Inland bearer instruments (other than deposit certificates for overseas stock)	3 times transfer duty
Overseas bearer instruments (other than deposit certificates for overseas stock or bearer instruments by usage)	Twice transfer duty
Bearer instruments excluded above	10p per £50 or part

Contract notes

Value of stock not exceeding £100	Nil
£100.01 to £500	10p
£500.01 to £1,500	30p
in excess of £1,500	60p

Conveyances or transfers on sale

Ordinary rate—For consideration:

not exceeding £5	10p
£5.01 to £100—for every £10 or part	20p
£100.01 to £300—for every £20 or part	40p
in excess of £300—for every £50 or part	£1

Reduced rate for 'certified transactions':

not exceeding £25,000	Nil
£25,001 to £30,000—for every £50 or part	25p
£30,001 to £35,000—for every £50 or part	50p
£35,001 to £40,000—for every £50 or part	75p

Leases

For definite term less than 1 year of furnished dwelling house at rent in excess of £500 per annum	£1
For any other definite or indefinite term (rent)	Ad valorem duty from 0 to 24% on sliding scale by reference to average rent
For any other definite or indefinite term (premium)	As for conveyances or transfers on sale

Life assurance policies

For two years or less	5p
Other policies—sum assured:	
not more than £50	Nil
between £50 and £1,000	5p per £100 or part
over £1,000	50p per £1,000 or part

Purchased life annuities and superannuation annuities

5p per £10 or part

Unit trust instruments

On value of property subject to the trusts	25p per £100 or part

Voluntary dispositions

As for conveyances on sale

There are many other heads, a number of which attract only a fixed duty of 50p. There are numerous exemptions and reliefs from each head. Where a deed (i.e. a document under seal) does not come within a specific head it normally attracts a 50p duty, but certain deeds of covenant to pay a fixed annual sum to charities or others are specifically exempt.

Adjudication and valuation (SA 1891, s 12)

Adjudication is the process whereby the Commissioners assess the amount of duty, if any, payable on an instrument. Adjudication may be voluntary or compulsory. Any person may voluntarily request the Commissioners to express their opinion as to whether an instrument is chargeable, and if so, to state the amount of duty payable. In certain instances legislation provides that adjudication is compulsory, for example in the case of voluntary dispositions, and where exemption is claimed from capital and stamp duty because a demerger is an 'exempt distribution' (see chapter 29).

Having considered the instrument the Commissioners will either stamp the document 'adjudged not chargeable with any stamp duty' or they will assess the duty due and on receipt will stamp the document 'adjudged duly stamped'. An adjudication stamp is normally conclusive evidence against third parties of due stamping.

Bearer instruments

Bearer instruments are little used, but they have a particular significance in relation to share acquisitions because it is provided that no duty is payable on renounceable letters of allotment where the rights are renounceable not later than six months after issue. This enables a considerable stamp duty saving to be made when a company is being sold to a purchaser who acquires its shares. New equity shares are issued out of reserves on renounceable letters of allotment and the existing equity shares are con-verted into low value shares, for example deferred ordinary shares. The major part of the company's value is then transferred on the renounceable letters of allotment which, when renounced in favour of the purchaser, attract no duty (see chapter 28).

Contract notes (F(1909–10)A 1910)

Contract notes are issued by brokers on the sale or purchase of marketable securities.

Contract notes relating to options to buy or sell and to the exercise of such an option bear duty at half the normal rates.

Duty on contract notes can be denoted by an impressed stamp or an adhesive stamp cancelled by the issuing broker writing his initials and date over the name. Many brokers arrange with the Commissioners to use franking machines and prepay the duty.

Conveyances and transfers on sale (FA 1963, s 55 and Sch 11; FA 1958, s 34)

Instruments relating to sales of all types of property (other than property passing by delivery) are covered under this heading, and transactions such as the release of an interest in property, the surrender of a lease, or a deed of family arrangement where cash adjustments are made by way of (inter alia) compensation are included.

The nil or reduced rates of charge apply only to certified transactions. A certificate cannot be given for a lease where the rent exceeds £300 per annum or for the transfer of stock or marketable securities, or units in a unit trust. An instrument is certified at a particular amount if it contains a statement that the transaction contained therein does not form part of a larger transaction or series of transactions whose value exceeds the certified amount.

Certificates are also required for the following transactions (see below):

(a) Equality money paid on an exchange or partition.
(b) Voluntary dispositions.
(c) Premiums paid under leases.

Exchange or partition

Where an instrument effects an exchange or partition of freehold land, and consideration ('equality money') exceeding £100 is given, ad valorem duty is payable on the equality money at conveyance-on-sale rates. Where the equality money is less than £100 a fixed duty of 50p is payable.

In the current depressed housing market many house builders are prepared to accept a purchaser's existing house on a trade-in basis. Where they do so considerable savings on stamp duty can be effected, as duty will only become payable if the equality money exceeds £25,000 (provided that a certificate of value is obtained—see above).

Voluntary dispositions

Any conveyance or transfer operating as a voluntary disposition inter vivos is chargeable with the same duty as if it were a conveyance or transfer on sale. Outright gifts and transfers at inadequate consideration are always voluntary dispositions. Inadequate consideration is deemed to exist where a substantial benefit accrues to the transferee either by reason of the inadequacy of the sum paid or by reason of other circumstances. Thus a bona fide arm's length sale at inadequate consideration may be liable as a voluntary disposition.

Unless specifically exempted voluntary dispositions must be adjudicated and the general basis for valuation is the price paid between a willing buyer and seller. Specific exemptions include conveyances of property to non-profit making bodies incorporated under Act of Parliament who hold property as an open space or for the benefit of the nation. Other exempt transactions are conveyances where no beneficial interest passes and conveyances made for nominal consideration to secure the repayment of a loan.

Premiums on leases of land and buildings

Where a premium is paid on a lease for a definite term exceeding one year or for an indefinite term the premium is treated as the consideration on a conveyance or transfer on sale and chargeable accordingly. The reduced rates for certified transactions apply to the premium unless the rent payable under the lease exceeds £300 per annum.

Surrenders of leases

Where a lease is surrendered, duty is payable on any consideration paid by the landlord as for a conveyance on sale. If no consideration passes a fixed duty of 50p is charged. Where the provisions of a lease can only be altered by surrender and re-grant, for example the alteration of the term, the re-granted lease will bear the appropriate duty but no duty will be paid on the surrender of the old lease.

Trusts

No stamp duty is charged on the creation of a trust by will.

When a trust is created in lifetime the stamp duty charged will depend on the way the trust is declared and the property vested.

There will be a minimum 50p stamp on any written declaration of trust. Property that is vested in the trustees by way of conveyance or transfer will usually attract ad valorem duty as a voluntary disposition. Property that can be vested in some other way, for example cash, does not require an instrument and will not attract duty if the trust is declared orally. If the trust is declared in writing prior to the transfer there will be a 50p declaration of trust stamp. If the property is vested before the trust is declared the trust document will attract ad valorem duty as a transfer of beneficial interest.

It is therefore common to avoid ad valorem duty by establishing a trust with only a minimal amount. Later transfers of property into the trust may or may not attract ad valorem duty, depending on the nature of the property.

Once a trust has been created the trustees are subject to stamp duty in the same way as any other person. Thus if they purchase shares they will pay the stamp duty on the contract note.

If a new trustee is subsequently appointed the deed of appointment attracts a fixed duty of 50p.

Ad valorem duty does not arise on a transfer of trust property to a beneficiary, although a 50p duty may be payable.

Termination of a trust will usually attract duty only at the fixed rate of 50p.

Capital duty (FA 1973, s 47)

Capital duty is charged at the rate of £1 for every £100 or part thereof on chargeable transactions by capital companies if the place of effective management is in Great Britain, or the registered office is in Great Britain and the place of effective management is outside the EEC. UK-registered companies whose place of effective management is in the EEC will thus not be chargeable, since they will usually be subject to a comparable charge in the EEC state concerned.

Payment is due on or before the expiry of one month following the date of the transaction. Failure to pay by the due date renders the person responsible for payment liable to a fine of 5% of the duty plus a further 5% for every month that the duty remains unpaid.

Capital company (FA 1973, s 48(1))

The definition of capital company covers UK limited companies and limited liability partnerships, EEC companies and companies dealt with on a stock exchange in the EEC. Unit trusts are expressly excluded.

Chargeable transactions (FA 1973, Sch 19)

The main examples of chargeable transactions are the formation of a capital company or an increase in its capital (other than by bonus issue).

The amount on which duty is payable is normally the value of the assets contributed by members. There are exemptions and reliefs where issues of or increases in capital take place on the redemption of preference shares, or on company reconstructions, or following previous reductions of capital as a result of losses, or under the demerger provisions of FA 1980, Sch 18.

9
Value added tax: general principles

Basis of charge (VATA 1983, ss 1, 2)

Value added tax (VAT) is charged on the supply of goods and services in the UK and on the import of goods and certain services into the UK. It applies where the supplies are taxable supplies made in the course of business by a taxable person.

References are to Value Added Tax Act 1983 unless otherwise stated.

Taxable supplies (s 3 and Sch 2)

All supplies of goods and services (including goods taken for own use) are taxable supplies, apart from items which are specifically exempt (see below). Goods for own use are valued at cost. Business gifts are taxable supplies (valued at cost) except where the gift is valued at £10 or less and does not form part of a series of gifts to the same person.

Exempt supplies (s 17 and Sch 6)

Exempt supplies are broadly supplies of:

Land	Betting, lotteries and gaming (except
Insurance	takings from gaming and amuse-
Postal services (but not telephones)	ment machines)
Education	Health services
Finance services	Burial and cremation

Who is a taxable person (Sch 1)

You are liable to be registered for VAT if the taxable turnover of all your business activities is expected to exceed £18,000 in the next twelve months. You are required to notify Customs and Excise immediately and will be registered from the date you became liable to register.

Liability to register also arises at the end of a quarter if turnover exceeded £6,000 in that quarter, or £18,000 in that and the previous three quarters, unless Customs and Excise are satisfied that the turnover in that quarter and the next three will not exceed £18,000. You must notify Customs and Excise within ten days from the end of the quarter and will be registered from twenty-one days after the quarter end.

See also below as regards voluntary registration.

Notification is made on form VAT 1 and a certificate of registration VAT 4 is then issued showing the VAT registration number.

There are provisions for groups of companies to have group registration if they wish.

Customs and Excise have discretion to exempt someone who makes only zero-rated supplies (see below) from registration if that person does not wish to be registered.

Cancellation of registration

Cancellation of VAT registration may be requested if you can show that your tax-inclusive turnover in the next twelve months will be £17,000 or less, or if you have been registered for two years or more and your tax-inclusive turnover in each of those years has been £18,000 or less. This will not apply if there are reasonable grounds for believing that taxable supplies will exceed £18,000 in the next year.

Rates of tax (s 9)

VAT is currently charged at only two rates, a standard rate of 15% and the zero rate.

Zero rate (s 16 and Sch 5)

The main zero-rated items are:

Food, except where supplied in the course of catering, or where it is pet food, or a 'non-essential' item such as chocolate, ice cream, alcoholic and fruit drinks or crisps
Water and sewerage services
Books (but not stationery)

Newspaper advertisements
Construction of buildings (but not repair or maintenance)
Children's clothing and footwear
Fuel and power (except petrol)
Transport (but not taxis or hire cars)
Drugs and medicines on prescription
Exports

How the System Works (ss 14, 15)

Each person in the chain between the first supplier and the final consumer is charged tax on taxable supplies to him (input tax) and charges tax on taxable supplies made by him (output tax). He pays over to Customs and Excise the excess of output tax over input tax, or recovers the excess of input tax over output tax. The broad effect of the scheme is that businesses are not affected by VAT except in so far as they are required to administer it, and the burden of the tax falls on the consumer. This is, however, modified by the rules relating to turnover thresholds and exemption, because businesses that do not make taxable supplies have to recover VAT suffered by them in the prices they charge.

VAT repayments are likely to arise where most supplies are zero-rated. The effect of the zero rate is that the person is making taxable supplies, albeit charged at a nil rate, and can therefore recover input tax suffered. If you make exempt supplies you are outside the scheme and cannot recover input tax (except under the partial exemption rules—see below).

You can recover input tax not only on goods for resale but also on expenses such as telephones and stationery and on capital items. You cannot, however, recover input tax on cars, other than for resale, or on business entertaining, other than of overseas customers. Output tax must likewise be charged on all taxable supplies, including for example sales of fixed assets like plant and machinery. Where business cars are sold, VAT is only payable on the excess if any of the selling price over cost.

If your business petrol bills include petrol for private use by employees an apportionment must be made to exclude the non-business proportion.

If you offer a cash discount you charge VAT only on the discounted amount whether the discount is taken or not.

Second-hand goods (s 18)

In general second-hand goods are taxable on the full selling price, but there are special schemes for cars, caravans and motor cycles, boats and outboard motors, works of art and antiques. Subject to certain conditions VAT is charged under the special schemes only on the excess of selling price over cost.

Imports (s 19)

VAT is chargeable on imports when they are entered for home use, so that the UK trader must account for tax on them at that time. If you are a registered trader you are entitled to deduct the tax as input tax in the same return, so that the net effect is nil, unless you are affected by the rules for partial exemption (see below). If the goods are for resale, output tax will be accounted for in the normal way when they are sold.

Voluntary registration

Voluntary registration may be applied for even though your turnover is below the statutory limits. You will then charge VAT on your supplies and recover input tax suffered. This may be beneficial if your customers are mainly taxable persons, but not where they are the general public. Registration will bring the burden of complying with the administrative requirements of the scheme, so may not be thought worthwhile even though a price advantage may arise. See example 1.

Example 1

You are in business as a handyman and pay input tax of £500 on phone, stationery etc. Your turnover is £10,000, including £500 to cover the tax suffered.

If you register voluntarily for VAT, you need only charge £9,500 for the same supplies and your turnover will then be:

£9,500 + 15% VAT £1,425 = £10,925.

You will pay to Customs and Excise £1,425 less £500 = £925, leaving you with £10,000 as before. If your customers are the general public your prices to them will be £925 higher, but if they are taxable persons they will recover £1,425, so that their net price will be £9,500.

Exemption and partial exemption (SI 1980/1536 Pt V)

If you make only exempt supplies you do not charge VAT but you cannot recover input tax charged to you, so your prices must include an element to recover the VAT suffered. Some businesses make both taxable and exempt supplies and are thus partially exempt.

If you are partially exempt you can recover all input tax suffered despite the exempt supplies if your exempt outputs are:

(a) Less than £200 per month on average; or
(b) Less than 50% of your total outputs and less than £8,000 per month on average; or
(c) Less than 25% of your total outputs and less than £16,000 per month on average; or
(d) Less than 5% of your total outputs.

If exempt supplies exceed these limits only a proportion of the input tax suffered may be claimed. The proportion is usually either a straight fraction of taxable outputs to total outputs, or, where some input tax can be specifically identified as relating to taxable supplies, the whole of that input tax plus the fraction of the remainder that taxable outputs bear to total outputs. If neither method is suitable you may agree with Customs and Excise a special method adapted to your own circumstances.

Special schemes for retailers

The normal VAT procedure requires records to be kept of every separate transaction. Retailers would find it virtually impossible to keep such detailed records, so there are various special schemes—nine in all—which enable retailers to calculate output tax in a way that suits their particular circumstances.

Losses and bad debts (s 22)

If goods are lost or destroyed before being sold, output tax is not chargeable.

You cannot recover VAT charged on a supply where the customer fails to pay unless he is formally declared insolvent. In that event you can reclaim the VAT charged and will then claim in the insolvency for the VAT exclusive amount.

Records and returns (Sch 7)

You are required to supply tax invoices in respect of taxable supplies, to keep a VAT account showing the results for each tax period, and to make returns to Customs and Excise showing the VAT payable or repayable.

Tax invoices (SI 1980/1536)

You must provide and keep a copy of a tax invoice showing the following:

Identifying number
Tax point (see below)
Your name, address and VAT registration number
Customer's name and address
Type of supply (e.g. sale, hire purchase, rental)
Description of goods or services supplied, and for each type of goods, the quantity, rate of tax and tax exclusive amount payable
Total amount payable excluding VAT
Rate of cash discount offered
Total tax chargeable

Retailers may provide a less detailed invoice omitting the customer's name and address and the amount (but not the rate) of VAT, if the tax inclusive price is £50 or less. Copies of these less detailed invoices need not be kept.

Tax point (time of supply) (ss 4, 5)

The basic tax point is normally when goods are made available or services are performed, unless they are invoiced and/or paid for earlier, in which case the earlier date is the tax point. Where goods or services are invoiced within fourteen days after supply the later date is the tax point, and if you invoice monthly you can adopt a monthly tax point.

VAT account, tax periods and tax returns

The results for each tax period must be summarised in a VAT account. Returns are made to Customs and Excise on form VAT 100 for each tax period, showing the VAT payable or repayable and certain statistical information.

A tax period is normally three months, but if you regularly claim VAT repayments (for example because you make mainly zero-rated supplies) you may have a one-month period if you wish. The advantage of earlier repayments in those circumstances must be weighed against the disadvantage of having to complete twelve returns annually.

Quarterly return dates are staggered over the year depending on your business classification. You can ask for the dates to be changed to coincide with your accounting period.

Changes in circumstances

Where your circumstances change you are required to notify Customs and Excise. Some changes require cancellation of your registration, others merely an amendment.

Your registration will require cancellation when you cease business, or take in a partner, or revert from a partnership to a sole proprietor, or incorporate or disincorporate your business, or cease to make taxable supplies. You must notify Customs and Excise within ten days of the change. In some circumstances it is possible to transfer your registration number to the new business.

Many changes require amendment to your registration, such as changes in the composition of a partnership, change of business name, changes in a group of companies, change of address and so on. Such changes must be notified within twenty-one days.

Selling a business as a going concern

If you sell all or part of a business as a going concern you do not normally have to account for VAT on the sale consideration, and the purchaser does not have any input tax to reclaim. This does not apply when you merely sell assets, rather than an identifiable part of the business which is capable of separate operation. The sale of a family company is dealt with in chapter 28.

Administration and appeals (Sch 8)

VAT is administered by Customs and Excise. If you disagree with their decision as to the VAT payable or various other matters, such as registration or cancellation of registration, use of a retailer's scheme etc., you may appeal to an independent VAT tribunal within thirty days of the decision. Normally any tax in dispute must be paid before the tribunal hearing, but this requirement may be waived to avoid hardship. VAT tribunals normally hear appeals in public. If you are dissatisfied with the tribunal decision further appeal is possible (see chapter 10).

10
Dealing with the Revenue

Revenue officials

Income tax, corporation tax and capital gains tax are administered by the Commissioners of Inland Revenue (also called the Board of Inland Revenue). The Board operates through its appointed officials, inspectors of taxes and collectors of taxes. Inspectors are responsible for sending out tax returns, making assessments and dealing with disputes. Collectors are responsible for collecting tax due as notified to them by the inspectors. Capital transfer tax is also administered by the Board of Inland Revenue, but through the medium of the Capital Taxes Office. Likewise development land tax, although under the control of the Board, is administered by the Development Land Tax Office, and stamp duties are administered by the Board through the Office of the Controller of Stamps.

Value added tax is under the control of the Commissioners of Customs and Excise, operating through the VAT Central Unit and through local VAT offices under collectors of customs and excise.

Returns of income and capital gains (TMA 1970, ss 7, 8, 113)

Tax returns are usually required to be submitted annually, although PAYE taxpayers with no other sources of income may receive them less frequently. The official time for the submission of a return is 30 days from its receipt. If you do not receive a return and you have income (other than wages or salary) or gains chargeable to tax, you must notify the inspector within twelve months of the end of the tax-year. The return for a married man deals with the joint income of himself and his wife, even if an election has been made for the wife's earnings to be taxed separately. If, however, a couple have applied for separate assessment (which relates to the entire income and not just the wife's earnings) separate returns may be required from each.

The 1983/84 return requires details of:

Your income from all sources for 1982/83
Your allowable outgoings for income tax during 1982/83
Capital gains—details of chargeable assets acquired and disposed of during 1982/83. If disposal proceeds do not exceed £10,000 and gains do not exceed £5,000 it is sufficient to state this in the 'gains' section and no further details need be given unless required by the Revenue.

Claim for allowances for 1983/84. For details of available allowances see chapter 3.

Other returns

Capital transfer tax

In the case of lifetime transfers a return must be made by either transferor or transferee. Returns are strictly not required until twelve months after the end of the month in which the transfer takes place, but interest on overdue tax runs from earlier dates (see chapter 7), so returns should be lodged accordingly.

In the case of death, the return is made in conjunction with the application for a grant of probate (where there is a will) or of administration (where there is no will or where the named executors cannot or will not act). Again a twelve-month return period is allowed, but interest runs from six months from the end of the month of death, and the need to obtain a grant in order to deal with the affairs of the deceased ensures an earlier return in most cases.

A return does not have to be made of chargeable transfers not exceeding £10,000 in any tax-year, provided that the cumulative total of those transfers and other chargeable transfers within the previous ten years (but after 26 March 1974) does not exceed £40,000. A return may, however, subsequently be required.

Similarly an account need not be submitted for a deceased's estate under £40,000 (£25,000 for deaths before 1 April 1983), provided that no trust is involved, that not more than 10% of the estate, or £1,000 if higher, is situated outside the UK, and that there have been no chargeable transfers in the deceased's lifetime. The Revenue again reserve the right to call for an account subsequently.

Development land tax

Notice of disposal of an interest in land must be given to the DLT Office within twelve months unless the Stamp Duty Office has already been notified. Notification of a project of material development must be given to the DLT Office within 30 days after commencement (or up to 60 days prior to commencement if desired).

Late submission of returns

The late submission of a return will not usually attract a penalty, but if a return is so late that it prevents an assessment being issued in time for the tax to be paid on the normal due date, the Revenue may contend that this amounts to negligence and may in consequence require the taxpayer to pay interest from the date on which the tax would have been payable had a return been made on time. This is particularly likely in the case of capital gains, which the Revenue are less likely to be aware of in the absence of a return than continuing sources of income.

Assessments and additional assessments; error or mistake claims

Income tax, corporation tax, capital gains tax, development land tax (TMA 1970, ss 29–41)

Assessments to income tax, corporation tax and capital gains tax are issued by inspectors of taxes (or sometimes, for assessments relating to close companies, by the Board). Development land tax assessments are issued by the Board.

If the inspector or Board discover that any profits or gains chargeable to tax have not been assessed, or have been insufficiently assessed, he or they may make an additional assessment.

The normal time limit for making an assessment or additional assessment is six years from the end of the tax-year to which it relates. If a taxpayer dies, assessments cannot be made later than three years after the tax-year of his death.

Special rules apply in cases of fraud, wilful default or neglect. These are dealt with on page 81 below.

If the individual or corporate taxpayer makes an error or mistake in a return causing an overpayment of tax, relief may be claimed at any time up to six years after the tax-year in which the assessment was made. Such a claim is not possible where no return has been submitted. Furthermore, when such a claim is made, it enables the Revenue to reconsider other aspects of the taxpayer's affairs if they think fit.

Capital transfer tax (FA 1975, Sch 4(6)(23)(24)(25))

Notification of the amount of capital transfer tax due is contained in a notice of determination issued by the Board. Adjustments for tax underpaid or overpaid, with interest thereon, may be made subsequently but not later than the expiry of six years from the date of payment, or if later the date payment was due. In cases of fraud, wilful default or neglect the period of six years starts at the time the fraud etc. became known to the Revenue.

Value added tax (FA 1972, s 31)

If a taxpayer fails to make returns, or the Commissioners feel returns are incomplete or incorrect, they may issue assessments of the amount of tax due. Such assessments must be issued before the expiry of two years from the end of the return period, or if later, one year after the facts come to light. In no case can assessments be made later than six years after the end of the return period or three years after the taxpayer's death, except in cases of fraud, wilful default or neglect, when an assessment may be made at any time, or, if a taxpayer has died, up to six years after his death. If a taxpayer finds he has made a mistake causing tax to be overpaid or underpaid he corrects it by showing an overdeclaration or underdeclaration in his next return. There is no other error or mistake procedure and no time limits are stipulated.

Stamp duty (Stamp Act 1891, s 12)

The Board may be required to state whether an instrument is liable to stamp duty and if so how much duty is payable. There is a right of appeal to the High Court.

Remission of tax because of official error

Where the Revenue discover that they have undercharged a taxpayer, although they have been given full information at the proper time, they will by concession not collect some or all of the underpayment according to the following scale (operative from 22 April 1983):

Taxpayer's gross income	Proportion of underpayment not collected
Up to £7,500	All
£7,501 to £9,500	75%
£9,501 to £12,000	50%
£12,001 to £14,500	25%
£14,501 to £20,500	10%
Over £20,500	No remission

The income limits are increased by £2,000 for taxpayers who, at the date of notification, are aged 65 or over or are in receipt of the national insurance retirement or widow's pension.

Due dates of payment and interest on overdue tax

Due dates of payment and interest provisions vary for the different taxes and are dealt with in detail for each tax in chapters 3 to 9.

Appeals (Income tax, corporation tax, capital gains tax, development land tax—TMA 1970, s 31; Capital transfer tax—FA 1975, Sch 4(7); Stamp duty—Stamp Act 1891, s 13; Value added tax—FA 1972, s 40, SI 1972/1344 rules 4 and 18)

Normally appeals must be made within thirty days from the date of issue of the assessment, except in relation to stamp duty where the prescribed period is twenty-one days. The appeal must state the grounds on which it is made (for example that the tax is estimated and not in accordance with information already or to be supplied). Late appeals may be allowed if the inspector or the Board is satisfied that there was a good reason for the delay.

Postponement of payment of tax

Tax still has to be paid on the normal due dates even though an appeal has been lodged, except that in relation to income tax, corporation tax, capital gains tax and development land tax an application may be made to postpone payment of all or part of the tax. The postponement application is separate from the appeal itself and must state the amount of tax which it is considered has been overcharged and the grounds for that belief. The amount to be postponed will then be agreed with the inspector or decided by the Appeal Commissioners (see below). Any tax not postponed will be due thirty days after the date of the decision as to how much tax may be postponed, or on the normal due date if later.

The appeal itself may be settled by negotiation with the inspector or, failing that, by following the appeal procedure to the Commissioners and thence if necessary to the courts. Once the appeal has been finally determined any underpaid tax will be payable within thirty days after the inspector issues a notice of the amount payable. Any overpaid tax will be repaid. Although a postponement application may successfully delay payment of tax it will not stop interest being charged against the taxpayer if the tax later proves to be payable (see the due date and interest provisions in chapters 3 to 6).

Appeal procedures

If an appeal is not settled between the taxpayer and the inspector it is listed for hearing by the Appeal Commissioners. There are two types of appeal commissioners, General Commissioners and Special Commissioners. Certain specialised appeals are heard by the special commissioners and other appeals normally by the general commissioners, although it is possible for a taxpayer to elect to have a non-specialised appeal heard by the special commissioners. The decisions of the commissioners on matters of fact are normally binding on both parties. If either taxpayer or the Inland Revenue is dissatisfied with a decision on a point of law, they may ask the commissioners to 'state a case' for the opinion of the High Court. Further appeal is then possible to the Court of Appeal and, where leave is granted, to the House of Lords. It should be noted, however, that the decision to take an appeal to the commissioners on a point of law must be weighed very carefully because of the likely heavy costs involved, particularly if the taxpayer should be successful at the earlier stages and lose before a higher court.

Additional and extended time limit assessments to income tax, corporation tax and capital gains tax (TMA 1970, ss 34–37)

The Revenue are able to issue an additional assessment for a year within the normal six-year time limit without alleging any culpability on the taxpayer's part. They may 'discover' that an assessment is inadequate through considering facts already in their hands, by say comparing gross profit rates from year to year, or through new facts, such as the existence of a previously undisclosed bank deposit account, or even because they change their minds on how something should be interpreted. However, to reopen years outside the six-year time limit, the Revenue have to show fraud, wilful default or neglect. If the case is one of neglect only, they must be able to show a continuing history of neglect with no gap of more than six years within it. In cases of fraud or wilful default, however, they may reopen the position for any year.

If the Revenue consider a case to be one of fraud, wilful default or neglect then, unless they are considering a prosecution, they will usually invite the taxpayer to cooperate in establishing the understated income or gains. If he does so, they will then not normally have to resort to their statutory powers to call for documents and to enter and search premises.

Establishing the tax lost

The Revenue investigation will include some or all of the following for the appropriate period, the effect of one on another being considered:

(a) A full review of the business accounts.
(b) A double-entry type reconstruction of the private affairs, establishing whether increases in private wealth can be substantiated.
(c) A business model based on a sample period, adapted for changing circumstances and compared with the results shown by the business accounts.
(d) A living expenses review and comparison with available funds to establish prima facie additional income.

At the conclusion of the review, if the need for a revision of profits, income or gains has been established, the calculation of tax underpaid follows automatically.

Interest and penalties (TMA 1970, ss 88, 95, 96)

Where culpability arises interest runs from the date on which the tax ought to have been paid. The Revenue have statutory powers to apply to the commissioners for interest certificates and to take penalty proceedings against a taxpayer when it has been established that tax has been lost through his negligence, wilful default or fraud. These powers are quite separate from their powers to take criminal proceedings for an offence against the Crown.

Penalties are additional to payment of tax and interest, and the maximum penalties are as in the table below.

The Revenue have power to mitigate both interest and penalties.

Alternative to an interest certificate and penalty proceedings

Instead of formal proceedings being taken for interest and penalties, the taxpayer will usually be invited to make an offer to the Board of Inland Revenue in consideration of their not taking such proceedings. If that offer is thought reasonable and likely to be accepted by the Board, it will be submitted to them by the district office or enquiry branch. Sometimes it will be accepted locally.

The amount of the offer will in fact be negotiated between the Revenue and the taxpayer and will comprise the calculated tax and interest plus a penalty loading, the penalty being reduced principally on three counts:

(a) Whether the initial disclosure was voluntarily made by the taxpayer or

Non-compliance	Penalty
Failure to notify liability within one year after end of tax-year (TMA 1970, ss 7, 10)	£100
Failure to submit income tax or capital gains tax returns within required period (TMA 1970, s 93)	£50 and £10 a day for every day failure continues after Commissioners or a Court have made an order for delivery of the return, plus an amount equal to the tax charged if failure continues beyond the end of the year following that in which the notice was served
Failure to submit corporation tax return (TMA 1970, s 94)	Broadly as for income tax and capital gains tax
Negligence or wilful default in any return or accounts	£50 and the equivalent of the tax lost
Fraud in any return or accounts (TMA 1970, ss 95, 96)	£50 and twice the equivalent of the tax lost

induced or partly induced by communication from the Revenue.

(b) The size and gravity of the offence.

(c) The degree of cooperation by the taxpayer.

The acceptance of a taxpayer's offer by the Board creates a binding contract, and if the taxpayer fails to pay the Revenue are able to proceed for the amount due under the contract itself without any reference to the taxation position, although the terms of the contract allow them to repudiate it if they wish in the case of non or late payment. This established procedure is used in the vast majority of cases, and has points both in the taxpayer's and in the Revenue's favour, in that the taxpayer may be treated less harshly than if proceedings were taken, and the Revenue are spared the trouble of taking those proceedings.

Special situations

Death of a taxpayer limits the Revenue's right to reopen earlier years to the six years before that in which he died, and moreover restricts their right to raise assessments to the three years after the end of the year of assessment in which the death occurs (TMA 1970, s 40).

Partnerships involve a joint income tax liability on trading profits (but not on other income or chargeable gains), an innocent partner having no defence against the Revenue in respect of his share of the trading profits. Where a partner has died, the principle of joint liability will cause his share of profits to remain subject to review while the liability of his estate is limited to the six earlier years, putting an added burden on the surviving partners for the years before the normal six years.

Companies and company directors. While the liabilities of a company and its directors are entirely separate, they will be looked at together in cases of suspected culpability. Unexplained wealth increases or funding of living expenses will generally be regarded as extractions from the company, and, under his duty to preserve the company's assets, the director must account to the company for the extracted funds. The director is spared the liability at personal rates on the extracted funds, but is required to repay the extractions to the company, the company's accounts having to be rewritten accordingly and the extractions being subject to tax at corporation tax rates, since they must represent additional company profits. The company is also accountable for tax at the basic rate on the grossed-up equivalent of the extractions unless they are repaid, that liability attracting interest until repaid and being reckoned in the tax due to the Revenue when calculating penalties.

Tax points

- If you delay sending in a return which will trigger a tax liability of which the Revenue are otherwise unaware, this will invariably cause the Revenue to seek interest and perhaps penalties. Neither the interest nor the penalties are allowable in calculating your tax liability.

- If you are guilty of known irregularities, a payment on account of the tax eventually to be accounted for will reduce the interest charge and also help to demonstrate your cooperation.

- If you are aware of irregularities in your affairs you should disclose them fully to the Revenue before they make a challenge. You will thereby obtain the maximum penalty mitigation when an offer in settlement is eventually made.

11
Employments—persons liable, assessable earnings and allowable deductions

Basis of charge (TA 1970, s 181; F(No 2)A 1975, s 38)

Income from an office or employment is charged to tax under Schedule E, tax normally being collected through the PAYE scheme. Employment under a contract *of service*, chargeable under Schedule E, must be distinguished from a contract *for services*, entitling the provider to payment for his services against his invoice or fee note, chargeable under Schedule D, Case I or II. The distinction is sometimes difficult to draw and depends on various factors, such as the extent of control exercised over the work done. The difference is important both to the payer, since, if the self-employed status of the payee is successfully challenged by the Revenue, the payer may be held responsible for non-compliance with the PAYE and national insurance regulations, and to the payee, because of the differences in the allowable expenses and in the timing of tax payments. Most agency workers are required to be treated as employees. Responsibility for the operation of PAYE usually rests with the agency but if the client pays the worker direct the responsibility falls on him. Sub-contractors in the construction industry are treated as self-employed but are subject to special rules (see chapter 47).

Pensions and social security benefits (TA 1970, ss 219 and 219A)

Tax is also charged under Schedule E on pensions, whether from your employer or from the state, and on many other social security benefits. Available allowances frequently cover the tax liability on taxable benefits, and certain benefits are exempt. A summary of the main taxable and exempt state benefits is given in the table below.

Persons liable (TA 1970, s 181)

The extent of an individual's liability to tax on earnings depends on his country of residence, ordinary residence and domicile. Broadly, residence requires some physical presence in the country in the tax year, ordinary residence means habitual residence and domicile is the country you regard as your permanent home.

SUMMARY OF MAIN STATE BENEFITS	
TAXABLE	EXEMPT
Retirement pensions	Wounds or disability benefits
Widow's allowance and widowed mother's allowance	War widow's pension
Widow's pension	Mobility allowance (from 1982/83)
Statutory sick pay	Sickness benefit, maternity benefit and death grant
Job release allowance for periods beginning earlier than one year before pension age	Job release allowance to men aged 64 or over or women aged 59 or over
Supplementary benefit to unemployed*	Child benefit
Supplementary benefit to strikers*	Attendance allowance
Unemployment benefit*	Invalidity benefits
	Family income supplement
* Paid gross initially with any tax due being collected later, for example via a subsequent employer	Supplementary benefit (other than as listed as taxable)
	Christmas bonus for pensioners

Visitors to the UK are liable to tax on the full amount they earn in the UK from a UK employer. If a visitor is not in the UK long enough to be classed as resident he is not entitled to personal allowances. If a visitor is domiciled abroad and his employer is not UK-resident only half his earnings are assessable, but the assessable proportion increases to three-quarters when he has been resident in the UK for nine out of the previous ten tax years. The provisions charging visitors to tax may be varied by double taxation agreements.

Someone who is resident, ordinarily resident and domiciled in the UK is charged to tax on his world wide earnings, although there is a permitted deduction for earnings during 'long' or 'short' absences abroad.

The treatment of earnings abroad for both UK citizens and visitors is dealt with in chapter 44, which also explains residence, ordinary residence and domicile more fully and deals with the question of double taxation.

Assessable earnings (TA 1970, s 183)

Tax is charged on 'emoluments', which covers wages, salaries, commissions, bonuses and certain benefits in kind. If your employer pays a debt for you the amount so paid is also taxed as your emoluments.

The charge is on your earnings of the tax year, whether received in that year or not. For most wage and salary earners the assessable earnings will coincide with the weekly, monthly or quarterly payments in the tax year, but if you receive periodic bonus payments an adjustment will sometimes be required to allocate your earnings to the correct tax year.

A director's remuneration is frequently voted on an annual basis. The Revenue will usually seek to charge a director on the earnings of the accounts year ended in the tax year, to enable them to raise assessments earlier. This practice has no legal foundation and you may refuse to accept it, but it will usually be to your advantage if your earnings are rising. See example 1.

Example 1

Remuneration of year ended 31 December 1983		£10,000
Remuneration of year ended 31 December 1984		£16,000
Assessable under Schedule E in 1983/84 on accounts basis:		£10,000
Assessable on an actual basis: $3/4 \times £10,000$	7,500	
$1/4 \times £16,000$	4,000	£11,500

Allowable expenses and deductions (TA 1970, ss 189, 192, 411; FA 1970, Ch II)

Relief is available for expenses incurred wholly, exclusively and necessarily in the performance of the duties of your employment and for travelling in the performance of those duties. Relatively few expenses satisfy this stringent rule. Some expenses which would not are specifically allowable by statute.

Travelling expenses from home to work are not allowed since they are not incurred in performing your duties. Travelling expenses on business journeys are allowed, together with the cost of subsistence when away from home. (Strictly only the extra cost of living away from home qualifies, but the Revenue will normally allow the whole cost where you have continuing financial commitments at home.)

For most manual workers flat rate expenses allowances have been negotiated for the upkeep of tools and special clothing, although this does not preclude a higher claim being made. The cost of normal clothing is not allowed even if it costs more than you would normally pay and you would not wear the clothes outside work.

If it is *necessary* for you to work at home you will be able to claim a proportion of the cost of light, heat, phone etc. The allowable proportion of such expenses is generally the subject of negotiation with the inspector.

Other allowable expenses include contributions to an approved pension scheme, and most professional subscriptions that are relevant to your job. The cost of business entertaining (other than of overseas customers on a reasonable scale) is not allowed, but the disallowance may fall on you or on your employer depending on how payment is made. The disallowance falls on you if it is paid out of your salary or out of a round sum allowance. If you receive a specific entertaining allowance from your employer or are specifically reimbursed for entertaining expenses no charge will fall on you and the disallowance falls on your employer.

You can claim a deduction against your earnings for:

> Contributions to a personal pension plan if you are not covered by an employer's scheme (see chapter 18).
> Capital allowances if you have to buy equipment, such as a car, for use in your job (restricted by any private use proportion) (FA 1971, s 47 and Sch 8(5)).
> Interest on money borrowed to finance the purchase of such equipment (restricted by any private use proportion)—for the three tax years following the tax year of purchase (FA 1972, Sch 9(12)(13)).

Directors and higher-paid employees (FA 1976, s 69)

The rules for assessable emoluments and allowable expenses are more onerous if you are in 'director's or higher-paid employment'. All directors are covered by these special rules unless they (together with their close family and other associates) own not more than 5% of the ordinary share capital and either work full time for the company or are employed by a non-profit making or charitable organisation. Directors who are excluded on these grounds are nonetheless included if they are higher-paid.

'Higher-paid' means earning at the rate of £8,500 per annum or more, earnings being calculated for this purpose by including all expenses payments plus the cash equivalent of all benefits and before deducting allowable expenses. Any private motoring expenses such as petrol, repairs, insurance, AA subscription, which are met by your employer, either directly or by reimbursement or through the provision of vouchers or credit cards, must be included in the calculation of earnings as well as the car and car fuel scale charges (see below).

Expenses payments and reimbursed expenses

The strict application of the rule for allowable expenses would require all expenses payments to employees to be treated as wages, leaving the employee to claim relief for the allowable part thereof. To avoid a lot of unnecessary work, expenses payments that do no more than cover expenses that are 'wholly, exclusively and necessarily incurred in the performance of the duties of the employment' are not treated as pay under the

PAYE scheme except where the employee is in director's or higher-paid employment. If, however, the allowance received exceeds the amount so expended the excess counts as pay.

For directors and higher-paid employees, expenses allowances are treated as pay unless the employer obtains from the Revenue a dispensation enabling them to be excluded. The most common expenses for which a dispensation is granted are travelling and subsistence allowances on an agreed scale. Dispensations are never given for round sum expenses allowances nor for entertaining expenses.

Benefits-in-kind for the lower-paid

If you are not in director's or higher-paid employment you are normally only assessed on those benefits which can be turned into cash, and the assessable amount is the realisable value. For example, if you are given a suit that cost your employer £100 but which is valued second hand at only £10, you are assessed only on £10. You escape tax on the benefit of use of a car because you cannot convert it into cash.

Benefits-in-kind for all employees—specific charges

Benefits assessed on all employees, whether in director's or higher-paid employment or not, are the provision of living accommodation and vouchers (see below).

Living accommodation (FA 1976, s 63A; FA 1977, s 33; FA 1983, s 21)

If your employer provides you with living accommodation you are charged to tax on its annual value (i.e. letting value) less any rent you pay. There is no charge, however, if

(a) you are a representative occupier, for example a caretaker, or
(b) it is customary in your employment to be provided with living accommodation, or
(c) the accommodation is provided for security reasons.

If you are exempt under one of these headings the exemption also covers rates. Except where the accommodation provided by a company falls within (c) above, a director cannot qualify for exemption unless he does not own more than 5% of the ordinary share capital and either he works full-time for the company or the company is a non-profit making or charitable body.

Lower-paid employees also escape tax on the provision of other benefits such as heating, lighting and the use of furniture, because they cannot be converted into cash.

If you are in director's or higher-paid employment you are chargeable on the value of other benefits relating to the accommodation whether or not you are chargeable on the annual value, but if you are exempt from the charge on annual value the charge for other benefits cannot exceed 10% of your earnings excluding the benefits in question.

The charge for living accommodation is to be increased from 1984/85 where the accommodation cost more than £75,000. The formula for calculating the extra charge over and above the annual value is:

((Cost less £75,000) × Appropriate %) less rent paid in excess of annual value, if any.

The appropriate percentage is the official rate of interest chargeable on beneficial loans (currently 12%). See page 92 below.

Vouchers (F(No 2)A 1975, ss 36, 36A, 37)

The vouchers rules apply to all employees and are wide-ranging.

Cash vouchers are treated as pay under the PAYE scheme at the time the voucher is provided.

The cost of providing transport vouchers (for example season tickets) and other vouchers (including cheques) and the cost of goods or services obtained through the provision of credit cards, although not treated as pay at the time they are provided, are nonetheless taxable, and your employer is required to provide details to the Revenue at the year end. Employees of passenger transport undertakings like British Rail who are not in director's or higher-paid employment are exempt from tax on transport vouchers.

There is still a derisory exemption of 15p per day for luncheon vouchers, providing they are available to all employees, non-transferable and used for meals only. Any excess over 15p is taxable, details being notified to the Revenue by your employer at the year end. No tax arises on free canteen meals that are provided to staff generally so the luncheon voucher rules discriminate against employers who are too small to have their own canteen.

Benefits-in-kind for directors and higher-paid employees (FA 1976, ss 60–72)

If you are a director or higher-paid employee you are charged to tax on all expenses payments received (unless covered by a dispensation, see page 89 above) and on the cash equivalent of virtually all benefits provided either direct to you or to your family or household.

The main benefits that are not chargeable to tax are:

>   Meals in a staff canteen providing they are available to staff generally
>   Employer's pension contributions

Payment for medical treatment or the provision of medical insurance is chargeable unless it relates to treatment outside the UK when on a business trip.

The value of a benefit is normally the cost to your employer (including VAT where appropriate, whether recovered or not) less any amount made good by you.

Scholarships to employees' children are caught following FA 1983 (see chapter 2).

Special rules apply to the provision of cars and cheap loans (see below) and to share option and incentive schemes (see chapter 12).

Where you are allowed the use of any other asset that remains the property of your employer, you are charged to tax annually on 20% of its cost (10% if the asset was first provided before 6 April 1980). Should such an asset subsequently be given to you, you are charged to tax on the higher of its market value at the date of the gift and the original market value less the intervening charges made for its use. See example 2.

Example 2

Television set cost employer £500. Used by director for two years, then given to him when market value is £50.
Assessments:
  For use of asset, 20% × £500 =   £100 per annum
                                                             ‾‾‾‾

  On gift of asset, higher of   £50 and
                                £500 − (2 × £100)
                                = £300, i.e.   £300
                                                    ‾‾‾‾

If, as well as allowing you to use an asset, your employer meets current expenses on it, for example pays the running expenses of a boat or aeroplane, you bear tax on those expenses as well.

Motor cars (FA 1976, ss 64, 64A, 65 and Sch 7)

The benefit of private use of a car is charged on a scale basis, with an additional charge being made if you are also provided with car fuel for private use. The scale charges are shown at the front of the book.

Any contribution you make to your employer for the use of the car is deducted from the car scale charge, but there is no reduction in the car fuel charge for a contribution to the cost of fuel. To escape the fuel charge you must reimburse the whole cost of private fuel.

If your annual business miles are 18,000 or more both the car scale charge and the fuel scale charge are halved.

If your annual business miles are 2,500 or less you are charged one and a half times the car scale benefit, but the fuel scale charge is not increased.

If you are provided with more than one car (for example a car for your spouse) the second and subsequent cars are charged at one and a half times the scale benefit whether you do 2,500 business miles in them or not, but again the fuel scale charge for the additional car(s) is not increased.

The scale charges cover the whole benefit obtained from the use of a car, except the expense of providing a chauffeur, which is charged in addition. If a car is provided for only part of the year (for example in the year when you start or cease employment) the scale charge is proportionately reduced. It is also proportionately reduced if the car is incapable of being used for a period of thirty consecutive days or more.

It is possible to escape tax on the benefit of use of a car if it is deemed to be a pool car, but the conditions are restrictive. A pool car is one where the private use is merely incidental to the business use, the car is not normally kept overnight at an employee's home, and the car is not ordinarily used by only one employee to the exclusion of other employees.

Cheap loans (FA 1976, s 66)

If by reason of your employment you are provided with a loan interest-free or at a rate of interest below the official rate (currently 12%) you are charged to tax on an amount equal to interest at the official rate less any interest paid.

There is no charge if the benefit amounts to £200 or less, or if you would have been entitled to tax relief on the interest if you had paid it. There is, for example, no tax charge on a loan of up to £30,000 to buy your only or main residence.

If the loan is written off you are charged on the amount written off whether you are still employed or not. (This does not apply to loans written off on death or to stop loss arrangements on employee profit sharing schemes where the shares were acquired before 6 April 1976, see chapter 12.)

Summary of Benefits Provisions

| BENEFIT | TAX CHARGE | |
	DIRECTORS AND HIGHER PAID EMPLOYEES	OTHER EMPLOYEES
Use of car	Scale charge Scale charged reduced by half if business miles 18,000 or more Scale charge increased by half if business miles 2,500 or less, and also for second and subsequent cars	Not assessable

Car fuel for private motoring	Scale charge Scale charge reduced by half if business miles 18,000 or more	Cost to employer less employee contribution
Living accommodation	Annual value (unless exempt)	Annual value (unless exempt)
Provision of services and use of furniture in living accommodation	Cost of services plus 20% of cost of furniture (restricted to 10% of other earnings if exempt from living accommodation charge)	Not assessable
Use of other assets	20% of cost	Not assessable
Vouchers other than luncheon vouchers	Full value	Full value
Use of credit cards	Cost of goods and services obtained	Cost of goods and services obtained
Medical insurance	Cost to employer	Not assessable
Beneficial loans	Interest at official rate (12%) less any interest paid, but no charge if benefit £200 or less	Not assessable
Loans written off	Amount written off	Amount written off
Free or subsidised canteen meals	Not assessable if available to all employees	Not assessable
Pension provision	Not assessable	Not assessable

Forms P11D

These returns are required at the year end under the PAYE scheme (see below). They summarise the benefits and expenses payments in respect of directors and higher-paid employees. They are increasingly subject to close scrutiny by the Revenue as to their accuracy, through e.g. visits to business premises and directors' homes, and a close inspection of the position as regards loans to directors. Care should therefore be taken to ensure that all sections of the form are correctly completed, and in particular that all allowable expenses of the employee met by the employer are returned, a

Example 3

An employee was paid a salary of £12,000 per annum in 1983/84.

He is provided with a 1500 cc company car which is completely run by the employer, including the provision of private petrol. He did 10,000 business miles and 5,000 private miles.

He received an overnight allowance which amounted to £649 and in respect of which a dispensation had been granted to his employer by the Revenue.

He paid hotel and meals bills on business trips amounting to £1,539 and spent £250 on entertaining customers. These expenses were reimbursed by his employer. His telephone bill amounting to £150 was paid by his employer. Two thirds of this was agreed business use.

He received a round sum expenses allowance of £1,200 out of which allowable expenses £200 are agreed.

Following Revenue agreement of an expenses claim by the employee the assessable earnings are:

	£	£
Salary		12,000
Scale charge for use of car		425
Scale car fuel charge		425
Overnight allowance (covered by dispensation)		—
Hotel and meal bills reimbursed		1,539
Entertaining expenses reimbursed		250
Telephone account paid by employer		150
Round sum expenses allowance		1,200
		15,989
Less: Hotel and meal bills reimbursed	1,539	
Entertaining expenses reimbursed (disallowed to employer)	250	
Proportion of telephone account agreed as relating to employment	100	
Other allowable expenses	200	2,089
Assessable emoluments		£13,900

claim being made by the employee in his annual tax return for the corresponding deduction.

Substantial penalties may be imposed for failure to submit a form P11D, or for submitting an incorrectly completed form.

PAYE

Tax under Schedule E is normally collected through the PAYE scheme, and no assessment is raised unless there is a significant underpayment. Employers deduct tax (usually on a cumulative basis) and national insurance contributions (on a non-cumulative basis) from the weekly or monthly pay, using tables supplied by the Revenue. The total amount deducted in each tax month (ending on the 5th), together with the employer's national insurance contributions, is due for payment within fourteen days, i.e. by the 19th. If the cumulative tax paid by an employee exceeds the amount due the excess is refunded to him and is deducted from the amount due to the Revenue from the employer.

For details on national insurance contributions see chapter 14.

All the necessary documentation is supplied by the Revenue. Basic guidance is provided on the Blue Card P8.

Code numbers

The tax calculation is made using code numbers notified by the Revenue on form P9 or using the specified emergency procedure where no code number is received. Once a code number is issued it remains in force from year to year until the Revenue notify a change.

Your code represents the tax allowance you are entitled to, such as personal allowances and allowable expenses in employment, less a deduction to cover small items of other income like bank interest, or to adjust underpayments in earlier years. The code number is the amount of your allowances less the last digit. For example if your allowances total £1,785 your code number is 178.

Most codes are three numbers followed by a suffix H, L, P, or V. H denotes higher personal allowance, L lower personal allowance or wife's earned income relief. V denotes higher age allowance and P lower age allowance. The suffixes enable the Revenue to implement changes in these allowances by telling employers to increase the codes by a specified amount.

Some codes have a prefix D or F instead of a suffix. The number following the D or F prefix relates to the tax rate to be used, for example D1 represents tax at 45% and F54 tax at 27%. Prefix D is used if you have more than one employment and your total income will attract higher rate tax. Your allowances are given against the earnings from your main employment and tax is deducted in other employments at higher rates according to the D code in use. The D code procedure represents an estimate of higher rate tax liability and an adjustment is necessary at the year end when the precise income is known. Prefix F enables tax to be collected on an excess of an employed pensioner's state pension over available allowances. Other codes are BR, which means basic rate tax applies, OT, which means no allowances are available, and NT, which means no tax is to be deducted.

Tax tables

Tables A, B and C work on a cumulative basis. Table A shows the cumulative free pay each tax week or month for the various code numbers, Table B the tax due on taxable pay to date up to the basic rate tax band and Table C the tax due at higher rates. Tables D and F are non-cumulative, Table D being a higher rate tax ready reckoner for use with Table C for D codes and Table F a tax ready reckoner for F codes.

Records and year end returns

Employers must keep records of pay, tax, employees' and employer's national insurance contributions and the amount of any statutory sick pay (see chapter 15). Details must be provided to the Revenue at the year end.

Employers may either use deductions working sheets P11 (New) supplied by the Revenue and official end of year return forms P14, or use their own pay records and notify the totals on forms P14, or use their own pay records with substitute end of year returns, or keep computerised records and make end of year returns on magnetic tape.

Form P14 is in three parts, two being sent to the Revenue (one of which is for the Department of Health and Social Security) and the third constituting the form P60 for the employee showing the total pay and tax deducted in the year. The forms to be sent to the Revenue at the year end are—

Two copies of form P14 (or substitutes)
Form P35 showing the total tax and national insurance contributions for each employee
Forms P11D showing details of expenses payments and benefits provided to directors and higher-paid employees
Forms P9D showing expenses payments in excess of £25 to lower-paid employees that have not been treated as pay (other than reimbursed business expenses and expenses paid in accordance with a scale agreed with the Tax Office).

Changing jobs

When you leave your job, your employer should give you two copies of form P45 and send one copy to the Revenue. The P45 shows the total pay and tax to date in the tax year and the code number in use. You pass on the form to your new employer when you start another job so that he can continue to deduct tax on the correct basis. Wages in lieu of notice and statutory redundancy pay are not treated as pay, but they may be subject to tax under special rules (see chapter 16).

If you do not produce form P45 to your new employer he will ask you to complete form P46, and, if your pay exceeds the tax threshold of £34 a week, he will give you a coding claim form P15.

The P46 procedure enables employers to deduct tax on a cumulative basis straight away if you are a school leaver who has not drawn unemployment benefit, so that you get the benefit of the unused single personal allowance from the beginning of the tax year to the date you start work. Otherwise you will usually be allocated a single person's allowance, code 178L, on a non-cumulative basis (called week 1 or month 1 basis), which means you get only one week's (or month's) proportion of the allowance against each week's (month's) pay. If you do not certify on form P46 that the employment is your only or main employment the employer will give you a coding claim form P15 and deduct tax at the basic rate from the whole of your pay.

Once the Revenue receive the coding claim form P15 they can establish what your correct code number is and they will notify the number to you and your employer. Any tax overpaid will then be refunded.

Forms P46 are sent to the Revenue unless the employee earns less than £34 a week and certifies on the form that he is a school leaver who has not drawn unemployment benefit or that the employment is his only or main employment. Forms P46 for such employees must be retained by the employer for three years, together with details of the employee's name, address and amount of pay.

Tax points

- The fringe benefits charges on directors and higher-paid employees are often not high compared with the benefit received, and there is no national insurance liability in respect of benefits in kind. It is thus usually more effective to pay a lower salary plus benefits than a higher cash figure with the employee providing the benefits himself out of taxed earnings.

- Benefits do, however, limit the employee's free choice of what to spend his money on, so sometimes the cash may be preferred.

- It is more tax efficient for the cost of employees' training courses and examinations to be met by the employer than by the employee because it is tax allowable to the employer but not to the employee. Those in director's or higher-paid employment will be assessed on a benefit in kind, but this will usually be insignificant compared with the benefit arising.

  It has also been established that a prize for examination success, even though provided by the employer, is not assessable as emoluments on the employee since it derives from passing an examination, not from the duties of the employment.

- Home to work travelling expenses are not allowable but the home and the workbase may be the same place. Those holding part time employments, such as consultants and tribunal members, should stipulate when they accept their employments that their place of employment is at their home or other workbase, so that their travelling expenses from that base will be allowable.

- Employers must be very careful to comply with the requirements of the PAYE scheme. For example, failing to apply the P46 procedure properly for new employees who do not produce form P45 could render the employer liable to account for tax which was not deducted from the amount paid.

  Forms P11D must be properly completed for each director and higher-paid employee; penalties apply if they are not.

- Watch the definition of 'higher-paid'. The requirement to include the cost of all expenses connected with a car as well as the car and car fuel scale charges brings many employees within the net whose salary is far less than £8,500.

12
Share option and share incentive schemes

Background

There is a minefield of legislation in this area, some intended to encourage genuine incentives through worker participation but much of it aimed at avoidance of income tax through share acquisition.

Share options

Directors and employees granted rights to acquire shares (TA 1970, s 186; FA 1982, s 40)

Where a director or employee acquires shares in the employing company, or an associated company, by reason of a right to acquire them (an option), an income tax charge arises on the difference between the open market value at the time of exercising the right and the cost of the shares, including any amount paid for the option. Similarly, where a right to acquire shares is assigned or released, an income tax charge arises on the consideration received less the cost of acquisition of the rights.

This prevents employees and directors being indirectly remunerated without an appropriate tax charge by the allotment of shares for less than they are worth. The tax charge cannot be avoided by the right being granted or the shares allotted to another person.

Where tax in excess of £250 is payable as a result of exercising an option to buy shares, it may be paid by three equal instalments over a three-year period, thus saving the director or employee from having to sell some of the shares to satisfy the income tax liability. An election for payment by instalments must be made within sixty days after the end of the year of assessment for which the tax charge arises.

The base cost of shares for capital gains tax is increased by any amount charged to tax under the option provisions and is thus equal to the open market value at the time of exercising the option.

Charge on granting a right to acquire shares (FA 1972, s 77)

If an option is capable of being exercised more than seven years after it is granted, a charge arises at the time the right is granted on the excess of market value of the option over cost. The tax paid may, however, be deducted from any tax arising when the option is exercised.

SAYE linked share option schemes (FA 1980, s 47 and Sch 10)

An exemption from the option charging provisions is given for approved savings-related share option schemes. No charge will arise on the difference between cost and market value when a share option is exercised, nor on the receipt of the right itself, where the cost of the shares is paid out of the proceeds of a linked SAYE scheme. The option will normally be exercised after five or seven years, when the SAYE contract ends. The present maximum monthly contribution is £50.

The scheme enables an option to be granted now to acquire shares at today's price, the shares eventually being paid for by the proceeds of a linked SAYE scheme. The employee does not get tax relief for the SAYE contributions but when the shares are taken up there is no tax charge on the excess of the market value over the price paid.

Various conditions must be complied with and in particular the scheme must be available to all directors and employees with five years' full-time service.

The capital gains tax base cost of the shares is the price paid by the employee.

Share incentives

Issue of shares at an undervalue (TA 1970, s 181)

The general charging provisions of Schedule E are wide enough to catch any issue of shares to a director or employee at an undervalue where the benefit arises out of the employment. The difference between the market value of the shares and the price paid by the employee or director is assessable as emoluments at the time of the issue of the shares.

Issue of shares partly paid up (FA 1976, s 67)

If shares are issued at a price equal to the current market value, with the price being paid by agreed instalments, no charge will arise under the general charging provisions since full market value is being paid, and this will apply even though the market value has increased by the time the shares are paid for. Any growth in value of the shares is liable only to capital gains tax.

There is, however, a charge on directors and higher-paid employees (see chapter 11) who do not pay the full price for shares immediately. They are deemed to have received an interest-free loan equal to the deferred instalments, and tax will be charged accordingly at the beneficial loans interest rate, currently 12% (see p 92). The loan will be deemed to be repaid as and when the instalments are paid. This charge will not apply if the interest would have qualified for tax relief if it had been paid, for example if the deemed loan was to acquire shares in a close or employee-controlled company (see p 16).

Share incentive schemes (FA 1972, s 79; FA 1973, Sch 8)

The tax charge on shares issued at an undervalue may be reduced if the shares are issued subject to restrictions, because the restrictions will depress the market value.

It is accordingly provided that, where shares are acquired in pursuance of a right conferred on or an opportunity offered to an individual as a director or employee of a company or an associated company, a tax charge arises either when the employee ceases to own the shares, or when any restrictions on them cease, or seven years after acquisition, whichever occurs first. The tax charge is on the excess of the market value of the shares at the time the charge crystallises over the acquisition cost. The employee is also charged to tax on the value of any benefit received that is not received by the majority of ordinary shareholders.

The charge does not apply:

> Where the shares are acquired as a result of an offer to the public.
> Where the shares are unrestricted shares issued as part of a profit sharing scheme open to all full-time employees aged 25 years or over with five or more years' service.
> Where the shares were not subject to special restrictions and the majority of the available shares of the same class were acquired other than under such arrangements.
> Where directors and/or employees acquire unrestricted shares of a class which gives them control over the company.

The charge is intended to apply only where advantages can be obtained from share acquisition as a director or employee rather than as a shareholder.

Any amount charged to tax under these provisions is part of the allowable base cost of the shares for capital gains tax.

Approved profit sharing schemes (FA 1978, ss 53–61 and Sch 9)

Favourable tax treatment is given to an approved profit sharing scheme under which a company appoints trustees and provides money for them to use to acquire shares in the company. The amount provided by the company is a tax deductible expense.

A director or employee is not charged to tax on shares appropriated to him by the trustees under the scheme. He is regarded for capital gains tax purposes as being absolutely entitled to the shares even though they are still held by the trustees, and any dividends arising are regarded as his for income tax purposes.

There is a limit on the value of shares that can be allocated to any one employee in any tax year. For 1983/84 the limit is 10% of the employee's salary for 1983/84 or 1982/83, but subject to a minimum limit of £1,250 and a maximum of £5,000.

A scheme will not receive Revenue approval unless it is available on similar terms to all qualifying employees—broadly those with at least five years' full-time service—but it is recognised that different levels of appropriation may apply to individuals on different salary levels. It must be demonstrated that the scheme does not have characteristics which discourage some of those eligible from participating.

No income tax charge arises if the shares are transferred to the employee after seven years. The shares must remain in the hands of the trustees for a minimum period which is generally two years, and a tax charge based on their market value on appropriation arises if the shares are disposed of within seven years, the charge being on the whole of the share allocation if the disposal is within four years, then reducing by 25% a year to 25% in the seventh year.

A similarly reducing tax charge will also arise if there is a capital receipt, as for example on a rights issue, within the seven years, but only if it exceeds a stipulated amount (broadly £20 per annum cumulatively up to a maximum £140).

The income tax charge has no effect on the capital gains tax base cost. Where shares are disposed of within or after the seven-year period the capital gains tax base cost is the market value at the time the shares were appropriated to the employee.

While such schemes appear attractive, there are drawbacks for unquoted companies in that the company cannot be selective in the employees who participate; there may not be a ready market for the shares if the employee wants to sell them; an immediate market valuation is not available; and the effect on established shareholders has to be considered.

Tax points

- It is important to remember that the income tax charge arising from a share option does not depend upon the shares being sold. It arises when the option is exercised, when no actual cash gain will have been realised. The shares acquired under the option then have a capital gains tax base value equivalent to their market value at the time of acquisition, any future increase being liable only to capital gains tax.

- There is no clearance procedure under FA 1972, s 79 (Share incentive schemes) and since this section taxes growth in the value of shares, as distinct from an advantage when they are purchased, it makes the schemes particularly vulnerable to Revenue attack.

- Business expansion relief is not available to directors and share-holders who take up shares in their employing company.

- In the case of unquoted companies, the value of shares will have to be agreed with the Revenue Shares Valuation Division.

13
Directors of small and family companies

Directors and shareholders

In family companies directors and shareholders are usually the same people, and they can benefit from the company in various ways, e.g.:

Payment of remuneration.
Provision of benefits.
Distribution of income through dividends.

The payment of remuneration and the provision of benefits will be allowed as a deduction in calculating the company's taxable profits. There will, however, in most instances be a liability for payment of employer's and employee's national insurance contributions in respect of the remuneration, although not on benefits.

Dividends are not an allowable deduction in calculating the company's profits, but the basic rate of income tax thereon in the hands of the shareholder is imputed from the company's corporation tax, effectively reducing the true rate of corporation tax on distributed profits.

Dividends are unearned income in the hands of the shareholder, affecting his liability to investment income surcharge, while remuneration and benefits are earned income. A combination of remuneration and dividends can be devised to suit any particular circumstances. See example 1.

A dividend is particularly tax-efficient where there is no taxable profit in the current year (possibly because of capital allowances), so that the advance corporation tax can be carried back and recovered against earlier corporation tax (see example 2).

Retention of profits within the company or payment as remuneration or dividends

Retention of profits within the company will increase the net assets and hence the value of the shares if they are subsequently sold on the basis of underlying assets. Having already suffered corporation tax, the retained profits will thus swell the value of the shares for capital gains tax purposes.

Reducing retentions through paying remuneration or dividends may therefore ultimately reduce the shareholders' chargeable gains, but this must be weighed against the immediate tax cost.

A further influence on whether or not to pay remuneration is the level of profit before and after such payment, and in particular whether *not* making payment would leave the company's profits in the marginal tranche taxable at 55½% (see chapter 4). If so, it may well be considered preferable to take remuneration, even if taxed at the highest personal rate of 60%, rather than to leave the profit in the company to be taxed at 55½% and also possibly to increase a future capital gains tax liability.

Effect on earlier years (TA 1970, s 177)

A decision on whether to pay remuneration or leave profits to be charged to corporation tax should not be taken by reference to the current year in isolation. The payment of remuneration may convert a trading profit into a trading loss, which, after being set against any non-trading profits of the current year, may be carried back against the total profits of the preceding accounting period of the same length. Any part of the loss that arises through first-year allowances on plant can be carried back a further two years (see chapter 26).

Example 1

Company makes profit (before director's remuneration) of £10,000 in year to 31 March 1984. Director has available personal allowances of £3,000 and pays mortgage interest of £2,000 (not within the MIRAS scheme, see chapter 3).

If profit is taken as	salary only £	salary and dividend £
company's tax position is:		
Profits	10,000	10,000
Salary	(8,973)	(1,700)
Employer's national insurance (11.45%)	(1,027)	(195)
Taxable profits	—	8,105
Corporation tax at 38% (assumed)		3,080
Cash dividend		5,025
ACT thereon (set against corporation tax liability)		2,154
		7,179

example 1 continued overleaf

example 1 continued

Director's tax position		
Salary	8,973	1,700
Dividend	—	7,179
		8,879
Mortgage interest	(2,000)	(2,000)
Personal allowances	(3,000)	(3,000)
Taxable income	3,973	3,879
Tax thereon @ 30%	1,192	1,164
Tax credit on dividend		(2,154)
Tax refund		(990)
Disposable income:		
Salary	8,973	1,700
Employee's national insurance (9%)	(808)	(153)
Dividend	—	5,025
Tax/tax refund	(1,192)	990
	6,973	7,562
Saving through paying dividend		£589

An extra saving of approximately £270 could be made by fixing the salary at £1,689, thus avoiding employer's and employee's national insurance. The right to short term and possibly long term national insurance benefits would however be affected.

Looking into the future

If all current-year profits are used to pay remuneration, there will be nothing against which to carry back any later losses. The expected future performance or anticipated capital expenditure available for first-year allowance should therefore be taken into account in considering whether to pay additional remuneration for the current year.

Other circumstances of the directors

With the current attractive investment opportunities because of small workshops allowances (see chapter 22) and the business expansion scheme (see chapter 29), directors may be able to create substantial available allowances to set against income. These can be used to extract income from a company in a tax efficient way.

Example 2

In 1983/84 a director invests £25,000 of his private funds in a very small workshop which is to be let to a qualifying tenant, thus entitling him to an industrial buildings allowance of £25,000 to set against his income. He has available personal allowances of £3,000 and pays mortgage interest of £2,000 (not within the MIRAS scheme—see chapter 3).

In that year the company pays him remuneration of £10,000 and a dividend of £14,000. Company's recent results are:

Year to 31 March 1982	Profit (all income)	£30,000
Year to 31 March 1983	Profit (all income)	£10,000
Year to 31 March 1984	Loss (after first-year allowances of £14,000)	(£20,000)

Company's tax position:

Year to 31 March	1982	1983	1984
	£	£	£
Profit (loss)	30,000	10,000	(20,000)
Carry back losses	(10,000)	(10,000)	20,000
	20,000	—	—
Corporation tax @ 40% (maximum ACT set off £6,000)	8,000	—	—
ACT paid	—	—	(6,000)
ACT carried back	(6,000)	—	6,000
Final corporation tax payable	£2,000	—	—

Director's tax position:

Remuneration	10,000
Dividend (£14,000 + £6,000)	20,000
	30,000
Less: Industrial buildings allowance	(25,000)
Mortgage interest	(2,000)
Personal allowances	(3,000)
Taxable income	Nil
Tax credit repayable	£6,000

Pensions (FA 1970, Ch II and Sch 5; TA 1970, ss 226–228)

The company may have its own pension scheme, either through an insurance company or self-administered. Provided that the benefits under the scheme are within the limits laid down by the Revenue, the company's contributions are allowable in calculating its taxable profit, and are not taxable on the director.

If there is no such scheme, the director may pay premiums himself under a personal pension plan (retirement annuity contract), and although the allowable premium is limited annually to $17\frac{1}{2}\%$ of his earnings, it is possible to bring forward unused relief from the previous six years, enabling a large payment to be made in a single year. A large payment under this heading is deductible against earnings, thus enabling equivalent remuneration to be taken from the company without tax arising thereon. The premium payment might be funded by a loan-back facility arranged by or in conjunction with the insurance company. Since the income and gains of both company and personal pension funds are usually exempt from tax, paying pension contributions rather than taking salary and investing it privately will be a more tax-efficient method of saving for the future. For further details on pensions see chapters 17 and 18.

Limits on allowable remuneration

Remuneration, like any other trading expense, must be incurred wholly and exclusively for the purposes of the trade. If it is regarded as excessive in relation to the duties, part may not be allowed as a deduction in calculating corporate profits. This should be borne in mind when considering payments of remuneration to members of a director's or shareholder's family, particularly a working wife, which, when viewed in conjunction with a separate earnings election (see chapter 37), may cause the Revenue to question the level of remuneration.

Employing children in the family company may be useful, particularly if they are not otherwise using their personal allowance, but again this is subject to the requirement that the work done must be sufficient to justify the amount paid. If they are under sixteen you must also comply with the regulations as to permitted hours of work, which vary according to local bye-laws. Payments by a farmer to his very young children have been held to be 'pocket money' and disallowed.

Waiving an entitlement to remuneration (FA 1976, s 91)

There is no income tax on remuneration which is not received, thus facilitating the waiving of an entitlement to remuneration to assist in a difficult period of trading, or because of a high personal tax rate. It is also specifically provided that no capital transfer tax liability arises from such a waiver. The waiver might enable the company to pay higher remuneration to other directors or family members (provided as always that it is justifiable under the 'wholly and exclusively' rule).

Benefits in kind provided by the company

Directors and higher-paid employees (i.e. those earning £8,500 or more per annum) are charged to tax on the cash equivalent of benefits in kind. Directors are caught by these provisions no matter how little they earn unless they do not have a material interest in the company (a material interest being more than 5% of the ordinary share capital, including shares owned by close family and certain other people) *and* either work full-time or work for a non-profit making or charitable body.

Benefits may take the form of the outright gift of an asset or of the provision of an asset for personal use, the ownership remaining with the company. The company is allowed to deduct the cost of providing benefits in calculating its taxable profit. The charge on the director/employee is broadly the cost to the company, including VAT where appropriate (whether recovered or not), or, if the asset remains the company's property, the 'annual value' of its use. The detailed provisions for calculating the charge are in chapter 11.

Now that family trading companies are not required by the 'close company' provisions to distribute trading profits, and with a corporation tax rate on profits up to £100,000 of only 38% compared with a top personal rate on earned income of 60% (see chapter 4), it will often be worthwhile to retain funds in the company to buy assets for the directors' use rather than the directors being provided with funds enabling them to purchase the assets personally.

Gifts of company assets to persons who are not directors or employees (TA 1970, s 284; FA 1975, s 39)

Gifts of company assets to directors and employees are covered by the benefits rules mentioned above and explained in detail in chapter 11. If an asset is given to a shareholder who is not a director, its cost is treated as a distribution, the appropriate amount of advance corporation tax being payable by the company and the gross equivalent being included in the shareholder's taxable income.

If a gift is made to someone who is neither a director/employee nor a shareholder nor connected with them, an apportionment of its value is made among the shareholders for capital transfer tax purposes, the shareholders then being deemed to have made personal transfers of the amount apportioned to them.

Loans from the company (TA 1970, s 286; FA 1976, s 66; Revenue Statement of Practice SP 7/79)

Directors and higher-paid employees who overdraw their loan accounts or who receive specific loans from the company, either interest-free or at a beneficial rate, are treated as having received remuneration equivalent to interest on the amount advanced at the 'official rate' (currently 12%) less any interest paid. This does not apply if the notional interest amounts to £200 or less, nor if the interest would have been tax deductible if the director or employee had paid it, for example on loans up to £30,000 to buy the principal private residence (see chapter 3). Where a director or employee receives an advance for expenses necessarily incurred in performing his duties the Revenue do not treat the advance as a loan, provided that

(a) the maximum amount advanced at any one time does not exceed £1,000,
(b) the advances are spent within six months, and
(c) the director or employee accounts to the company at regular intervals for the expenditure.

If the loan or overdrawing is written off by the company, the director or employee is treated as having received an equivalent amount of remuneration at that time. This applies to any loan obtained through the employment, and not just one at a rate of interest below the 'official rate'. Where the loan is made by a close company and the director or employee is also a shareholder, the liability on amounts written off is calculated differently, as indicated below.

If a company is a close company (broadly one controlled by its directors or by five or fewer people), loans and advances to shareholders (including shareholders who are directors or employees) give rise to a tax liability on the company (unless the loan does not exceed £15,000 and is made to a full-time working director or employee who does not have a material interest (see above) in the company). The company has to pay tax at the ACT rate (currently 3/7ths) on the amount of the loan or overdrawn account balance, the tax being recoverable as and when the overdrawn amount or loan is repaid to the company. Should the company not account to the Revenue for the tax at the appropriate time, interest arises thereon at the rate applicable to overdue tax.

If the close company writes off the loan, the shareholder is liable to tax at excess rates (including investment income surcharge if applicable) on the gross equivalent of the amount written off, the basic-rate tax being treated as having been already accounted for by the company.

As well as the tax aspects, comprehensive legislation was introduced in the Companies Act 1980 on directors' loans. In essence loans in excess of £2,500 are not permitted unless they fall within some very limited exceptions, one of which is a loan to enable a director properly to perform his duties, where the loan is sanctioned by the company in general meeting (but for relevant companies, which broadly means public limited companies and members of groups that include public limited companies, such a loan cannot exceed £10,000). A relevant company which breaches the rules may be liable to both criminal penalties and civil remedies. If a company is not a relevant company only civil remedies are available, enabling a company to avoid the contract and making the directors jointly and severally liable for any loss the company suffers as a result of the transaction. Family companies will usually not be relevant companies so that they will normally be exposed only to civil remedies.

Liabilities in connection with directors' remuneration

Remuneration is regarded as paid when it is credited to the director's account and the liability of the company to account for PAYE and national insurance arises at that time. The credit should therefore be made net of employee's tax and national insurance contributions. Drawings from the account can be made without any further liability once the PAYE and national insurance have been accounted for to the Revenue. From 6 April 1983 if a company does not deduct PAYE from the remuneration paid to a director, the amount that should have been deducted is treated as extra remuneration and taxable accordingly (FA 1983, s 22).

Where a director receives payments in advance or on account of future remuneration this has to be treated as pay for tax and national insurance purposes at the time of the advance, unless the advances are covered by a credit balance on the director's loan account (or unless the advances are on account of expenses as indicated above).

It used to be possible to reduce national insurance contributions by paying remuneration at uneven rates and irregular intervals. This has been prevented from 6 April 1983 by changes in the method of calculating earnings limits. The detailed provisions are in chapter 14.

If employers fail to deduct and account for PAYE and national insurance contributions when due they may incur penalties. It is also provided in the Social Security Act 1975, s 152, that if a company is convicted of failing to pay national insurance contributions and does not then comply with a court order for payment, any director who knew, or could reasonably have been expected to have known, of the company's failure to pay the contributions is jointly and severally liable for payment. If the company is in liquidation, a director who makes such a payment cannot replace the DHSS as a preferential creditor, and ranks as an unsecured creditor.

Tax points

- Always look at the combined company/director/shareholder position in considering the most appropriate way of dealing with pre-remuneration profits.

- Look at all relevant years and not just the current year.

- Make effective use of company or personal pension funds, which will grow faster than individual investments because of their tax exemption.

- Where a director's wife is also a director, benefits in kind can often be provided to her at reasonable cost to the company and the benefit assessed on her is treated as her earned income against which wife's earned income relief is available if not already used. If, however, she were a lower-paid employee the benefits assessment would be made on the husband and taxed at his marginal rate.

14
National insurance contributions—employees and employers

Background

A large part of the cost of the social security system is funded from contributions made by people currently earning money either as employees or as self-employed persons. The level of a person's contributions and the regulations relating to its collection depend upon which 'class' of contribution is to be paid.

Employees and their employers pay Class 1 contributions which are earnings-related and are payable as a percentage of earnings. Payments made by employees are known as 'primary' contributions, those by employers as 'secondary' contributions.

Persons liable to pay Class 1 contributions (SSA 1975, ss 2, 4)

Unless specifically exempted (see below), all 'employed earners' and their employers must pay Class 1 contributions. An 'employed earner' is a person gainfully employed either under a contract of service or as the holder of an office with emoluments chargeable to income tax under Schedule E (see chapter 11).

DHSS leaflet NI 39 'National Insurance and contract of service' outlines a number of criteria which are taken into account in deciding whether or not a person is employed. Thus, for example, an employer exercises control over the work of an employee whereas a self-employed person is normally his own master. Also, whereas a self-employed person is in business and usually takes a degree of financial risk in attempting to make a profit, an employed person receives a wage in return for doing work which he is instructed to do.

In addition, certain people are specifically brought within the liability to Class 1 contributions, including office and similar cleaners, most agency workers (including 'temps' but excluding outworkers and entertainers), wives employed in their husbands' businesses and vice versa, ministers of religion paid chiefly by way of stipend or salary, and certain part-time lecturers and teachers.

Certain employees and their employers are exempted from payment of Class 1 contributions. These are

(a) people employed outside Great Britain and its Continental Shelf,
(b) people aged under 16,
(c) people whose earnings are below the weekly lower earnings limit (£32.50 for 1983/84),
(d) a wife employed by her husband for a non-business purpose and vice versa,
(e) people employed for a non-buisiness purpose by a close relative in the home which they both inhabit,
(f) returning and counting officers and people employed by them in connection with an election or referendum, and
(g) certain employees of international organisations and visiting armed forces.

Earnings (SSA 1975, s 3)

Class 1 contributions are calculated on gross pay, which is broadly the same as pay for income tax, but before deducting superannuation contributions. They are not charged on benefits in kind or on tips that are received directly rather than via the employer.

Contracted-out employees

Pensions for retirement, widowhood and invalidity consist of two parts, a basic flat-rate pension, and an additional pension related to the level of the employee's earnings.

Employees who are members of occupational pension schemes which meet the requirements of the Occupational Pensions Board can be 'contracted-out' of the additional pension for retirement and part of the additional pension for widowhood by their employers. Contracted-out employees are still eligible for the basic pension from the state but obtain their additional pension from their employer's occupational pension scheme. To help defray the cost of setting up and running a separate pension scheme, contracted-out employees and their employers pay reduced rates of Class 1 contributions.

Contribution rates (SSA 1975, ss 1, 3, 4)

No national insurance contributions are payable by either employee or employer if weekly earnings are below the lower earnings limit (£32.50 for 1983/84). If weekly earnings exceed that amount, both employee's and employer's contributions are payable on the *full amount* up to the upper earnings limit (£235 per week for 1983/84), beyond which no contributions are payable. See example 1.

Example 1

A single man's weekly earnings in 1983/84 are (*a*) £32, or (*b*) £34.

		(*a*)	(*b*)
		£	£
Total earnings		1,664	1,768
Tax		—	—
Employee's national insurance		—	160
Net earnings		£1,664	£1,608

Earnings of £2 a week more thus leave the employee worse off, and also cost the employer an additional £207 in secondary contributions.

Employers' contributions include a 'national insurance surcharge', which is payable by all employers except charities. The surcharge is reduced from 1.5% to 1% in respect of earnings paid after 1 August 1983.

CONTRIBUTION RATES FOR 1983/84 EARNINGS UP TO £235 PER WEEK

	Employee	Employer To 31.7.83	Employer From 1.8.83
Not contracted-out:			
Standard rate	9%	11.95%	11.45%
Reduced rate	3.85%	As for standard rate	
Contracted-out:			
Standard rate			
On first £32.50 a week	9%	11.95%	11.45%
Between £32.50 and			
£235 a week	6.85%	7.85%	7.35%
Reduced rate	3.85%	As for standard rate	

Employee contributions

Reduced rate

Women who were married or widowed as at 6 April 1977 had a right to choose on or before 11 May 1977 to pay Class 1 contributions at a reduced rate. Entitlement to pay reduced rate contributions is evidenced by a certificate (Form CF 380, CF 380A or CF 2AR(TO)) which must be handed over to the employer to enable him to deduct contributions at the correct rate.

The reduced rate for 1983/84, which is the same for both contracted-out and non-contracted-out employees, is 3.85% on earnings up to £235 per week.

Women who pay reduced rate contributions are not eligible to receive contributory benefits, but they can claim retirement pension, death grant and widow's benefit on the contribution record of their husbands, and they are entitled to receive statutory sick pay.

The election to pay reduced rate contributions is effective until it is cancelled or revoked. A woman will lose the right to pay reduced rate contributions

(a) if she is granted a decree absolute of divorce or nullity, in which case the right is lost immediately,

(b) if she pays no reduced rate Class 1 contributions and has no earnings from self-employment for two consecutive tax years, or

(c) if she becomes widowed and is not entitled to widow's benefit or industrial or war widow's pension. The right to pay reduced rate contributions is not lost until the end of the tax year in which the husband dies, or the end of the following tax year if he dies between 1 October and 5 April.

Revocation, which must be in writing, can be made at any time and will, in most instances, take effect from the beginning of the tax year following the one in which it is given.

People over pensionable age

No contributions are payable by an employee who is over pension age (65 for a man, 60 for a woman), although the employer is still liable for secondary contributions where earnings reach or exceed the lower earnings limit, such contributions always being at non-contracted-out rates.

Employees who are not liable to pay contributions should apply for a certificate of age exception (form CF 384). This should be given to the employer as authority for the non-deduction of the Class 1 contributions from earnings.

More than one employment

Where a person has more than one employment he is liable to pay primary Class 1 contributions in respect of each job.

If, at the end of a tax year, an employee has paid more than the prescribed maximum contributions for that year, the DHSS will automatically refund any overpayment of 50p or more. Alternatively, the employee may obtain an earlier refund by submitting form CF 28F together with evidence of excess payments, e.g. a P60.

To avoid having to pay contributions in all employments throughout the year and being refunded any excess after the end of the year, an employee may apply to defer some of his contributions or to pay a year's contributions in advance. An application form for deferment of contributions can be found in DHSS booklet NP 28—'More than one job?', and if deferment is granted a certificate (form RD 950) will be sent to the employers concerned (except those paying the emoluments upon which the maximum contributions are calculated) authorising them not to deduct the employee's contributions.

As an alternative to applying for deferment of contributions an employee may pay the maximum contributions in advance. Where this is done all employers will be instructed not to deduct primary contributions.

The maximum contributions for 1983/84 are:

All employments non-contracted-out	All employments contracted-out	Reduced rate
£1,120.95	£873.36	£470.52

Where an employee has both contracted-out and non-contracted-out employments the amount to be paid in advance is £1,120.95 where earnings from contracted-out jobs are expected to be less than the upper earnings limit, and £873.36 where such earnings are expected to exceed the upper earnings limit.

Irrespective of whether employee contributions are deferred or paid in advance, the various employers concerned must pay the full amount of the secondary contributions.

To prevent abuse of the system the following 'anti-avoidance' provisions have been included in the legislation:

(a) where a person has more than one job with the same employer, earnings from those employments must be aggregated together and contributions calculated on that aggregate;

(b) where a person has jobs with different employers who 'carry on business in association with each other' and the earnings from at least one of the jobs are below the lower earnings limit, all earnings from 'associated' employers must be aggregated together for the purpose of calculating contributions.

These aggregation rules will not be enforced if it can be shown that to do so would be impracticable.

Income from self-employment

The position of the employee who also has income from self-employment is examined in detail in chapter 24.

Company directors

It is not uncommon for a director to receive a salary under a service contract in addition to receiving fees for holding the office of director. Furthermore, it is not unusual for a director to receive his emoluments in irregular amounts at irregular time intervals, for example a fixed monthly salary together with a bonus after the year end, once the results of the company are known.

Prior to 6 April 1983 the application of monthly or weekly upper earnings limits meant that it was possible for companies to minimise liability to national insurance contributions simply by paying fees and bonuses in unequal amounts. This practice has led the DHSS to introduce new provisions regarding the Class 1 contributions liability of directors.

From 6 April 1983 directors in employment at the beginning of a tax year will have an annual earnings period coinciding with the tax year. Persons appointed during a tax year will have a pro-rata earnings period comprising the number of weeks from the date of appointment to the end of the tax year. No Class 1 contributions are due if the director's earnings are less than the annual lower earnings limit (1983/84 £1,689.96) or the pro-rata limit for directors appointed during a tax year. For a pro-rata earnings period the appropriate multiple of the weekly limit is used.

All earnings paid to a director during an earnings period must be included in that earnings period (irrespective of the period to which they relate). Earnings include fees, bonuses, salary, payments made in anticipation of future earnings, e.g. advances on future bonuses to be declared when a company's results are finalised, and payments made to a director which were earned while he was still an employee.

If a director resigns during a tax year all payments made to him between the date of resignation and the end of the tax year relating to his period of directorship must be aggregated with his other 'directorship earnings' of that tax year.

Earnings in respect of a time when a person was a director, paid in a tax year after the directorship ended, are not aggregated with any other earnings of the year in which payment is made. Instead, they are assessed independently on an annual earnings basis, and Class 1 contributions accounted for accordingly.

Many directors have payments in anticipation of future earnings, e.g. a payment on account of a bonus to be declared when the company's results are known. From 6 April 1983 liability for Class 1 contributions arises when the payments are made (subject, of course, to the lower earnings limit). The advance bonus payments are aggregated with all other earnings of the annual earnings period. When the bonus is voted (probably at the annual general meeting) the balance, if any, will become liable to Class 1 contributions in the tax year in which the annual general meeting is held. Once a bonus is voted for a past period it is deemed to be paid unless exceptionally it is not placed at the directors disposal. This is the case regardless of whether or not it is left in the company or placed in an account on which the director can draw as and when he chooses.

To the extent that advances to directors are covered by a credit balance on directors' loan account no Class 1 liability will arise as these advances are deemed to be reductions in the loan account.

Unpaid national insurance contributions and company liquidations

The Social Security Act 1975 provides that where a limited company fails to pay over Class 1 contributions to the DHSS, the directors of the company become jointly and severally liable in respect of unpaid contributions which they know (or ought to have known) should have been paid.

In a recent case it was held that directors who pay over money in satisfaction of a debt to the DHSS as a result of proceedings brought under the Social Security Act 1975 cannot replace the DHSS as preferential creditors by the process of subrogation. Directors of companies which are about to go into liquidation should thus ensure that national insurance liabilities are cleared before placing the company in liquidation.

Tax points

- If an employee has several employments he can get back national insurance contributions in excess of the annual maximum, but the employer cannot. Consider having the employee engaged by only one company, which makes a charge to the other companies for his services and related employment costs. Don't overlook the addition of VAT to the service charge.

- If your spouse pays maximum contributions in a separate job and also does some work in the family business run by you, you cannot get back employer's national insurance on the earnings. It may be more sensible to pay your spouse less than the weekly limit and increase your own earnings. This has to be considered in the light of your joint total earnings level and possible effect on separate taxation of wife's earnings where applicable. See page 264.

- Remember that national insurance does not work on a cumulative basis like income tax. If average earnings will not exceed the lower earnings level, try to ensure that the actual earnings in any week do not do so, otherwise both employer and employee will be liable to pay contributions thereon.

- If your company is likely to go into liquidation, make sure all national insurance liabilities are first paid up to date, otherwise as a director you will be personally liable for payment and your payment will not rank as a preferential debt.

15
Statutory sick pay

Background

Statutory sick pay (SSP) was made law by the Social Security and Housing Benefits Act 1982. As from 6 April 1983 most employees are entitled to receive SSP from their employers for up to eight weeks of sickness absence in any one tax year. SSP is paid at one of three flat rates, according to the employee's average weekly earnings, and is subject to deductions for income tax and national insurance contributions. Employers can recoup the direct cost of SSP by deducting amounts paid from their monthly remittances of national insurance contributions and PAYE to the Collector of Taxes.

When an employee is being paid SSP he has no entitlement to state sickness benefit. Employees who are not entitled to SSP and employees who have exhausted their annual SSP entitlement may claim sickness, and later invalidity, benefit.

Employees entitled to receive SSP

The definition of an employee is the same as that of an 'employed earner' for Class 1 national insurance contributions (see chapter 14). One effect of this definition is that married women and widows paying reduced rate Class 1 contributions are entitled to SSP.

All employers and employees must participate in the operation of SSP and neither party can opt out of the scheme. An employee is entitled to SSP for each job he has, so that if an individual is employed by two different employers he will be paid SSP by each employer for any day off work through illness.

An employee is entitled to SSP unless he/she falls into one of the excluded groups outlined in Schedule 1 to the 1982 Act.

Excluded employees

Employees who, at the beginning of a 'period of incapacity for work' (see below), fall into one of the following categories are excluded from entitlement to SSP.

(a) People over state pensionable age (men 65, women 60).

(b) Those who have claimed certain state benefits within the 57 days before falling ill. The benefits concerned are:
  (i) sickness benefit;
  (ii) invalidity benefit or non-contributory invalidity pension;
  (iii) maternity allowance;
  (iv) unemployment benefit, where prior to claiming the claimant was receiving either of the benefits in (ii).
An employee who has received one of these benefits will receive a letter from the DHSS notifying the employer of the period of exclusion.

(c) Those whose average weekly earnings are below the lower earnings limit for national insurance contributions (see chapter 14).

(d) A person who has not begun work under his contract.

(e) Those who become ill during a stoppage of work at their place of employment during a trade dispute, unless the employee can prove that he is not participating in, or directly interested in, the dispute.

(f) A pregnant woman during her 'disqualifying period' of eighteen weeks beginning eleven weeks before the expected week of confinement.

(g) Those who have received eight weeks SSP from their current employer in the current tax year or in one continuous period of illness spanning two tax years. This latter exclusion does not prevent an employee receiving a total of eight weeks SSP in the second tax year if he should subsequently fall ill later in that year.

(h) Those who fall ill while working outside the EEC.

(j) Those who fall ill while in prison or in legal custody.

(k) Those contracted to work for a period not exceeding three months (e.g. seasonal workers). If, however, an employee works on beyond the three months (even though the contract is not formally extended) he will be entitled to SSP thereafter. Moreover, if an employee starts work under a new contract within eight weeks of an earlier contract with the same employer, and the contracts together produce a contract of thirteen or more weeks, the employee will be entitled to SSP.

Where an employer receives notification of illness from an employee who falls into an 'excluded' category, he must issue the employee with an exclusion form SSP 1(E). Failure to issue an exclusion form within seven days of the formation of a 'period of incapacity for work' (see below) is a criminal offence.

Qualifying conditions

For SSP to be payable three qualifying conditions must be met:

  (i) there must be a 'period of incapacity for work' ('PIW');
  (ii) there must be a 'period of entitlement' ('PE'); and
  (iii) there must be one or more 'qualifying days'.

Incapacity for work

A PIW is a period of four or more consecutive days of incapacity for work, counting rest days and holidays as well as normal working days. A person may be deemed incapable of work on the advice of a doctor or medical officer of health (e.g. where a pregnant woman is advised to stay at home during an outbreak of German measles at her place of work), but a day counts towards a PIW only if the employee is, or is deemed to be, 'incapable by reason of specific disease or bodily or mental disablement of doing work which he/she can reasonably be expected to do under the contract of employment'. The incapacity must exist throughout the day, nightshift workers falling ill during a shift being treated as working only on the day in which the shift began.

If two PIWs are separated by a period of less than fourteen days, they are linked together and treated as one single PIW. See example 1.

Example 1

An employee is incapable of work through illness from Thursday 1 March to Monday 5 March inclusive and from Sunday 11 March to Thursday 15 March inclusive.

The two PIWs of five days are separated by less than fourteen days and are therefore treated as a single PIW of ten days.

Period of entitlement

SSP is only payable when days of incapacity fall into a PE, which is a period beginning with a PIW (see above) and ending with whichever of the following first occurs:

(a) the period of incapacity ends and the employee returns to work;
(b) the employee reaches his maximum entitlement to SSP;
(c) the employee's contract of employment ends;
(d) the employee goes abroad outside the EEC;
(e) the employee is detained in legal custody;
(f) a pregnant woman employee starts her 'disqualifying period' (see above).

Where a PE ends for any reason other than the return of the employee to work, the employer must issue transfer form SSP 1(T) to the employee to enable the employee to claim sickness benefit. The transfer form must be issued two weeks before the employee's entitlement to SSP is likely to or will end. If the employee goes sick after having been entitled to six weeks SSP in a tax year (or in a continuous period of illness spanning two tax years), or if the employee's entitlement suddenly ends (e.g. through being taken into legal custody), it must be issued immediately. It is a criminal offence not to issue the transfer form within seven days of the required date.

Qualifying days

SSP is payable only in respect of 'qualifying days'. These are days of the week agreed between the employer and employee and will normally be those days on which the employee is required to work. Employer and employee may, however, come to other arrangements if they wish. There is an overriding rule that there must be at least one qualifying day each week even if the employee is not required to work during that week.

SSP is not payable for the first three qualifying days in any PIW not linked to an earlier PIW. These are 'waiting days'. See example 2.

Example 2

An employee with qualifying days Monday to Friday each week, who had not been ill during July, was incapacitated for work on the days ringed in August.

M	T	W	Th	F	Sa	Su
①	②	③	④	⑤	6	7
8	9	10	11	12	13	14
15	16	17	18	19	20	21
㉒	㉓	㉔	㉕	26	27	㉘
㉙	㉚	㉛				

There are three PIWs, from the 1st to the 5th, from the 22nd to the 25th, and from the 28th to the 31st.

In the first, SSP is payable for the fourth and fifth days only.

In the second, which begins more than 14 days after the end of the first and is therefore not linked with it, SSP is payable for the fourth day only.

The third begins less than 14 days after the end of the second and is therefore linked with it. As there are three waiting days in the second PIW, SSP is payable for each of the three qualifying days in the third.

Amount of SSP

Average earnings

SSP is payable on a daily basis at a rate which is determined by the employee's average weekly earnings. 'Average earnings' are gross earnings (including bonuses and overtime) paid in the eight weeks immediately preceding the period of illness. Where an employee is paid monthly the weekly rate is computed by adding together the two salary payments prior to the illness, multiplying the result by six and dividing the total by 52. There are special rules where an employee is paid irregularly.

Rates

The weekly earnings bands and applicable rates of SSP from 6 April 1983 are as follows.

Average weekly earnings	Standard £65 and over	Middle £48.50–£64.99	Lower £32.50–£48.49
SSP weekly rate	£40.25	£33.75	£27.20
Annual maximum	£322.00	£270.00	£217.60

The daily rate of SSP applicable is the appropriate weekly rate divided by the number of qualifying days in the week (e.g. an employee who has five qualifying days in a week and who has average weekly earnings of £70 will receive SSP at a daily rate of £8.05 (£40.25 ÷ 5)).

Although there are no rules about when SSP must be paid out, in the normal course of events it would be paid on the employee's normal pay day.

Contractual remuneration paid to an employee can be offset against any SSP due for the same day. If the contractual remuneration is less than the SSP due, the employer must make up the payment to the appropriate rate of SSP.

Notification and evidence

Any system for the payment of SSP is triggered by the employee notifying his employer that he is unfit for work. An employer can draw up his own procedure for notification subject to the following limitations:

(a) reasonable steps must be taken to notify employees of the procedures; and
(b) it is not legal to insist that notification
  (i) is made by the employee in person, or
  (ii) is made by a particular time of day, or
  (iii) is made more than once weekly for the same illness, or
  (iv) is made on a document provided by the employer or by way of a medical certificate, or
  (v) is given earlier than the first qualifying day.

If no notification procedures have been drawn up, the employee should inform his employer in writing by the seventh day after his first qualifying day of absence. If an employee fails to notify within the laid-down time limits an employer may withhold SSP; if an employee is more than 91 days late with his notification he loses his right to SSP.

Having been notified by an employee of his illness, the employer must satisfy himself that the illness is genuine before paying SSP. The DHSS anticipates that employers will obtain 'self-certificates' for the first week of illness and medical notes for longer absences.

An employer may withhold SSP when notification is late, and he may refuse to pay SSP if he feels that the employee is not in fact sick. In both these instances the employer, if required by the employee, must provide written reasons for withholding or refusing to pay SSP. An employee who disagrees with his employer's actions has the right to appeal for an official decision.

Recovery of SSP by employer

Employers are able to recover the gross amount of SSP paid in any month from amounts due to be paid over to the Collector of Taxes in respect of Class 1 national insurance contributions. If SSP paid exceeds contributions due, the excess can be deducted from PAYE payable to the Collector; and if SSP paid exceeds both national insurance and PAYE payable the employer can either carry the excess forward or apply to the Collector for a refund.

It should be noted that 'secondary' Class 1 contributions (see chapter 14) paid by the employer in respect of SSP paid are not recoverable.

Employer's records

Employer's records are particularly important, as the information required to be kept may have to be made available to the DHSS. The form the records take is up to the employer, but the following information must be recorded:

(a) dates of employees' PIWs;
(b) details of qualifying days in each PE;
(c) details of days within each PIW for which SSP was not paid with reasons (including 'excluded categories', see above).

Records must be readily accessible to DHSS inspectors and must be kept for a minimum of three years after the end of the tax year to which they relate.

In addition to the records outlined above, the DHSS recommends that the following are also retained for further reference:

(i) medical notes and 'self-certificates';
(ii) an outline of the employer's SSP rules;
(iii) a record of all correspondence with the DHSS;
(iv) a record of when employees report absence through sickness;
(v) explanatory letters giving details of persons excluded because of their recent receipt of state benefits (see above).

16
Termination of employment

Lump sum payments (TA 1970, ss 187, 188 and Sch 8)

Such payments may arise in two different ways, as compensation for breach of the contract of employment or as ex gratia payments by employers. A payment will be taxable as emoluments under Schedule E in the normal way if it is a payment for services rendered. If not so taxable, it will be subject to special rules (see below).

A termination payment will generally be regarded as for services rendered only where it was specifically provided for in the contract of employment, or where the contract was made under an expectation that it would be received.

In the case of an ex gratia payment, however, since there is no obligation on the employer to make the payment, it will be more difficult to demonstrate to the Revenue that it was made in respect of the termination of employment rather than for services rendered.

For either type of payment, the following circumstances may give rise to further complication:

(i) Where the employer is also a shareholder, it may be difficult to demonstrate that the payment is not a distribution, with the consequential requirement for the company to pay advance corporation tax and with no deduction being given for the payment in calculating the employer's trading profit (see chapter 4).

(ii) Where the payment is made at the same time as a change in voting control, a clear distinction between the payment and the share transactions must be demonstrated if the payment is not to be regarded as part and parcel of the capital transaction.

(iii) If the employee continues with the employer in a new capacity, either as an employee or perhaps under a consultancy agreement, it becomes that much harder to demonstrate that the payment was not in respect of services rendered or to be rendered in the future.

Taxation of the lump sum

Provided that the payment is not caught either as taxable emoluments, or as a distribution, or as part of a capital transaction, it will be taxed according to the special rules for termination payments. Under these, the first £25,000 is exempt from tax. The tax on the next £25,000 is 50% of what it would be if it were treated as extra earnings of the tax-year in which the employment ceases. The tax on the next £25,000 is similarly reduced but by only 25%, and the remainder is taxed in full. See example 1.

Example 1

An employee received a termination payment of £100,000 in 1983/84. His other taxable income of the year (after allowances) is £10,000.

The tax on the termination payment is calculated as follows:

Tax on other taxable income of £10,000 @ 30%				£3,000

Tax on termination payment of £100,000:

On first	£25,000			—
On next	£25,000	4,600 @ 30%	1,380	
		2,600 @ 40%	1,040	
		4,600 @ 45%	2,070	
		7,100 @ 50%	3,550	
		6,100 @ 55%	3,355	
			11,395	
		Less 50%	5,698	5,697
On next	£25,000	1,000 @ 55%	550	
		24,000 @ 60%	14,400	
			14,950	
		Less 25%	3,737	11,213
On remaining £25,000		@ 60%		15,000
Total tax on termination payment				£31,910

Statutory redundancy payments, whilst not themselves taxable, are included within the first £25,000. Most payments in lieu of notice will be covered by the first £25,000 and thus not charged to tax unless, exceptionally, they are taxable as emoluments under Schedule E in the normal way.

Exemptions

Some payments are completely exempt from tax, for example those on death in service or in respect of disability, or where the service has been predominantly abroad. There is partial exemption for shorter periods of work abroad, and also where the employee is not domiciled in the UK and the employer is not UK-resident (i.e. where the earnings are foreign emoluments, see chapter 11).

Lump sums received under approved superannuation schemes are exempt. They may be boosted by agreed special contributions from the employer to the fund prior to the termination of employment (see chapter 17).

Application of PAYE

The employer must deduct and account for PAYE on the excess of chargeable termination payments over £25,000.

Since the application of normal PAYE procedures will not give the relief which has been described, it is wise to negotiate a special reduction with the Revenue before the payment has to be made, so that the PAYE payment will equate more closely with the tax due.

Tax position of the employer

In deducting any expense in determining the employer's profits, it must be shown that the expense was wholly and exclusively for the purposes of the trade. There is no special rule for termination payments, but it will usually be easier to demonstrate that they meet this requirement when they are compensation rather than ex gratia payments, and when the trade is continuing rather than when it is not.

It is specifically laid down that an additional payment up to three times any amount paid under the statutory redundancy pay provisions is allowable as a deduction in computing the employer's profits. Any rebates received under the statutory redundancy scheme must be brought into account to reduce the cost to the employer.

It may be particularly difficult for the employer to obtain a deduction where the payment is ex gratia and is associated with a sale of the shares or a change in voting control, or where it is an abnormally high payment to a director with a material interest in the company.

Expenses incurred in obtaining a termination payment

Some employees may incur expenses, for example fees to advisers, in obtaining a termination payment. These will not reduce the assessable earnings or lump sum payment for tax purposes as they will not have been wholly, exclusively and necessarily incurred in the performance of the duties of the employment.

Tax points

- An ex gratia payment to a director or shareholder of a close company is especially vulnerable to Revenue attack, on either or both of the following grounds:

(a) It is not a deductible trading expense.

(b) It is a distribution of profits.

- If an ex gratia payment by a close company is not allowed in calculating profits, the Revenue may contend that each shareholder has made a proportionate transfer of value for capital transfer tax. There is a specific exclusion where the payment is allowed in computing profits.

- Unless the income after termination will be equally high, the tax cost of a substantial termination payment may be lower if the termination occurs shortly after 6 April rather than before, so that the income from the terminated employment will be minimal.

- It is essential that proper documentation and board minutes are available so that the nature of payments can be demonstrated to the Revenue.

17
Company pension schemes

Background

Since 1978 all employers have been required to make provision for employee's pensions, either under the State scheme or by 'contracting out' (see chapter 14 for details). 'Contracted-in' employees receive a basic pension and an additional earnings-related pension from the State. 'Contracted-out' employees receive the basic pension from the State but the additional pension comes from their employer. Contracting out is not permitted unless the benefits provided are at least equal to the additional earnings-related pension that would have been received under the State scheme (called the 'guaranteed minimum pension'). In most cases the benefits are better. Few occupational schemes provide for any inflation-proofing of pension, whereas the additional pension under the State scheme is increased annually in line with increases in the retail prices index. It is therefore provided that the State will pay inflation increases on the guaranteed minimum pension element of a contracted-out occupational pension whether or not the employer's scheme provides for inflation-proofing, so that the contracted-out employee will never get less than he would have received under the State scheme.

Many employers, particularly family companies, remain contracted in to the State scheme and provide their own pension scheme in addition. The employee then gets full benefits under the State scheme (and pays full contributions) plus the additional benefits provided by his employer's scheme.

Revenue approval for employers' schemes (FA 1970, ss 19–26)

A pension scheme gains automatic Revenue approval if it conforms precisely to the statutory conditions. The Revenue may, however, approve a scheme which does not precisely conform and many schemes receive this discretionary approval. The Revenue issue Practice Notes on the manner in which they exercise their discretion, and specialist pensions advisers are able to structure schemes so that they will receive the approval of the Superannuation Funds Office.

Taxation advantages of Revenue approval

(a) The employer's contributions are deductible in calculating business profits.

(b) The employer's contributions are not treated as a benefit in kind to the employee.

(c) An employee's own contributions are deductible in calculating his taxable earnings.

(d) A tax-free lump sum can be paid from the scheme to the employee on retirement.

(e) The eventual pension is treated as earned income in the retired employee's hands.

(f) Provision can be made for a lump sum to be paid on an employee's death in service, which is usually free of taxation.

(g) The fund itself is not liable to income tax or capital gains tax.

Retirement age

Approval is usually given for a retirement age not earlier than 60 for men and 55 for women, and although earlier ages can be approved for certain occupations a lower age is not normally approved for a director of either sex who, together with defined family and trustees, owns or controls more than 20% of the company voting rights.

Maximum contributions

There is no specific upper limit on the amount that an employer may contribute, subject only to the requirement that the benefits provided as a result are within the permitted levels and the contributions are not excessive in relation to those benefits. If for example an employee joins a scheme late it is possible to make contributions of several times the employee's current remuneration in order to fund the maximum benefits. Inflation-proofing may be provided for. Special irregular contributions may be made by the employer in addition to the normal annual contributions. Such irregular contributions may, if they are very large, have to be spread forward over a maximum of five years in calculating the employer's profits, rather than all the relief being given in the year of payment.

It is not necessary for an employee to be required to contribute to a scheme, but where he does the contributions (including any additional or special contributions to obtain additional benefits) must not exceed 15% of his remuneration.

Maximum benefits for employees

Basis for calculating maximum benefits

Maximum benefits are measured in terms of 'final pensionable remuneration'. Final pensionable remuneration is the greater of the remuneration in any one of the five years before retirement (with averaging for fluctuating payments) or the average of total remuneration for any period of three or more consecutive years ended in the last ten years before normal retirement date. Remuneration includes taxable benefits in kind.

Unless the 'final remuneration' is that of the twelve months ending with normal retirement date, each year's remuneration included in the calculation may be 'dynamised', i.e. increased in proportion to the increase in the cost of living index for the period from the end of the year up to normal retirement date.

A director who, together with his defined family and trustees, controls more than 20% of the employing company's voting rights must use a final remuneration calculation with at least a three-year averaging of earnings, but the increases from indexing may be taken into account.

Maximum pension

The maximum pension payable is 2/3rds final remuneration, at the rate of 1/60th for each year's service up to 40 years. This may be increased for late entrants who are unable to complete 40 years' service, so that the maximum can apply after 10 years' service. Inflation-proofing may be provided for within the funding of the scheme. Part of the pension may be commuted for a lump sum (see below).

Pensions from other schemes

Benefits at the 1/60th per year rate may usually be provided regardless of any pension benefits earned in previous occupations. Where, however, the 1/60th rate is increased because of late entry, retained benefits from previous employment, including self-employed pension plans, must be taken into account in determining the maximum benefits payable.

Lump sums

Part of the maximum available benefits may be commuted to a lump sum not exceeding one and a half times final remuneration, at the rate of 3/80ths final remuneration for each year's service. Again provision is made for late entrants, so that the maximum may arise after 20 years' service, but lump sums from earlier employments must be taken into account. If dynamised final remuneration is used to calculate the pension, it may also be used to calculate the lump sum.

Provision for dependants

Provision for dependants may be made both in respect of death in service and for death after retirement. Inflation increases may be provided for in both cases. A pension to a surviving spouse may continue for the spouse's lifetime, but children's pensions must cease when they reach age 18 or cease full-time education.

Death in service

When an employee dies in service, a lump sum not exceeding four times final remuneration (which is defined in a more generous way than for other benefits) may be paid without attracting capital transfer tax. The pension scheme trustees usually have discretion as to who receives the payment, but they generally act in accordance with the employee's known wishes. In addition the employee's own contributions to the pension scheme may be repaid with interest.

Pensions may also be paid to the surviving spouse and/or dependants. The pension paid to any one person cannot exceed two thirds of the maximum pension the employee could have received if he had retired on incapacity grounds at the date of death (with potential service up to normal retirement age being taken into account). The total pensions to spouse and dependants cannot exceed the total incapacity pension the employee could have received.

Death after retirement

Provision may be made for an employee's pension to continue for a set period after retirement despite his earlier death. Separate pensions for spouse and dependants can also be provided, subject to the individual pensions not exceeding two-thirds of the maximum pension that could have been approved for the employee and the total pensions not exceeding the whole of that maximum. Lump sum benefits will not normally be permitted.

Changing employment (FA 1970, Sch 5)

When you change employment, then depending on the rules of the employer's scheme, you may either have a deferred pension which will become payable on retirement, or a transfer payment into a new scheme, or be 'bought back' into the State scheme through a payment by the employer. Where there is a deferred pension, the amount paid on retirement must be at least equal to the guaranteed minimum pension that would have been paid under the State scheme.

Refunds of contributions are not usually available except for contributions made before April 1975 or for short periods of employment, but where they are made tax is deducted at the rate of 10%.

Self-administered pension schemes

A self-administered pension scheme gives maximum flexibility in managing a fund, but the pension scheme trustees must invest in the best interests of the members in order to provide their pension benefits.

In particular loans to pension scheme members or their families are forbidden, but loans to the company itself, or to buy shares in it, may be permitted. Specialist advice is essential.

Tax points

- Contributions by employers to approved pension schemes are one of the few non-taxable benefits for directors and higher-paid employees, so generous funding of a scheme is particularly beneficial to them.

- A family company can have a pension scheme for its controlling directors and the contribution limits are less restrictive than those for self-employed pension plans.

- A family company could eliminate taxable trading profits by contributions to an approved scheme, and perhaps create a trading loss for carry back.

- Over-funding an approved scheme will result in contributions being returned to the company. They will be included as a trading receipt in the corporation tax computation.

18
Providing your own pension

Qualifying individuals

Those who are self-employed, or who are not members of an employer's pension scheme, may effectively build a personal fund for themselves by paying premiums within stipulated limits to one or more insurance companies, the premiums being accumulated by the insurance company in a fund free of income tax and capital gains tax. A person who has both pensionable and non-pensionable earnings may pay premiums in respect of the non-pensionable earnings, and husband and wife who each have non-pensionable earnings may make separate pension provision in this way.

Permissible benefits (TA 1970, s 226)

The retirement benefits must commence not later than age 75 nor earlier than age 60, except where the occupation is one in which earlier retirement is customary, for example entertainers and athletes, in which case the Revenue may approve a scheme with an earlier retirement date.

At retirement a tax-free lump sum is permitted, which may not exceed three times the annual pension remaining after such commutation. The pension itself is taxed as earned income.

Instead of taking benefits from the company with whom the policy was taken out, the taxpayer may elect at retirement that the accumulated fund be transferred to another company or companies, thus taking advantage of the most favourable annuity rate available.

It is possible to guarantee payment of the pension for up to ten years even if the taxpayer dies within that time. Should death occur before retirement the premiums are refunded, with or without interest and bonuses. The refund may be to the personal representatives or to the widow. Alternatively the contract may provide for the death benefits to be held in trust, with the monies payable at the trustees' discretion. If paid to the personal representatives, the sum refunded will form part of the estate for capital transfer tax purposes, but if paid to the surviving spouse or held in trust capital transfer tax is avoided.

Allowable premiums (TA 1970, ss 227, 227A, 228)

Premium limits are fixed by reference to 'net relevant earnings'. For a self-employed person this means his adjusted profits, after deducting capital allowances, stock relief, losses and any excess of business charges (such as patent royalties) over general investment income. For an employee, net relevant earnings are his non-pensionable earnings, including benefits, but after deducting expenses allowable against those earnings. The maximum premiums which may be allowed as a deduction from relevant earnings in any one tax year are presently $17\frac{1}{2}\%$ of the net relevant earnings, plus any unused relief for the previous six years. The percentage limit is increased for taxpayers who were born before 1933 as follows:

Year of birth	%
1916 to 1933	20
1914 or 1915	21
1912 or 1913	24
1910 or 1911	$26\frac{1}{2}$
1908 or 1909	$29\frac{1}{2}$
1907	$32\frac{1}{2}$

The opportunity of using unused past relief can substantially reduce or even eliminate the net relevant earnings for the tax-year, but, as indicated in example 1 below, it is not necessary to utilise all the unused past relief in one year. Any premium paid uses up first the available relief for the current year, then any unused relief for the previous six years, earliest first.

Backdating of premium payments to earlier years (TA 1970, s 227)

A premium payment made in one tax-year may, by election before the end of that tax-year, be treated for all purposes as a payment in the previous tax-year (or, if there were no net relevant earnings in the previous year, as a payment made two years earlier). Thus in example 1 below the premium payment of £2,550 could have been paid wholly or partly in 1984/85 and by election treated as relating to 1983/84. This gives a breathing space to establish what the maximum allowable premium is for a particular year, and also to provide the cash resources to make the payment. It is a useful provision since it is not possible to carry forward an excess of premium payments over the allowable limit for relief in a later year.

Funding the premium payments

Two often expressed objections to personal pension provision are, first, the cost of funding and, second, the inability to utilise the fund until retirement. Although it is not possible for a lender to take a charge on a personal pension fund, several insurance companies have arrangements under which a lender will make an appropriate advance to a taxpayer with a sufficiently large accumulated fund, or who is paying regular premiums to a fund, probably based in the latter case on a multiple of recurrent premiums.

Example 1

			£
Net relevant earnings in 1983/84			10,000
17½% thereof		1,750	

Unused relief for earlier years:

	Appropriate percentage of net relevant earnings, say	*Less* premiums already relieved for that year, say	
1982/83	3,500	2,000	1,500
1981/82	2,500	2,200	300
1980/81	2,900	1,700	1,200
1979/80	3,000	1,000	2,000
1978/79	2,000	500	1,500
1977/78	2,200	1,400	800

Maximum relief available for year 1983/84   9,050

The minimum premium payment required for 1983/84 in order to avoid wasting any unused relief would have to be:

17½% of £10,000 (relevant earnings for 1983/84)	1,750
Unused relief for 1977/78	800
	£2,550

The unused relief for 1978/79 to 1982/83 inclusive would then be available to increase the funding limit for 1984/85.

The terms of the advance are usually that interest is payable year by year but capital repayments are taken from the eventual tax-free lump sum on retirement. Whether security is required often depends upon the trade or profession carried on by the taxpayer.

The loan could itself be used to fund premium payments, so that in example 1 a substantial part of the £9,050 maximum premium payment might be funded from a loan made in conjunction with the pension premium arrangements.

Tax relief on the interest paid will be available if the borrowing is for a qualifying purpose, such as the acquisition of a dwelling, a business property or a partnership share (see chapter 4), but not otherwise. There will thus not be any relief in the case of a loan used to pay pension premiums.

Life assurance and pensions for dependants (TA 1970, s 226A)

The return of premiums on death prior to retirement is in itself a form of life assurance. The amount refunded is the gross premiums, usually with reasonable interest, whereas the cost to the payer was net of tax relief, a cash profit thus automatically arising. Clearly the longer the premiums have been paid the greater the capital sum on death before retirement or lump sum following retirement.

To cover the eventuality that death might occur before a reasonable sum has been built up, the taxpayer may also pay a premium to provide a lump sum on death before age 75. Such a policy may be written in trust, which has the advantage of making the sum quickly available instead of waiting for a grant of representation, and also avoids the sum assured swelling the estate for capital transfer tax. Relief for premiums paid is given at the taxpayer's marginal rate on earned income rather than at the life assurance rate of 15%.

Alternatively or additionally, a premium may be paid to provide a pension for dependants.

The allowable premiums for the term assurance and/or dependants' pensions are subject to a limit of 5% of net relevant earnings, the 5% being part of, and not additional to, the $17\frac{1}{2}$% limit (see above).

Late assessments and investigation settlements (TA 1970, s 227A; Revenue Statement of Practice SP 9/80)

Assessments are sometimes determined more than six years after the tax-year to which they relate, usually owing to the fraud, wilful default or neglect of the taxpayer (see chapter 10). Where an assessment becomes final and conclusive more than six years after the tax-year to which it relates, a taxpayer may utilise any unused relief created by the assessment to cover a premium paid in excess of the $17\frac{1}{2}$% limit (see above) for the year of payment, provided that he both pays the premium and makes an election within six months after the assessment becomes final and conclusive. Relief is then given against the earnings of the year of payment. (Only the premium related to the unused relief need be paid within the six-month period. The normal premium under the $17\frac{1}{2}$% limit could be paid in the following year and carried back.)

Strictly this relief is only available where assessments are formally determined, but the Revenue will allow it where an investigation settlement is concluded by their acceptance of an offer in respect of tax, interest and penalties rather than by the formal determination of assessments, provided that certain conditions are satisfied.

Tax points

- Term assurance within TA 1970, s 226A for the self-employed and those in non-pensionable employment gives relief at up to 60%, compared with the 15% relief available for life assurance.

- Consider surrendering a life assurance policy to provide funds for a retirement annuity premium, replacing life cover with tax-efficient term assurance under the retirement annuity rules. But remember that a term assurance can only provide a lump sum on death before age 75, not on surviving to a certain age as with an endowment policy.

- An inheritance or unexpected windfall may be used to fund an exceptional premium payment supported by current earnings and unused past relief.

- Even though earnings have been eliminated by personal reliefs, they still qualify as relevant earnings for the calculation of premium relief. Thus a working wife may have paid very little tax on modest earnings because of the wife's earned income relief, but those earnings can nonetheless create unused relief to support a premium payment in a later year when perhaps the earnings are more significant and of a size sufficient for the set-off to be beneficial.

19
Choice of business medium

Non-tax considerations

When starting in business the main alternatives are to become a sole trader, to form a partnership with others or to form a limited liability company. A sole trader or partner is liable for the debts of the business to the full extent of his personal assets, and can in the extreme be made bankrupt. A company shareholder's liability is normally limited to the amount, if any, unpaid on his shares. Protection of private assets is usually one of the main reasons for commencing a new venture in the form of a company. However, lenders and landlords frequently require directors to give a personal guarantee in respect of the company's obligation, which reduces significantly the benefit of limited liability. There are also major compliance requirements for a company under the Companies Acts, including the need to prepare and publish audited accounts.

The general commercial and family considerations must be weighed alongside the comparative tax positions when choosing what form the business is to take.

Comparative income tax and national insurance position for the unincorporated trader and the company director

A trader's profits are taxed at a marginal rate of 60% on taxable earned income in excess of £36,000, whether they are retained or withdrawn. (A husband and wife partnership could however effectively double this threshold by an election for separate taxation of the wife's earnings (see page 264), at a cost of losing the extra £1,010 of married man's allowance.) In addition, flat rate class 2 national insurance contributions of £4.40 per week are payable, together with class 4 contributions of 6.3% on profits between £3,800 and £12,000, giving a maximum class 4 liability of £516.60. In a husband and wife partnership both would have to pay class 4 national insurance contributions. They would also both have to pay class 2 contributions unless the wife elected not to do so on or before 11 May 1977 and holds a certificate of exemption.

A controlling director/shareholder can decide whether profits are taken out in the form of remuneration and/or dividends or retained within the company for taxation at corporation tax rates. The corporation tax rates for the year to 31 March 1983 are 38% on income profits up to £100,000, 52% on income profits in excess of £500,000 and on all other profits, and an effective marginal rate of 55½% on income profits lying between those two levels. Retained company income profits of up to £100,000 thus suffer tax at only 38%. Retentions will, however, swell the company's assets and may have either later income tax consequences, if distributed as dividends, or capital gains tax implications. The capital gains tax aspect is dealt with below. The total national insurance cost is higher with a company, because the individual employee pays national insurance at 9% on weekly earnings up to £235, and the company pays national insurance on those earnings at 11.95% from 6 April 1983 to 31 July 1983 and 11.45% thereafter (the company's contributions, however, being deductible in calculating its taxable profits). These rates apply equally to husband and wife directors, unless the wife elected before 11 May 1977 to pay reduced contributions, in which case she pays 3.85% instead of 9%. The company's liability is unaffected.

In rounded terms the national insurance comparison is of a maximum contribution of approximately £750 payable by a trader as against £2,500 payable by employee and employer. Some national insurance benefits, however, in particular unemployment benefit and earnings-related retirement pension, are not available to the self-employed. A further consideration where a wife or husband does not work full time in a business is that the earnings as a director or employee are required to be 'wholly and exclusively for the purposes of the trade' and may thus be challenged by the Revenue as excessive. There is no such requirement for a wife or husband who is a partner and who does take some part in the running of the business.

In example 1 the tax liability in the short term is considerably lower for the company. Although the long-term aspect could swing the balance the other way, it is possible that, through changes in tax rates, exemptions etc., the future tax liability may never materialise. A problem shelved may be a problem solved.

Timing of tax payments (TA 1970, ss 4, 115, 243)

Individuals (including partners) are normally assessed to tax on the basis of the profits earned in the accounts year ending in the previous tax-year, but at the rates in force during the year of assessment itself. The tax is generally payable in two equal instalments on 1 January in the tax-year and on 1 July following. Depending on the choice of accounting date, there can be a gap of anything from nine to nearly twenty-one months between earning the profits and paying the first instalment.

Companies, on the other hand, are charged to corporation tax at the rate in force during the accounting period when the profits are earned, and new companies are always required to pay the tax nine months after the end of the accounting period, except where assessments are issued late, in which case the due date is 30 days after the issue of the assessment. Furthermore

141

Example 1

A trader expects to make a consistent profit of £50,000 before tax and national insurance. His personal requirements are approximately £13,000 per annum.

The comparative tax position is:	Trader		Company
Profits/remuneration	50,000		20,000
Personal allowances, say	3,000		3,000
Taxable income	47,000		17,000
Tax thereon: 14,600 @ 30%	4,380	14,600 @ 30%	4,380
21,400 @ 40–55%	10,565	2,400 @ 40%	960
11,000 @ 60%	6,600		
	21,545		5,340
Class 2 NI (flat rate)	229	Employee's NI	1,100
Class 4 NI	517		
	22,291		6,440
Company's tax:			
Profits		50,000	
Less: Director's remuneration		(20,000)	
Company's NI thereon		(1,419)	1,419
Taxable profits		28,581	
Tax thereon @ 38%			10,861
Total tax and NI liabilities	£22,291		£18,720
Balance remaining:			
Drawn or undrawn profits	27,709	Net remuneration	
		(20,000 − 6,440)	13,560
		Retained profits	
		(28,581 −	
		10,861)	17,720
			31,280

Possible further tax liabilities on company retentions:
If distributed as unearned income, maximum of
45% on £17,720 (basic rate tax being imputed
from company's corporation tax) £7,974
If taxed as capital gains, 30% on £17,720 £5,316

director's remuneration will be taxed under the PAYE scheme immediately it is paid or credited to the director's loan account.

Unincorporated businesses thus have considerable cash flow advantages. They may also benefit from lower tax rates and thresholds in the year of assessment compared with those in force when the profits were earned, although the converse is of course equally true.

Effect of basis period rules for individuals (TA 1970, ss 116, 117)

The profits of an unincorporated business are assessed to tax more than once in the opening years of a new business, with a corresponding drop out of profits for an equivalent time when the trade ceases. The ways in which these rules work and can be used to advantage are dealt with in chapter 21. Partnerships are a particularly flexible form of business in this connection, because the introduction of a new partner, or the retirement of an existing one, can be treated either as the cessation of one trade and the commencement of another, or as the continuance of a single trade, as the partners choose.

No such planning opportunities are available to a company, whose profits are taxed once and once only.

Losses (TA 1970, ss 168–171, 177; FA 1978, s 30; CGTA 1979, s 136; FA 1980, s 37)

If a new business is expected to make losses in its early years, it is a good idea to bear in mind the different loss reliefs available to individuals and to companies. (These are dealt with more fully in chapters 25 and 26.)

Reliefs available to individuals in respect of trading losses are generous. Losses incurred in any of the first four tax-years of a new business may be carried back to set against any income of the previous three tax-years, earliest first, and a tax repayment obtained, enhanced by a tax-free repayment supplement. For losses in later years (or instead of a carry-back claim for opening-year losses) a claim may be made under TA 1970, s 168 to set them against the total income of the tax-year in which the loss is sustained or the next following year, resulting in the discharge or repayment of tax. There is additional flexibility for married couples, who can avoid wasting personal allowances by restricting claims to the lossmaker's income. The losses may be boosted, or indeed created, by capital allowances and stock relief. Unrelieved trading losses may always be carried forward to set against future trading income.

If trading losses are sustained in a new company, they may only be set against any current profits the company has, such as bank interest or chargeable gains, or carried forward against the company's later trading profits. Trading losses of an established company may be set against the profits if any of the same accounting year, then against the total profits of the previous accounting year, with any balance being carried forward. If the losses derive from first-year allowances on plant the carry-back period is extended to three years, latest first.

Funds introduced to a limited company by working directors to support early and subsequent losses, either as share capital or on director's loan account, do not qualify for any immediate relief (but see p 16 as regards relief for interest payable). There are two relieving measures for shares and loans, but they are only available when shares are disposed of or when money lent becomes irrecoverable.

(a) A capital loss on the disposal of shares subscribed for in an unquoted trading company can be relieved against income in the same way as a loss under TA 1970, s 168.

(b) The loss of money advanced by a director to the company on loan account (or by way of a payment to cover a bank guarantee) may be deducted against the director's capital gains.

The first measure gives relief at income tax rates, but only when the director's shares are disposed of, probably because the business has failed. The second measure is also only likely to be available at the point where the director's involvement with the company has ceased. The flexibility of having provided money on loan account compared with being locked in as share capital results in relief at the probably lower capital gains tax rate, and also requires some current or future chargeable gains against which the loss may be set.

Pensions

If you are self-employed, you are entitled to tax relief at your top rate of tax on earned income in respect of premiums paid to provide an annuity when you retire. The maximum allowable premium is $17\frac{1}{2}$% of your profits, although there are provisions to allow unused relief in any year to be carried forward for six years. Company directors/employees in non-pensionable employment can also take advantage of these provisions, but it is usually preferable for a family company to operate its own pension scheme.

Company pension schemes are less restrictive in that the only limit on the company's contributions is that the retirement benefits provided must not exceed certain limits. The company scheme can be contributory or non-contributory, the company's contributions being deductible in arriving at the company's taxable profits and the individual's contributions, if any, being allowed against his earned income.

For details on company and individual pension schemes see chapters 17 and 18.

Capital gains (CGTA 1979, ss 124, 126; FA 1980, s 79)

Where chargeable gains are realised which cannot be eliminated by available reliefs, the first £5,300 of the total gains in 1983/84 are exempt from tax for individuals, tax being charged at 30% on the remainder. Companies are not entitled to any exemption and pay an effective 30% on the full amount. Furthermore, the effect of gains is to swell the value of the company's assets by the after-tax amount. This will eventually result in a double tax charge, because the gain will be reflected in the value of the shares, and will be realised either when the individual disposes of his shares or on liquidation of the company.

Whether or not a business is incorporated, the increase in the value of its assets over time may lead to chargeable gains in the future, and in the case of a company this will be particularly true where assets are swelled by profit retentions. Death is an effective, albeit unwelcome, way of escaping capital gains tax liabilities. Legatees effectively take over the assets at their market value at the date of death and thus get a tax-free uplift in base cost.

Less drastically, two important reliefs lessen the capital gains tax impact.

Subject to certain restrictions, gains are exempt up to a maximum of £50,000 if you are over 65, or a pro-rata proportion of £50,000 if you are between 60 and 65, on the disposal of a business, or of an interest in a business, or of shares in your family company. (A family company is one in which your personal shareholding is at least 25%, or in which your family hold 51%, of which your own share is at least 5%.) Under proposed legislation, the limit is to be increased to £100,000 with effect for 1983/84.

If you make gifts of chargeable assets the gifts are treated as disposals at open market value, which may give rise to chargeable gains. Tax on the gains may, however, be deferred by a joint election by you and the donee, so that the donee effectively takes over your base cost. For the over 60s this relief may be used to cover any gain remaining after the retirement exemption.

See chapter 5 for a fuller treatment of these provisions.

Unincorporated and incorporated businesses are equally able to take advantage of these two reliefs. From a capital gains tax point of view the tax disadvantage of incorporation is therefore restricted to the double charge on any gains the company makes, and the charge when shares are disposed of on that part of their value that reflects retained profits. This latter point has to be weighed against the benefit of a possibly lower tax rate at the time the profits were retained, leaving the company with more liquid funds to invest in the business.

Capital transfer tax (FA 1976, Sch 10)

A gift of a business or of an interest in a business, or a gift of shares out of a controlling holding, qualifies for business property relief of 50% of the value of the gift. There is also an annual exemption for the first £3,000 of total chargeable transfers and a tax-free threshold for cumulative transfers which is currently £60,000 and is index-linked. Gifts made more than ten years earlier drop out of the cumulative total. Capital transfer tax is thus well on the way to becoming as avoidable a tax as estate duty was.

If you want to pass on your business gradually to other members of the family the company format has the edge in terms of flexibility, since it is easier to transfer shares than to transfer a part of an unincorporated business. You should, however, bear in mind that if your own shareholding, together with that of your spouse, falls below 50%, any subsequent transfers will only qualify for business property relief of 30%.

Raising finance (FA 1983, s 26 and Sch 5; F (No 2)A 1983, s 5 and Sch 1)

The new business expansion scheme gives a company an advantage over an unincorporated business in attracting funds from outside investors. Apart from a few excluded businesses, such as leasing or financial services, the scheme offers tax relief at all rates, including investment income surcharge, for investment between 6 April 1983 and 5 April 1987 in new share capital of an unquoted trading company. The maximum amount for which an individual can obtain relief in this way in a tax-year is £40,000. The company need not be a new company. There is a minimum investment of £500 in any one company, but this limit does not apply when the investment is made through a Revenue approved investment fund. The detailed rules are in chapter 29.

Tax points

- Don't let the tax tail wag the commercial dog. Consider *all* aspects of alternative business forms.

- If profits are high enough to attract a personal income tax rate of 60%, operating through a company will reduce the tax rate on retentions to 38% on profits up to £100,000. There are long term factors to consider, but these may well be outweighed by the short-term advantage.

- Unincorporated businesses have cash flow advantages over companies when it comes to paying tax.

- A slow start is particularly advantageous to an unincorporated business because of the multiple assessment of the early profits. A transfer to a company when the business has prospered can be timed to maximise the benefit of the corresponding profits that escape tax.

- The loss rules for individuals, particularly the three year carry-back of new business losses, make an unincorporated start an attractive proposition where there is heavy initial expenditure, either on revenue or capital items. The business can later be converted to a company if this is considered appropriate. But there are anti-avoidance provisions to be watched in FA 1976, s 41 where loss claims incorporate first-year allowances on plant.

- A company with growth potential will attract funds from investors because of the tax advantages to them of the business expansion scheme.

20
Calculation of business profits: individuals and companies

Background (TA 1970, ss 108, 109, 526)

Trading profits are charged to tax under Schedule D, Case I. Profits from carrying on a profession or vocation are charged under Schedule D, Case II. In most instances the rules used in calculating assessments are the same under both Case I and Case II, and 'trade' should therefore be read as including 'profession or vocation' unless the contrary is indicated. However, the charge under Case I is extended beyond what would normally be regarded as trading. The word trade is defined as including 'every trade, manufacture, adventure or concern in the nature of trade'. The definition is thus wide enough to cover activities which have only some of the characteristics of a trade, and will embrace occasional transactions and those to which an investment motive cannot be attributed.

Important indicators of possible trading are the nature of the asset itself (whether it is income producing, or something you get enjoyment from owning, which will indicate investment rather than trading), your reason for acquiring it, how long you owned it, whether you worked on it to make it more saleable, your reason for selling and how often such transactions were undertaken.

General rules for computing profits (TA 1970, s 130)

Whether the business is that of an individual trader, a partnership or a company, profits are calculated according to normal commercial accounting rules unless they conflict with statute law as interpreted by the courts. The two most important rules for expenses are firstly that they be wholly and exclusively for the purposes of the trade, and secondly, that they be of a revenue, and not capital, nature.

'Wholly and exclusively'

An expense is inevitably outside the 'wholly and exclusively' rule if it is for both business and private purposes, but part of a mixed expense may be wholly and exclusively for the purposes of the trade and thus be a valid deduction in calculating profits.

Some of the miles travelled in a car are wholly and exclusively for business, others are purely for private purposes, and others again may be partly both. No part of a business trip combined with a holiday satisfies the rule, even though the business benefits, but a conference fee within that trip might qualify. The same applies to mixed business and living accommodation, where again it may be possible accurately to separate the business and private areas. See example 1.

The Revenue might sometimes allow concessional relief for a part of mixed expenses but they are under no obligation to do so.

Example 1

A trader's recorded mileage in a twelve month period of account was as follows:

Purely business journeys	5,000
Purely private journeys	4,000
Home to business	2,000
Journeys with a combined business and private purpose	1,000
	12,000

Allowable business proportion is 5/12ths.

A company employer may incur expenses from which directors or employees derive a personal benefit. Such expenses are allowed to the company, with an appropriate benefits assessment on the director or employee using the particular facility (see chapter 11). The wholly and exclusively rule may, however, cause a disallowance of directors' fees or wages, particularly where they are paid to members of the family who do not work full-time and the payment is excessive in relation to the work done.

Capital or revenue

A capital expense may not be deducted in calculating profits, although many items of capital expenditure may attract capital allowances (see chapter 22). The usual definition of a capital expense is one made 'not only once and for all, but with a view to bringing into existence an asset or an advantage for the enduring benefit of the trade'. Thus expenditure on renovating newly acquired premises to make them fit for use in a trade is capital, whilst the ongoing expenditure on maintaining the premises is revenue. The distinction is often hard to draw, and has led to a large body of case law.

The same considerations apply in deciding whether a particular profit is income chargeable under Schedule D, Case I or II or a capital profit (see chapter 5).

Allowable and non-allowable expenses (TA 1970, ss 134, 411; FA 1980, s 38)

The principles outlined above provide a broad guide to what expenses are allowed. Some specific examples are given in the table below, including items specifically allowed or disallowed by statute.

Allowable	Not allowable
Wages and directors' fees	Drawings (including drawings in
Employer's national insurance	the form of partners' interest on
contributions	capital and salaries)
Rent of business premises	Self-employed national insurance
Repairs	contributions
Premium for grant of lease, but	Cost of improvements, extensions,
limited to the amount	additions
assessed on the landlord as	Depreciation (capital allowances
extra rent (see chapter 33),	are available on certain assets—
spread over the term of the	see chapter 22)
lease	Living expenses and private
Interest on money borrowed	payments
Cost of raising loan finance	Legal expenses on forming a
(excluding stamp duty), for	company, drawing up
example debentures (not	partnership agreement,
share capital)	acquiring assets such as leases
Advertising	Fines and legal expenses connected
Business travel	therewith
Bad debts written off and	Business entertaining expenses
provision for specific bad	(except on a reasonable scale for
debts	overseas customers)
Legal expenses on debt	Gifts to customers, except gifts with
recovery, trade disputes,	a conspicious advertisement that
defending trade rights,	cost not more than £2 per person
employees' service	per year
agreements and, by	Charitable subscriptions and
concession, renewing a short	donations (unless exceptionally
lease (i.e. 50 years or less)	the donation satisfies the wholly
Non-recoverable VAT, for	and exclusively rule)
example where turnover is	Donations to political parties
below VAT threshold	Taxation (but see opposite as
	regards VAT)

Goods for own use

A retail sole trader or partnership must include in sales the retail value of goods taken from stock for own use (the wholesale price being used for a wholesaler). Services are valued at cost, so no notional profit has to be included for services provided free of charge to, say, a relative. Where business is carried on through a limited company, the directors are charged on goods taken for their own use under the benefits-in-kind rules (see chapter 11).

Stock and work in progress—valuation (TA 1970, s 137)

Stock is valued at the lower of cost or realisable value, opening and closing stock being brought into the accounts in determining profit. Work in progress is similarly brought into account, and may be valued on any one of three bases, provided that the chosen base is used consistently:

(a) Cost.
(b) Cost plus overheads.
(c) Cost plus overheads plus profit contribution.

The value of a proprietor's or working partner's own time is not a contributory part of cost but effectively represents profit, so this element need not be included in a work-in-progress valuation.

When a trade ceases stock is valued at the price received if sold to a UK trader, and otherwise at open market value.

Stock relief (FA 1981, s 35 and Sch 9)

Relief is given for the effect of inflation on stock levels by reference to the increase in the 'all stocks index' over a period of account. The all stocks index is prepared by the Department of Industry. See Table at front of this book.

The relief is given whether or not stocks and work in progress actually increase in value, and even if the levels actually drop, so that there is an opportunity for converting stock into more liquid funds of working capital without any tax penalty.

The relief is calculated by applying the increase in the all stocks index to the value of opening stock and work in progress in a period of account, reduced by a de minimis limit of £2,000. In arriving at the figure any progress payments, etc. are deducted. See example 2.

Since relief is given by applying the all stocks index to the opening stock, it follows that there is no relief for stockpiling until after the end of the next period of account.

For a new business there is no opening stock. A notional opening stock is arrived at by using the closing stock figure and reducing it by the index increase in the period.

A claim for stock relief must be made by sole traders and partners within two years after the end of the tax year in which the period of account ends and by companies within two years after the end of the period of account.

Example 2

Period	1	2	3
	£	£	£
Stock at start of period	10,000	13,000	18,000
Stock at end of period	13,000	18,000	7,000
Stock increase (reduction)	3,000	5,000	(11,000)
Increase in all stocks index over period of account	10%	8%	9%
Stock relief:			
Opening stock	10,000	13,000	18,000
Less de minimis limit	2,000	2,000	2,000
	8,000	11,000	16,000
	×10%	×8%	×9%
Amount of stock relief available	£800	£880	£1,440

For both companies and individuals stock relief reduces profits, or creates or increases losses. The treatment of stock relief in relation to losses is dealt with in chapters 25 and 26.

If the stock relief claimed exceeds profits and loss relief is not available (or is not claimed), the unused relief may be carried forward to set against later trading profits, but there is a six-year time limit on the carry forward. The same applies to any part of a company's losses attributable to stock relief. Traders need not claim the full amount of stock relief available to them. This may be particularly relevant for non-company traders who might otherwise waste personal allowances.

If a trade ceases or is reduced to an insignificant level within six years after stock relief is given, the relief is clawed back by an addition to profits in the final period. Once six years have elapsed the relief cannot be clawed back, so that only the last six years' relief are subject to clawback at any one time.

Non-trading income and capital profits

Any non-trading income of sole traders and partners included in the business accounts is not part of the profits assessable under Schedule D, Case I. The precise nature of the income will determine under what head it is chargeable, for example bank interest under Schedule D, Case III and rent under Schedule A. In the case of a partnership, such income will usually be included in the accounts for the purposes of division between the partners, but it will have to be excluded from the trading assessment and appropriate assessments made under other Schedules or Cases. These will not be on a joint basis since the principle of joint assessment only applies to partnership trading profits and not to other income or to capital gains.

A company's non-trading income is also excluded from the Case I trading profit, but the company is charged to tax in a single assessment on all its sources of income plus its chargeable gains, as indicated in chapter 21.

Capital profits of sole traders and partners are liable to capital gains tax, subject to any available reliefs and to the annual exemption. See chapter 5.

Tax points

- Try to avoid duality of purpose in expenditure. Make sure you do not cloud a genuine business expense with a private element.

- If you are a retailer, use your business connections to make private purchases at lower cost, rather than taking goods out of your own stock and suffering tax on a notional profit.

- Progress payments received after the end of a period of account will not reduce the opening stock figure at the start of the next period, so progress payments received early in a new account rather than at the end of an existing account are preferable.

21
Assessment of business profits

Companies (TA 1970, ss 243, 244 and 247)

Although taxable business profits for individuals and companies are computed in the same way in most respects, the assessment of company profits is much more straightforward. A company's business profits are assessed along with any other profits the company has, such as interest, rents and chargeable gains, by reference to chargeable accounting periods. A chargeable accounting period can be as short as the company wishes but cannot exceed twelve months. If a company makes up a period of account for say fifteen months it is split into two chargeable accounting periods for tax purposes, the first of twelve months and the second of three months. Capital allowances and stock relief are deducted as expenses in arriving at the business profits. Corporation tax is charged at the rate(s) in force during the chargeable accounting period.

Example 1

A company made profits of £12,000 in the year to 31 December 1982. The small companies rate of corporation tax was 40% for the year to 31 March 1982 and 38% for the year to 31 March 1983.

	£
Corporation tax payable:	
3/12 × £12,000 = £3,000 @ 40%	1,200
9/12 × £12,000 = £9,000 @ 38%	3,420
	£4,620

The due date for payment of corporation tax by companies established after March 1965 is nine months after the end of the accounting period, i.e. 1 October 1983 in example 1, or 30 days after the assessment is raised if later. Companies in existence before April 1965, when corporation tax was introduced, retain the same time interval between the end of an accounting period and the payment date as they used to have for income tax. If the company in example 1 had been in business before April 1965 and had made up accounts to 31 December 1964, income tax would have been payable on 1 January 1966. Corporation tax for the year to 31 December 1982 would accordingly be payable on 1 January 1984 (or 30 days after the making of the assessment if later).

Individuals

Normal basis of assessment (TA 1970, s 115)

For the self-employed person or such persons in partnership, income tax on trading profits is payable in equal instalments on 1 January within the tax year and 1 July following it. Thus the tax for 1983/84 is payable in equal instalments on 1 January and 1 July 1984.

An individual (or partnership) is free to choose the annual date to which his accounts are made up and it is usual, but not compulsory, for accounts to be made up to a calendar month end. The assessment to tax for an established business is usually based on the trading profits of the accounting year which ended in the preceding income tax year. The 1983/84 assessment for an established trader could therefore be based on the result of any accounting period of twelve months ended in the previous tax year 1982/83, i.e. between 6 April 1982 and 5 April 1983, for example:

Year ended 30 April 1982
Year ended 31 May 1982
Year ended 30 November 1982
Year ended 31 March 1983

The earlier the accounting date in the tax year the greater the time interval between earning the profits and paying the tax on them.

Example 2

	Due date of payment of tax for 1983/84	Interval between end of accounting year and payment date
Year ended 30.4.82	1.1.84	20 months
	1.7.84	26 months
Year ended 31.10.82	1.1.84	14 months
	1.7.84	20 months
Year ended 31.3.83	1.1.84	9 months
	1.7.84	15 months

An established trader or partnership may wish to alter the interval by changing the previously adopted accounting date, see page 159 below.

Assessment in early years (TA 1970, ss 116 and 117)

Since there can be no previous year's accounts for a new business, the assessment for the tax year in which a business commences is based on the profit from the date of commencement to the following 5 April. If necessary, profits are apportioned on a time basis. The second tax year's assessment is based on the profits of the first twelve months, and assessments thereafter are normally based on the profits of the accounting year ended in the preceding tax year.

Example 3

Trade commenced on 1 January 1983. Profits are £3,650 for the year ended 31 December 1983 and £4,400 for the year ended 31 December 1984.

Year of Assessment	Basis period	Assessment £
1982/83	1.1.83–5.4.83 95/365ths × £3,650	950
1983/84	1.1.83–31.12.83	3,650
1984/85	1.1.83–31.12.83	3,650
1985/86	1.1.84–31.12.84	4,400

When the first accounts are prepared for a period other than twelve months, in the third year there may not be an accounting period of twelve months ended in the preceding tax year. In these circumstances the assessment for the third tax year is again based on the profit of the first twelve months trading.

Regardless of the dates to which accounts are made up, some profits are used more than once in establishing the assessments for the early years. In example 3 the first year's profits formed the basis of assessment for 27 tax months (3 months in 1982/83 and the whole of 1983/84 and 1984/85). This overlap is balanced by profits for an equivalent time escaping assessment when an established trade ceases (see p 157 below). If profits are increasing year by year the opening year rules and subsequent preceding year basis of assessment work in the taxpayer's favour, because the assessable profits will be less than the profits currently being generated. But if profits fall, the multiple assessment of the initial higher profits could cause hardship. The taxpayer is able to elect within six years after the end of the third year of assessment to have the assessments for both the second and third years (not just one of them) based on the actual profits made in those tax years rather than on the profits of the earlier period.

Capital allowances and stock relief in early years (CAA 1968, s 72; FA 1981, Sch 9)

Capital allowances for a year of assessment are based on qualifying

Example 4

Trade commenced on 1 January 1983. Profits of the 4 months to 30 April 1983 are £1,000, those of the year to 30 April 1984 are £15,000 and those for the year to 30 April 1985 are £2,400.

Assessments for the second and third tax years are as follows:

Year of assessment	Basis period			Assessments

Normal basis

			£	£
1983/84	1.1.83–30.4.83	£1,000	1,000	
	1.5.83–31.12.83	8/12 × £15,000	10,000	
				11,000
1984/85	1.1.83–31.12.83			
	(As for 1983/84)			11,000
				£22,000

With taxpayer's election

1983/84	6.4.83–30.4.83	1/4 × £1,000	250	
	1.5.83–5.4.84	11/12 × £15,000	13,750	
				14,000
1984/85	6.4.84–30.4.84	1/12 × £15,000	1,250	
	1.5.84–5.4.85	11/12 × £2,400	2,200	
				3,450
				£17,450

Clearly it is in the taxpayer's interest to elect for the 1983/84 and 1984/85 assessments to be on the basis of actual profits.

expenditure incurred in the accounting period which forms the basis period for that year (see p 162). The early accounting periods of a new trade can, however, form the basis periods of more than one year's assessment. Where this happens capital allowances for expenditure incurred in that period are given in the first of the tax years only.

Similarly stock relief for an accounting period is normally given in the tax year for which the accounting period is the basis period. However, where the profits of an accounting period form the basis of more than one year's assessment, the relief is given in the first of the tax years based on those profits.

If a new trade is very profitable the effect of these rules can be drastically to reduce the taxable profit of the first year, but to leave high profits assessable in the next two years. The effect can be mitigated by disclaiming some or all of the 100% first year capital allowances on plant but this means that only writing-down allowances of 25% will then be available on that plant in the future. An alternative is to try to plan the early capital expenditure so that it falls into different basis periods, for example by postponing some until after the end of the tax year in which the trade commences. Stock relief is not so easy to spread and it is only possible to do so by reference to the dates to which accounts are made up.

In some circumstances the bunching of capital allowances and stock relief can be beneficial by creating opening year losses which can be carried back three years (see chapter 25).

Assessment on cessation of trade (TA 1970, s 118)

The use of profits more than once in the opening years is balanced by the rules for assessment when a business ceases. The final assessment is based on the profit from the immediately preceding 6 April to the date of cessation, and replaces the assessment based on the 12 months account ended in the preceding year if that has already been issued. This means that some profits drop out of account and are never assessed at all. However, just as the taxpayer can elect which profits are used more than once for assessment at the start of the business, so the Revenue has the right at cessation to decide which profits escape assessment. The assessments for the two tax years before the final year may, if the Revenue so decides, be revised to the profits actually made in those tax years instead of the profits which would be assessed on the normal preceding accounting year basis. As with the taxpayer's election, this revision must be made for both tax years or for neither.

Example 5

A trader who has prepared accounts to 30 April for many years ceases to trade on 31 August 1983, the recent and final profits having been:

	£
Year ended 30.4.80	18,000
30.4.81	24,000
30.4.82	30,000
30.4.83	36,000
Four months to 31.8.83	8,000

example continued overleaf

---

example 5 continued

Assessments for the last three tax years are as follows:

Year of assessment	Basis period		£	Assessments £
1983/84	6.4.83–30.4.83	1/12 × £36,000		3,000
	1.5.83–31.8.83			8,000
				£11,000

and either
Normal preceding year basis

1982/83	1.5.80–30.4.81	24,000
1981/82	1.5.79–30.4.80	18,000
		£42,000

or
Revenue's revised actual basis

1982/83	6.4.82–30.4.82	1/12 × £30,000 2,500	
	1.5.82–5.4.83	11/12 × £36,000 33,000	
			35,500
1981/82	6.4.81–30.4.81	1/12 × £24,000 2,000	
	1.5.81–5.4.82	11/12 × £30,000 27,500	
			29,500
			£65,000

Although following revision by the Revenue the total assessments for 1981/82 and 1982/83 will be increased by £23,000, the profits of the 23 months from 1 May 1979 to 5 April 1981, amounting to £40,000, will not be assessed at all.

Choice of cessation date

A significant tax advantage can sometimes be obtained where a choice of cessation date is possible. A trade clearly ceases for tax purposes when trading comes to an end. There is also a cessation for tax purposes:

When a trader dies (although by concession, assessments can continue to be made on a preceding year basis if the trade is continued by the spouse).
When partners change in a partnership (although the partners may elect for assessments to continue on a preceding year basis, see chapter 23).

When a trader or partnership transfers a trade to a limited liability company (see chapter 27).

It will normally be advantageous to delay the cessation until a later tax year if profits are rising, since the escaping profits will be later higher profits, and to cease in an earlier tax year if profits are falling, since the later the cessation the smaller the escaping profits.

Capital allowances and stock relief in closing years (CAA 1968, s 72; FA 1981, Sch 9)

For capital allowances purposes, expenditure in the period for which profits escape tax on cessation is added to expenditure in the next period unless that is the last tax year, in which case it is added to expenditure in the previous period. This ensures that no qualifying capital expenditure and receipts are left out of account.

Example 6

	Normal basis	Revenue's revised basis
In example 5 the 'profits gap' was	1.5.81–5.4.83	1.5.79–5.4.81
It is added to the basis period for	1982/83	1981/82
Which then covers capital expenditure		
and receipts from	1.5.80–5.4.83	1.5.79–5.4.82

The result is a bunching of capital allowances for a long period in one tax year. In the final tax year there will usually be a balancing charge to claw back the excess of allowances given compared with disposal proceeds (see p 163).

Stock relief for a period of account which escapes assessment is given in the tax year following that in which the period of account ends, causing a similar bunching effect. In the last tax year there will be a charge to tax to claw back stock relief given in the previous six years (see p 151).

Change of accounting date (TA 1970, s 115)

A change of accounting date during the life of a business will cause profits at that time to escape assessment or be assessed more than once, with a corresponding adjustment to the length of the period for which profits escape tax when the trade ceases. This can provide an opportunity to reduce overall assessments as long as the change is commercially justifiable. The detailed provisions are beyond the scope of this book, but broadly the Revenue practice is to use a period of twelve months based on the new accounting date as the basis of the next year's assessment and to adjust the previous year's assessment according to the average profits over the total period concerned, unless the averaging adjustment would not make a significant alteration to the assessment.

Partnership

Although in general the rules for assessing a partnership are the same as those for sole traders, there are some special points to be considered about the way assessments are divided between partners and about the treatment of losses and capital gains. These are dealt with in chapter 23.

Pre-trading expenditure (FA 1980, s 39)

Some expenditure, for example rent and rates, may be incurred before trading actually commences. So long as it is a normal revenue expense and is incurred not more than three years before the trade commences, it may be treated by sole traders and partnerships as a separate loss of the first tax year of trading and loss relief may be claimed for it. The types of loss relief available are dealt with in chapter 25. Where the expenditure is incurred by a company it may be treated as an expense of the first trading period. The different treatment for individuals ensures that they do not get the benefit of deducting the expense several times over because of the assessment rules for the opening years (see page 155 above).

Post cessation receipts (TA 1970, ss 143–151)

Income may arise after a business has ceased which has not been included in the final accounts. This may be because of the nature of the business and is particularly relevant for barristers because their accounts are traditionally prepared on the basis of cash received rather than on the normal earnings basis. In all cases the income arising after cessation is assessed in the year of receipt under Schedule D Case VI, unless it arises within six years of cessation in which case the taxpayer may elect to have it treated instead as income of the last day of trading. An appropriate adjustment is then made to the final assessment on the business.

Tax points

- Choosing an accounting date early in the tax year not only gives more time for planning the funding of tax payments but also maximises the profits which escape assessment when the business ceases.

- Where possible plan your expenses in the opening years to maximise the benefit of the opening year rules. Expenses are effectively relieved as many times as the profits are assessed.

- Consider leasing plant (particularly cars) instead of buying, so that the early leasing charges reduce the assessments of several tax years. (Capital allowances reduce them once only.) An additional consideration is that VAT can be reclaimed on the leasing payments, whereas VAT on the cost of a purchased car can not.

- If possible postpone cessation of a trade to a date after the next 5 April if profits are rising, before that date if profits are falling. The maximum possible profits will then escape assessment.

22
Capital allowances

Background

Capital expenditure is not allowable in calculating income profits, but relief is given on certain capital expenditure by means of allowances when the expenditure is incurred and/or over the later years of the ownership of the assets.

The most important allowances available to companies and non-incorporated businesses are those in respect of expenditure on:

Plant and machinery
Industrial buildings
Agricultural buildings
Hotels
Buildings in enterprise zones, other than dwelling houses
Dwellings let under the assured tenancy scheme
Patents
Know-how
Scientific research

Allowances are also available to employees who have to provide plant and machinery for use in their employment, and to those letting property in respect of landlord's fixtures, fittings etc. The most common example of qualifying expenditure by an employee is that on provision of a car, but another might be a musical instrument purchased by an employee of an orchestra. A landlord of let property may obtain relief on such items as lifts.

If an asset is used partly for private purposes only the appropriate business fraction is allowed against the assessable income.

The following capital allowances are dealt with in more detail in other chapters:

Industrial buildings—See chapter 32
Agricultural buildings—See chapter 31
Dwellings let under the assured tenancy scheme—See chapter 33

Expenditure qualifying for relief (CAA 1968, ss 84, 85; FA 1971, s 45)

Capital allowances are available to the person incurring the expenditure, and if the expenditure is funded by means of a loan or bank overdraft the allowances can still be claimed in the usual way. Interest on such funding is, however, allowed as a business expense and not as part of the cost of the asset.

When an asset is purchased under a hire purchase agreement, the expenditure is deemed to be incurred as soon as the asset comes into use, even though ownership does not strictly pass until the option payment is made. The hire purchase charges are not part of the cost but are allowed as a business expense spread over the term of the agreement.

Subsidies or contributions from third parties must in general be deducted from the allowable cost. Regional development grants, however, are specifically excluded from this requirement and do not have to be deducted.

Any contribution for trading purposes towards another person's eligible expenditure which restricts the allowances available to the recipient will be treated as expenditure by the contributor, even though strictly he does not have an interest in the asset.

Basis periods (CAA 1968, ss 70–74)

Allowances are given by reference to the expenditure incurred in a basis period. For a company this is its chargeable accounting period, so that where a period of account exceeds twelve months, it is split into a twelve-month period or periods and the remainder, and relief for capital expenditure is given according to the chargeable period in which the expenditure is incurred.

For employees and landlords the basis period is the income tax year itself.

For traders and partnerships the basis period is the accounting period forming the basis of the assessment. Thus expenditure incurred by an established businessman in his year ended 31 December 1982 would qualify for relief in 1983/84, when the profits of the year to 31 December 1982 are assessed.

Because of the rules for assessments in the opening and closing years and on changes of accounting date, there may be overlaps and gaps in basis periods (see chapter 21). Where expenditure falls in the basis period for more than one assessment, it is regarded as being incurred in the first and not in any other. Where it does not fall in any basis period, it is regarded as incurred in the next period, unless the next period is the last tax-year of the business, in which case it is deemed to be incurred in the previous period.

Way in which allowances are given (CAA 1968, ss 70–74; FA 1971, ss 41, 44)

Allowances for companies are given automatically, whereas individuals must make a specific claim for them.

Some allowances need not be taken in full, e.g. first-year allowances on plant and initial allowances on industrial buildings. A company must specifically disclaim that part of any allowance not required within two years after the end of the accounting period for which the allowance is due. Individuals and partnerships merely restrict their claim to the required amount.

Individuals and partnerships, but not companies, may also claim only part of the 25% writing-down allowance on plant.

If a company makes a trading loss as a result of claiming the first-year allowance on plant, that part of the loss may be carried back for three years (see chapter 26). This extended carry-back is not available to individuals and partnerships, who are, however, able to use capital allowances to increase or create losses, and can carry back losses arising in the opening years of a new business for three years (see chapter 25).

Balancing allowances and charges

When an asset is sold, the proceeds are in most cases compared with the unrelieved expenditure, if any, and a 'balancing allowance' given for any deficiency. If the proceeds exceed the unrelieved expenditure, the excess is included in taxable income by means of a 'balancing charge'. Since the aim of a balancing charge is merely to claw back excess allowances, only the proceeds up to original cost have to be taken into account. Any excess over cost is dealt with under the capital gains tax rules (see chapter 5).

For plant and machinery, balancing allowances and charges are normally dealt with on a 'pool' basis (see below).

If an asset is withdrawn from a business for personal use or sold to a connected person, the amount to be included as sales proceeds is broadly the open market value.

Plant and machinery

What is plant and machinery?

Plant and machinery is not defined, and although 'machinery' is generally well understood, the question of what is and is not 'plant' has come before the courts many times. The main problem area lies in distinguishing the 'apparatus' *with* which a business is carried on from the 'setting' *in* which it is carried on. Items forming part of the setting do not attract relief unless they do so as part of the building itself, for example where it is an industrial building, or unless the business is one in which atmosphere, or ambience, is important. Lifts and central heating systems are treated as plant, while basic electricity and plumbing systems are not. Normal lighting in a shop is considered to be part of the building, but specific lighting to create atmosphere in a hotel has been held to be plant.

Certain items that are not plant are specifically allowable as such, for example expenditure by traders on fire safety, heat insulation in industrial buildings, and expenditure on safety at sports grounds.

CAPITAL ALLOWANCES

Allowances available

The allowances available are a first-year allowance of 100%, which is not given on all plant (see below), and a writing-down allowance of 25% per annum on unallowed expenditure.

Allowances are sometimes denied, or their use restricted, by various anti-avoidance provisions — see chapter 48.

First-year allowances (FA 1971, s 42; FA 1980, s 64)

The first-year allowance of 100% need not be taken in full, and any balance of unrelieved expenditure qualifies for the writing-down allowance in later years.

First-year allowance is not available on the following assets:

> Vehicles suitable for private use, except those hired out on a short lease, (see below) or let to someone receiving mobility allowance.
> Plant and machinery provided for leasing, except where the lessee would have qualified for the allowance if he had purchased the asset himself, or where the plant is let on a short lease (see below) or to someone receiving mobility allowance.
> Plant acquired from a connected person.

If the asset is disposed of without being brought into use, any first-year allowance given is withdrawn, and in the case of leased assets the allowance is withdrawn if the asset ceases to be used for a qualifying purpose within four years. First-year allowance is not available on plant purchased in the period in which a trade ceases.

Meaning of 'short lease' (FA 1971, s 43; FA 1980, s 64)

A 'short lease' for a car is one under which the car is normally hired to the same person for less than 30 consecutive days and for less than 90 days in any 12 months. For any other plant, 'short lease' means one under which either the 30 day/90 day rule applies as for cars, or the plant is normally let to the same person for less than 365 consecutive days and for an aggregate of not more than 2 years out of the period of 4 years from the time of first use.

Writing-down allowances (FA 1971, s 44)

Writing-down allowances are given at the rate of 25%, calculated by the reducing balance method, on any plant on which a first-year allowance is not available, and on any balance of expenditure on which a first-year allowance was not, or was only partly, claimed. See example 1.

In the first and last year of business, for individuals and partnerships, the writing-down allowance is reduced according to the length of the basis period, and it is also reduced proportionately for companies in respect of accounting periods less than 12 months.

164

Example 1

A trader makes up accounts to 31 December each year. In the year to 31 December 1982 (the basis period for 1983/84) he purchases plant for £4,000, but claims only 60% first-year allowance.

The allowances available are:		£
1983/84	Cost	4,000
	First year allowance 60%	2,400
		1,600
1984/85	Writing-down allowance 25%	
	(as part of pool allowance—see below)	400
Balance carried forward to 1985/86		1,200

Allowances then continue at 25% on the reducing balance.

Pooling expenditure (FA 1971, s 44)

All qualifying expenditure on plant and machinery is included in a single 'pool' except for the following:

Any asset with part private use.
Any car costing over £8,000.
Any other cars or plant for leasing on which first-year allowance is not available (see above)—all items under this heading are kept in a separate 'cars and leased assets pool'.

When plant is sold, any sales proceeds (up to but not exceeding the original cost) are deducted from the balance of pool expenditure before calculating the writing-down allowance. If the proceeds exceed the pool balance a balancing charge is made. A balancing allowance will not arise except on a cessation of trade where the total sale proceeds are less than the pool balance. See example 2.

Assets with part private use (FA 1971, Sch 8(5))

Any asset that is privately used by the sole proprietor or by a partner in a business is dealt with separately. This does not apply to assets used by directors of family companies. The use of company assets for private purposes by directors or employees does not affect the company's capital allowances position, but results in a benefits charge on the director/employee (see chapter 11).

The calculation of allowances and charges on privately-used assets proceeds in the normal way, but the available allowance or charge is restricted to the business proportion. The most common privately-used asset is a car, on which only writing-down allowances are available, but it could be say a van,

165

Example 2

A trader has the following transactions in plant in the years ended 31 December 1982 and 1983:

		£
June 1982	Proceeds of sales	3,000
November 1982	Purchase from associated business	1,000
June 1983	Proceeds of sales	9,000
December 1983	Arms length purchase	10,000

The pool balance brought forward at 1 January 1982 is £8,000.

The allowances are calculated as follows:

1983/84 (based on year to 31 December 1982)	
Pool value brought forward	8,000
Additions on which first-year allowance not available	1,000
	9,000
Less sales proceeds	(3,000)
	6,000
Writing down allowance 25% (reduces taxable profit)	(1,500)
	4,500
1984/85 (based on year to 31 December 1983)	
Sales proceeds	(9,000)
Balancing charge (increases taxable profit)	4,500
Additions	10,000
First-year allowance 100% (reduces taxable profit)	(10,000)
Balance carried forward	—

in which case the first-year allowance of 100% would apply, restricted by the private use proportion.

Cars costing more than £8,000 (FA 1971, Sch 8(10))

Each car that costs more than £8,000 is dealt with separately, and the available writing-down allowance is £2,000 or 25% of the unrelieved balance, whichever is less. If such a car is used privately the available amount is further restricted by the private proportion. When the car is sold a balancing allowance or charge arises.

Cars and leased assets pool (FA 1980, s 65)

Unless they qualify for first-year allowance or are treated individually because of private use or as cars costing over £8,000, all cars and assets for leasing are kept in a separate pool. The expenditure on the pool qualifies for writing-down allowances of 25%. Sales proceeds are deducted before the writing-down allowance is calculated, and a balancing charge is made if the sales proceeds exceed the pool balance. A balancing allowance will only arise on a cessation of trade where the total sales proceeds are less than the pool balance.

Transitional provisions for television sets (FA 1980, Sch 12)

First-year allowance used to be available on all assets provided for leasing. To lessen the impact of its withdrawal on the television rental industry, the first-year allowance on rental sets is being phased out, and will cease to be available for any type of set purchased after 31 May 1986. Once the available allowance is less than 100%, television sets are included in the cars and leased assets pool rather than the main pool.

Films (FA 1982, s 72)

Expenditure on the production and acquisition of films is treated as revenue expenditure and not capital expenditure, with the cost being written off over the income producing life of the film. An exception is currently made for British films, which qualify for 100% first-year allowance instead up to 31 March 1987.

Hotels (FA 1978, s 38)

Relief is available for construction costs in respect of a qualifying hotel or hotel extension. The hotel or extension must be of a permanent nature, be open for at least four months between April and October, and when open must have at least ten letting bedrooms offering sleeping accommodation. It must provide services of breakfast, evening meal, making beds and cleaning rooms. The relief works in the same way as that for industrial buildings (see chapter 32) except that the initial allowance is restricted to 20%, the annual writing-down allowance being 4% of cost.

Buildings in enterprise zones (FA 1980, s 74 and Sch 13)

When an area has been designated as an Enterprise Zone by the Secretary of State, expenditure incurred within ten years after the creation of the zone on any buildings other than dwelling houses qualifies for an initial allowance of 100%, or whatever lower amount is claimed. Any expenditure on which initial allowance is not claimed qualifies for writing-down allowances of 25% of cost (straight line method) until it is written off in full. Balancing allowances or charges apply on the disposal of buildings in enterprise zones.

Patents (TA 1970, ss 378–385)

Expenditure incurred in devising and patenting an invention (or an abortive attempt to do so) is allowable as a business expense. Where, however, you purchase patent rights the expenditure is relieved by way of capital allowances in equal annual instalments over seventeen years, or over the period for which the rights are acquired, whichever is less. So if you make up accounts to 31 March and purchase patent rights with 12 years to run for £1,800 in January 1983, you will get allowances of £150 per annum for 12 years, commencing in 1983/84 if you are an individual or in your accounting period ended 31 March 1983 if you are a company.

Patents allowances granted to non-traders can only be set against income from the patent rights and not against any other income.

Balancing charges and allowances arise in the usual way if all or part of the patent rights is sold, and a balancing allowance is given on any unallowed expenditure if the rights come to an end without subsequently being revived.

Although a balancing charge can never exceed the allowances given, there are specific provisions to charge a capital profit on patent rights as income rather than as a capital gain. The profit is not dealt with as part of the business profits but is charged under Schedule D, Case VI over six years in equal instalments, commencing with the tax-year of receipt, unless the taxpayer elects to have the whole sum charged in the year of receipt.

Know-how (TA 1970, s 386)

'Know-how' is defined as any industrial information or techniques which are likely to assist in a manufacturing process, or the working of a mine, or the carrying out of agricultural, forestry or fishing operations.

Capital expenditure on its acquisition for use in a trade is allowed by way of a writing-down allowance in equal instalments over six years.

If the trade ceases during the six years, relief for the unallowed expenditure is given by way of a balancing allowance. If know-how is sold the sale proceeds are treated as a trading receipt.

Scientific research (CAA 1968, ss 91, 92)

Capital expenditure for the purposes of scientific research is allowed in full, when incurred, in taxing trading income.

Proceeds of sale (not exceeding the allowance given) are treated as a trading receipt at the time of sale or when the trade ceases if earlier.

If the sale takes place in the same basis period as the expenditure is incurred any deficiency between the cost of expenditure and the proceeds is allowed as a deduction.

Tax points

- A specific claim for capital allowances must be made by individuals and partnerships, so it is important to ensure that the appropriate entry is made on the tax return and supported by computations.

- If claiming the maximum allowances means wasting personal allowances, you can reduce your claim. You will then get writing-down allowances on the disclaimed amount in future years.

- Alternatively you can use capital allowances to turn a trading profit into a loss which you can relieve against other income, but this may mean wasting personal allowances. If you are married and your spouse has income, you can protect personal reliefs by restricting the loss set-off to your own income (see chapter 25).

- Companies will not usually benefit from disclaiming allowances, except where they want to leave profits high enough to take advantage of reliefs which are only available in the current period, such as group relief for losses or double tax relief. The disclaimed allowances will then qualify for writing-down allowances in later years.

- If you are anticipating high profits, consider accelerating capital expenditure (borrowing the money if necessary) so as to get the allowances in an earlier tax-year.

- Watch the dates when you incur capital expenditure on commencing trading. If your profits are expected to be high, the allowances may reduce the profit of the first tax-year and leave high profits assessable in the following years (see chapter 21). If the allowances are high enough to turn a profit into a loss, this may be carried back against the income of earlier years.

- If you are a company, you save tax at $55\frac{1}{2}\%$ on any capital allowances that reduce profits lying in the marginal tranche between £100,000 and £500,000 (for financial year 1982).

- You normally only get 25% writing-down allowance when you buy cars. If you lease a car instead, you can usually set the whole of the leasing charge against your profit, subject to disallowance of any private element, but not where the car cost the leasing company more than £8,000. In that event your allowable hire charge is restricted to the proportion that £8,000 plus half the excess cost over £8,000 bears to the full cost. Thus if your hire charge is £2,500 and the car cost the leasing company £10,000, the allowable hire charge is restricted to £2,500 × (8,000 + 1,000) ÷ 10,000 = £2,250.

- When you buy or sell a group of assets, such as goodwill, plant and machinery, and trade premises, some will be subject to capital allowances at different rates and some will not qualify for allowances at all. It is essential to agree the price apportionment with the other party at the time of purchase or sale in order to avoid complications when you submit the tax computations.

- If there is doubt as to whether a contract for the purchase of plant is a hire purchase contract or a leasing contract, it is advisable to check with the finance company as to who is entitled to the capital allowances.

23
Partnerships

Assessment (TA 1970, ss 115–118, 152; CGTA 1979, s 60)

An assessment on the business profits of persons in partnership is made jointly in respect of all the partners. The assessment is calculated in the same way as an assessment on any self-employed person (see chapter 21). Thus the profits of an established partnership for the year ended 31 August 1982 will be assessed in 1983/84.

One assessment is made in the partnership name, any partner being liable for the whole of the tax if it is not paid. The liability of one of the partners, or of any group of partners, can never be separated from that of the other partners.

There is no joint assessment on non-trading income or on capital gains of the partnership. Here each partner is assessed on his share, and there is no recourse against the others in the event of non-payment. Thus an individual assessment on each partner will be made in respect of, for example, his share of partnership bank deposit interest, or of rent where there is co-ownership of land.

Division of assessments (TA 1970, s 26)

Profits assessable in a year of assessment are divided amongst the partners on the basis of the profit-sharing arrangements under the partnership agreement for the year of assessment itself. This may differ from the division of the actual profits on which the assessment is based where the preceding year basis of assessment applies. See example 1.

Example 1

A, B and C share profits equally in the year ended 30 November 1982. The profit is £12,000, each taking a £4,000 share. By 6 April 1983 they have amended the profit-sharing ratio to 2:1:1.

The 1983/84 assessment is divided as follows:
A £6,000   B £3,000   C £3,000.

Sometimes the profit-sharing arrangement may not be a straight split but may provide for interest on capital, partnership salaries or perhaps a system of slices by which profits are disproportionately divided. The division for tax purposes takes into account any variation of profit-sharing arrangements during a tax-year. See example 2.

Example 2

The profit of X, Y and Z for the year ended 30 September 1982 is £40,000, shared in the ratio 3:1:1, so that X has £24,000, and Y and Z £8,000 each.

They continue in this way until 5 October 1983, when the arrangements are changed to give interest on partnership capital amounting to £4,000, £1,000 and £700 per annum respectively, annual partnership salaries of £7,500, £12,000 and £10,000 respectively, with the balance being shared equally.

The division for 1983/84 is:

	Total	X	Y	Z
Profit to 5.10.83				
(½ of that of year to 30.9.82)	20,000			
Split 3:1:1		12,000	4,000	4,000
Profits from 6.10.83				
(½ of that of year to 30.9.82)	20,000			
Interest on capital	(2,850)	2,000	500	350
Partnership salaries	(14,750)	3,750	6,000	5,000
Balance remaining	2,400	800	800	800
Division for tax purposes	40,000	18,550	11,300	10,150
Whereas accounts profit was divided	40,000	24,000	8,000	8,000

Change of partners (TA 1970, s 154)

There is a cessation for tax purposes whenever a new partner is introduced or an existing partner leaves the partnership. The cessation rules apply to the tax-year in which the change takes place and the two previous tax-years, with the new business rules applying to the first three tax-years of the new partnership (see chapter 21). If, however, all those who were partners either before or after the change so elect in writing to the Revenue within two years after the date of the change, and there is at least one continuing partner, there is no deemed cessation and assessments continue on the normal preceding year basis.

Since, in calculating the tax payable by a partnership, an assessment is divided between the partners in the way in which they share profits in the year of assessment, it follows that where a continuation election is made on a change of partners, the division will be made between different persons from those who actually shared the profits. See example 3.

Example 3

Profits in the year ended 30 June 1982 £30,000, and in the year ended 30 June 1983 £45,000, were divided equally between the then partners A and B.

C is admitted as a partner on 1 July 1983. A, B and C share profits equally thereafter.

All three partners sign and submit to the Revenue an election for continuity within two years after 1 July 1983.

Assessments and their division, leading to the calculation of tax payable, become:

	Total	A	B	C
1983/84 £30,000				
(profits of year to 30.6.82)				
To 30 June 1983, say 3 months	7,500	3,750	3,750	—
1 July 1983 to 5 April 1984,				
say 9 months	22,500	7,500	7,500	7,500
	30,000	11,250	11,250	7,500
1984/85 £45,000				
(profits of year to 30.6.83)	45,000	15,000	15,000	15,000

C shares in the assessments based on the profits of £30,000 to 30 June 1982 and £45,000 to 30 June 1983 even though he did not share in those profits.

The partners cannot by agreement between themselves alter the statutory basis of allocation (as distinct from making other arrangements for the actual division of the profits) and hence the calculation of tax. They could agree to bear the calculated tax charge in a different way, so that for example C in example 3 did not bear any of the tax, not having received any of the profit, but this will not normally be done in an established partnership, since C will after all have received partnership income from 1 July 1983 onwards, and it is from this date that he is being included in the division of the assessment. He will get a compensating benefit when he leaves the partnership by escaping tax on some of his profit shares, assuming a continuation election is made on the occasion of that change of partners.

If a continuation election is not made on a change of partners, the Revenue option to assess the two years before the last year of the old partnership on an actual basis will be available, but, as indicated in chapter 21, some profits will still escape assessment, compensating for those assessed more than once at the beginning. The new business rules will, however, apply to the early years of the new partnership, and, if profits are rising, the profits of the old partnership that escape tax will be less than those of the new partnership assessed more than once.

Stock and work in progress

The value of stock and work in progress is included in the business accounts. Profits are affected accordingly, and stock relief is available. A change in the basis of valuation may be necessary, for example when two firms amalgamate and one has a different basis of work in progress valuation from the other. The Revenue will not usually seek to tax an adjustment which makes the basis consistent.

Consultancy

An outgoing partner may perform consultancy services for the partnership. He will be taxed on the income either under Schedule E, if the services are provided under a contract of service, or under Schedule D, Case I or II, if performed under a contract for services. The payments will be an allowable deduction in calculating the taxable profits of the partnership so long as they satisfy the 'wholly and exclusively' rule (see chapter 20).

Trading losses (TA 1970, ss 168–175; FA 1978, s 30)

Chapter 25 deals with the calculation of the available loss reliefs and ways in which relief may be given. Relief for partnership trading losses may be claimed by each partner quite independently of the others. Thus one partner may decide to carry forward his share of the loss, another to set his against other income of the same tax-year, another to set it against any income of the next tax-year, another to carry back in the early years of his being a partner, and so on.

Where there have been changes in profit-sharing arrangements, the ability of partners to make different loss claims can result in relief being available in aggregate for an amount greater than the actual loss, because a claim under TA 1970, s 168, against other income of the tax-year of loss and the following year, requires losses to be split according to the sharing arrangements of the tax-year itself, while carrying forward a loss under TA 1970, s 171 requires a split on the accounts year basis.

The carry-back loss rules for the first four years of a new trade only apply to a new partner, not to the continuing partners, whether or not the change of partnership has been treated as a cessation and restart. There is an anti-avoidance provision blocking carry-back claims by a new partner if he is joining his spouse in a continuing business.

Partnership assets (CGTA 1979, ss 60, 63; Revenue Statements of Practice D12 (17/1/75) and SP 1/79)

When partners join or leave a partnership, this will involve a change in the persons who are entitled to share in the partnership assets. There is no capital gains tax consequence if an incoming partner introduces cash which is credited to his capital account. Nor is there normally any capital gains tax consequence when an outgoing partner withdraws his capital account. In the first instance an incoming partner is paying in a sum which remains to his credit in his capital account, whilst in the second instance an outgoing partner is only withdrawing what belongs to him.

If, however, before an outgoing partner withdraws his capital account, that capital account has been credited with a surplus on revaluation of partnership assets (e.g. premises or goodwill), the withdrawal will include a realised capital gain in respect of the excess on revaluation, and to that extent it is chargeable to capital gains tax.

This charge will arise not only on retirement, but whenever a partner's capital account includes a revaluation of chargeable assets and his profit-sharing entitlement is reduced. He is deemed to have disposed of a proportion of the chargeable assets equivalent to the drop in his profit-sharing entitlement.

A payment by an incoming partner to the existing partners for a share in the chargeable assets such as goodwill or premises will constitute a disposal by the existing partners for capital gains tax, and a cost for capital gains tax to the incoming partner. The same applies where cash passes on a variation of profit-sharing arrangements without a change in partners. It makes no difference whether the cash is left in the partnership (by a credit to the capital account of those disposing) or is withdrawn by them, or indeed is dealt with outside the partnership itself. The test is whether a partner receives consideration for reducing his share in the partnership. Conversely, if he does not receive consideration, whilst there is still a deemed disposal, the market value of the assets is not substituted, so that no gain is deemed to arise.

The same principle applies where consideration is received that is less than the market value of the share which is being disposed of. Any chargeable gain is calculated by reference to the consideration actually passing.

See example 4.

Annuities to outgoing partners (FA 1974, s 16 and Revenue Statements of Practice D12 (17/1/75) and SP 1/79)

An outgoing partner may be paid an annuity by the continuing partners consequent upon his retirement. This will be taxed in his hands partly as earned and partly as unearned income, the earned proportion being limited to 50% of the average of his best three year's assessable profit shares out of

Example 4

X and Y are in partnership. Z is admitted as an equal partner, introducing £15,000 as capital which is credited to his capital account. The £15,000 is neither a capital gains tax base cost for Z nor a disposal by X and Y. The partnership assets include premises worth £60,000, which cost £21,000 when acquired.

Consider the following alternatives:

(1) Before Z's admission, X and Y revalue the premises up to £60,000 by crediting each of their capital accounts with £19,500.

	£
On Z's admission they each make a chargeable gain of:	
Value of premises reflected in their capital account	
($\frac{1}{2}$ each)	30,000
Share of premises retained after Z's admission ($\frac{1}{3}$ each)	20,000
	———
Deemed disposal proceeds	10,000

Less cost:		
Cost was $\frac{1}{2}$ each × £21,000	10,500	
Cost is now $\frac{1}{3}$ each × £21,000	7,000	
	———	
Cost of part disposed of		3,500
		———
Gain (subject to any available indexation allowance)		£6,500
		———

Z's base cost is £20,000 ($\frac{1}{3}$ × £60,000), equivalent to the disposal proceeds of X and Y.

(2) The premises are not revalued on the admission of Z.

There is then no deemed gain by X and Y, and Z's base cost for capital gains tax is $\frac{1}{3}$ × £21,000 = £7,000.

(3) Z privately pays £20,000 (£10,000 each) to X and Y, representing his $\frac{1}{3}$rd share in the market value of the partnership premises.

X and Y are treated as receiving £10,000 each as in (1).

The base cost for future disposals in the case of (1) and (3) is:

	X	Y	Z
Original cost	10,500	10,500	—
On introduction of Z	(3,500)	(3,500)	7,000
Gains on which X and Y are assessable			13,000
	———	———	———
	7,000	7,000	20,000
	———	———	———

the last seven, after a retail prices index adjustment. Once the amount to be treated as earned income is established, it is itself increased in line with the retail prices index in later years.

The annuity ranks as a charge against income in the hands of the paying partners. They will deduct basic-rate income tax at source when making the payment and claim relief at higher rates and surcharge where appropriate by an adjustment in the assessment. Only that part of the annuity which ranks as unearned income in the hands of the retired partner is available to reduce the unearned income for surcharge purposes of those paying it.

The capitalised value of the annuity will not be regarded as an amount subject to capital gains tax in the hands of the recipient so long as the annuity falls within what is regarded as reasonable recognition for past services to the partnership. This is again based on the average of the best three year's assessable profit shares out of the last seven, not on this occasion index-linked. The annuity is considered reasonable if it does not exceed the fraction of that average amount obtained from the following table.

Years of service	Fraction
1–5	1/60 per year
6	8/60
7	16/60
8	24/60
9	32/60
10	2/3

Capital gains tax retirement relief (CGTA 1979, s 124)

A person disposing of an interest in a partnership is exempt from tax on gains of up to £50,000 (to be increased to £100,000 for 1983/84 onwards under proposed legislation) on the business assets if he is 65 years of age or over with ten years qualifying trading. Someone over 60 but under 65 is entitled to the exemption at the rate of £10,000 per annum, and, if there are less than ten qualifying years but at least one, the available exemption is further reduced according to the number of qualifying years.

Despite the description of the relief, actual retirement is not necessary, but there must be a disposal of an interest in the business as distinct from a mere sale of assets. See chapter 5 for fuller details of the relief.

Death of a partner

Where a partner dies in service:

(a) Any election which is made for continuity of assessments must be signed by his personal representatives, otherwise a deemed cessation cannot be avoided.
(b) Any chargeable gains arising on the disposal of partnership assets by

177

reason of the death are exempt like any other chargeable asset held at death.

(c) The annuity referred to earlier may be paid to his widow or dependants.

Capital transfer tax

The interest of a deceased partner in the partnership (including his capital account) ranks as relevant business property for the 50% business property relief unless the surviving partners are obliged to acquire his share, in which case it is regarded as an entitlement under a contract for sale and not therefore eligible for relief. Relief is not lost where there is an option as opposed to an obligation to acquire the share.

Capital transfer tax on a partnership share may be paid by ten annual instalments if it arises on death, or on a lifetime gift where the donee pays the tax, but if the share or part thereof is disposed of within the ten years by the transferee, the balance of the tax or the appropriate part thereof becomes payable immediately (see chapter 7).

Value added tax

Customs and Excise need to be notified on a change of partner, but not on a change of profit-sharing arrangements. The registration number will normally continue.

Stamp duty

A 50p stamp applies to the partnership deed if under seal. Partnership is not specifically dealt with in stamp duty legislation, but it will arise when the partnership transactions involve documents requiring to be stamped, for example on the purchase of land.

The division of assets on dissolution will not normally attract ad valorem duty, as distinct from any sale of assets liable as a conveyance or transfer or where the dissolution agreement requires stamping as a voluntary disposition because a gratuitous benefit accrues to one or more partners.

Miscellaneous

A *salaried partner* is to be distinguished from a partner who is allocated a salary as part of the profit-sharing arrangement. Senior employees are often made salaried partners in professional firms. They remain liable to income tax under Schedule E as employees, receiving a salary for the duties of their employment.

A partnership may include a *limited partner* under the Limited Partnership Act 1907. His liability for the partnership debts is limited, and he may not take part in the management of the partnership. His share of profits ranks as unearned income.

The share of a *sleeping partner* likewise ranks as unearned income. A *company* may be a partner with individuals. In this case the profit share of the company is liable to corporation tax and is excluded from an assessment to income tax on the partners who are individuals. The profits are computed for the period of account, the preceding year basis not applying, and the shares of the individuals are apportioned over the tax years comprised in the period of account.

The national insurance cost of employing a *wife* is usually greater than if she were a partner with the husband. Moreover, if she is a partner, capital gains tax retirement relief will apply to the disposal of her share as well as his. But this must be weighed against her taking on the legal liability associated with partnership.

Partnership itself, and matters arising, need not be governed by *formal written agreement*. In the absence of such agreement, sometimes indeed despite it, the Revenue will require other evidence of partnership, for example the name of, and operating arrangements for, bank accounts, VAT registration, names on stationery, contracts, licences etc.

The overseas aspect of partnerships is dealt with in chapter 44.

Tax points

- Failure to make a continuation election can be costly. To avoid the risk of a partner not being prepared to sign one, include a clause in the partnership agreement providing that an incoming or outgoing partner will sign an election if required to do so by the other partners, appointing each partner as power of attorney for the others under the partnership deed.

- An election for continuity does not, however, always pay, and a comparison of the alternatives should be made in respect of the old and new partnerships taken together.

  An agreement that a dissenting or disadvantaged partner is compensated for any extra tax suffered is always possible.

- Calculate annuities to retiring partners within the allowable capital gains tax limits, leaving them taxable only as income in the hands of the recipient and allowable to the payers.

- Because of the preceding year basis, tax is usually payable some time after the profits are earned. It is sensible to set aside sufficient monies from partnership funds to pay the liability on trading profits on 1 January and 1 July yearly, retaining an appropriate part from each partner's drawings for this purpose.

- In the opening years of a new business, consider employing an intended partner before his admission to the partnership. Profits which will form the basis of assessment for more than one year of assessment (assuming a continuation election is made) will then be reduced by deduction for his salary and for employer's national insurance contributions.

24
National insurance contributions for the self-employed

Background

A self-employed person who has attained the age of 16 must, unless specifically exempted, pay both Class 2 and Class 4 contributions. Class 2 contributions are payable weekly at a flat rate and entitle the contributor to most contributory benefits, but not unemployment benefit, invalidity pension, widow's benefit or the earnings-related portion of the retirement pension. Class 4 contributions are earnings-related and are payable as a percentage of earnings chargeable to income tax under Schedule D, Case I or II (see chapter 21). These contributions, which carry no entitlement to benefits of any kind, were introduced to ensure that self-employed persons as a whole pay their fair share of the costs of the social security system.

Class 2 contributions

Payment (SSA 1975, s 7)

Class 2 contributions are payable weekly and can be made by either:

(a) purchasing a special stamp from Post Offices which is then stuck on a contribution card; or
(b) making a transfer by direct debit out of a bank or National Giro account.

The weekly rates for 1982/83 and 1983/84 are:

1982/83	£3.75
1983/84	£4.40

Exempt persons

The following people are not liable to pay Class 2 contributions:

(a) men and women over state pension age (men 65, women 60);
(b) individuals working outside Great Britain throughout any contribution week;
(c) married women who chose on or before 11 May 1977 to pay reduced rate Class 1 contributions or to pay no Class 2 contributions;
(d) people with small earnings who obtain certificates of exception (see below);
(e) persons who are not 'ordinarily' self-employed (see below);
(f) persons, who for a full week, are
  (i) incapable of work, or
  (ii) in legal custody or prison, or
  (iii) in receipt of sickness, invalidity or injury benefit or maternity allowance; and
(g) individuals who, for any day in a particular week, are in receipt of unemployability supplement or invalid care allowance.

In the case of (f) and (g) the exemption is applicable only to the particular week concerned.

Small earnings

You may apply for a certificate of exception for a tax year if you can show that:

(i) your net earnings for the year of application are expected to be less than a specified limit; or
(ii) your net earnings for the year preceding the application were less than the limit specified for that year and that circumstances have not materially altered.

In this context 'net earnings' are earnings disclosed in the profit and loss account as opposed to taxable earnings. Where an accounting period overlaps 5 April earnings are apportioned on a time basis between tax years.

The limits referred to above are

1982/83	£1,600
1983/84	£1,775

Certificates of exception must be renewed each tax year and can be applied for on form CF 10 which is contained in DHSS leaflet NI 27A—'People with small earnings from self-employment'.

Persons not 'ordinarily' self-employed

When a person applies to pay Class 2 contributions he may be informed by the DHSS that they consider that he is not ordinarily self-employed and that there is therefore no liability to such contributions. There is no statutory definition of 'ordinarily self-employed' but the example quoted by the DHSS in leaflet NI 27A is of a person employed in a regular job whose earnings from spare-time self-employment are not expected to exceed £800 in a tax year.

If you are in this category, you do not have to apply for a certificate of exception. You would be eligible for relief under the small earnings rule anyway, but this lower limit avoids the need to apply for a certificate.

More than one self-employment

People who are self-employed have to pay only one Class 2 contribution per week irrespective of the number of self-employed jobs they may have. In establishing whether or not you are entitled to a certificate of exception on the grounds of small earnings, self-employed earnings from all sources are aggregated together.

Class 4 Contributions

Payment (SSA 1975, s 9)

Class 4 contributions are payable at a percentage rate on profits chargeable to income tax under Schedule D, Case I or II which fall between specified upper and lower earnings limits.

Contribution rates and limits for 1982/83 and 1983/84 are:

Year	Rate	On profits
1982/83	6.0%	Between £3,450 and £11,000
1983/84	6.3%	Between £3,800 and £12,000

In general 'profits' are computed in exactly the same way for Class 4 contributions as for income tax but certain special rules apply, for example losses allowed under TA 1970, ss 168, 169 (see chapter 25) against non-trading income for income tax are set only against Schedule D, Case I or II income for national insurance, and may thus be carried forward against future profits for calculating Class 4 contributions. Class 4 contributions are calculated and collected by the Inland Revenue together with income tax payable under Schedule D, Case I or II; the contributions are therefore payable at the same time as the income tax liability on the relevant profits, usually in equal instalments on 1 January in the tax year and on the following 1 July.

Exempt persons

The following people are not liable to pay Class 4 contributions:

(a) men and women over state pension age (men 65, women 60);
(b) individuals who are not resident in the UK for income tax purposes;
(c) trustees and executors who are chargeable to income tax on income which they receive on behalf of other people (e.g. incapacitated persons);

(d) 'sleeping partners' who supply capital and take a share of the profits but take no active part in running the business;

(e) divers and diving supervisors working in connection with exploration and exploitation activities on the Continental shelf or in UK territorial waters;

(f) persons under 16 on 6 April in a particular tax year who hold a certificate of exception for that year. Application for an exception certificate should be made on form RD 901; application need only be made once as any certificate granted will cover all the relevant tax years; and

(g) persons who are not 'ordinarily' self-employed (see under Class 2 above).

Partnerships and married persons

When computing the Class 4 liability of partnerships the Revenue will normally calculate each partner's liability separately but will collect the total liability in the partnership name, together with the income tax liability arising under Schedule D. Where a partner carries on a further trade or trades, the profits of all such businesses are aggregated for the purposes of calculating his overall Class 4 liability. Class 4 contributions are payable only up to the upper earnings limit regardless of how many businesses are involved.

Where a husband and wife are in partnership their Class 4 liability is calculated separately, although the liability is assessed on the husband. If, however, a husband and wife have elected either to be assessed separately for income tax purposes or to have the wife's earned income taxed as if she were a single person (see chapter 37) the election will also apply for Class 4 purposes, and the Class 4 liability of the wife will be assessed on the wife.

Self-employed and employed in the same tax year

Where a self-employed individual is also an employee he is liable to pay Class 1, 2 and 4 contributions. It is possible, however, to claim deferment of both Class 2 and Class 4 contributions if it can be shown that Class 1 earnings are likely to be substantial and that total contribution liability without deferment would exceed the maximum liability by more than £10.

For 1983/84, Class 4 contributions only will be deferred if total contributions are likely to be more than £10 in excess of £750.30.

Class 2 and 4 contributions for that year will be deferred if total contributions are likely to be more than £10 in excess of £1,123.14.

Application for deferment must be made on form CF 359, which is part of leaflet NP 18 'Class 4 NI Contributions'. Where deferment is granted responsibility for the computation and collection of Class 4 contributions is transferred from the Inland Revenue to the DHSS.

If you feel you have overpaid Class 4 contributions you may apply for a refund by writing to the DHSS and stating why it is felt that an overpayment has arisen. This could happen, for example, if you have several businesses and the total profits of those businesses have been incorrectly aggregated in arriving at your overall liability.

Tax points

- If you pay Class 2 contributions by direct debit, make sure you notify the DHSS of any weeks for which a contribution is not due, for example when you are receiving sickness benefit or working abroad, so that an adjustment can be made.

- If you are both employed and self-employed make sure you claim deferment if you are eligible. This is better than waiting till after the year end for a refund.

- If you are a married couple who both work in the business, consider whether it is better for the wife to be a partner or employee. From a national insurance point of view it would usually be better for her to be an employee if she earns less than £32.50 a week and to be a partner if she earns more. For income tax a wife's wages may be challenged as being too high for the work done, but this does not apply to the profit share of a wife who works as a partner.

- Remember that trading losses set off against non-trading income for income tax purposes are carried forward against trading profits for Class 4 contributions purposes.

25
Relief for trading losses: sole traders and partners

Loss reliefs available

There are various alternative ways in which relief for trading losses may be claimed:

Carry forward against later profits of same trade (TA 1970, s 171).

Set against general income of current year and following year (if trade still exists) (TA 1970, s 168).

In a new trade, carry back against general income of previous three years (FA 1978, s 30).

When a loss occurs on ceasing to trade, carry back against trading income of previous three years (TA 1970, s 174).

Calculation of loss

Trading losses are calculated in the same way as profits (see chapter 20). Where a loss occurs in a partnership, each partner may choose what loss claim(s) to make for his share of the loss quite independently from how the other partners relieve their loss shares.

Assessments (TA 1970, s 115)

The first thing a trading loss does is to fix the assessment based on the accounting period at Nil. See example 1. However, this does not give relief for the loss.

Loss carried forward (TA 1970, s 171)

The most straightforward way of obtaining relief for a loss is by carrying it forward to reduce later income of the same trade, so that in example 1 the loss of £7,000 would reduce the 1984/85 assessment to £1,000. The carry forward is only against profits of the *same* trade, so that a change in activity will cause relief to be denied.

There are disadvantages in carrying forward a loss. The trade may cease, or its nature change, before the loss is fully relieved. The relief is against the

---

Example 1

The results of a sole trader or the shares of a partner are as follows:

Year ended 31 December	1981	Profit £10,000
	1982	Loss (£7,000)
	1983	Profit £8,000

Assessments based thereon:

1982/83	£10,000
1983/84	Nil
1984/85	£8,000

---

first available profits and the size of those profits may leave insufficient income to utilise the taxpayer's personal reliefs, so that if the taxpayer in example 1 had personal reliefs in 1984/85 of £3,000 and no other income, reliefs of £2,000 would be wasted.

It is not possible to set off only £5,000 of the losses forward and leave £3,000 taxable profit to be covered by personal reliefs. There is also a considerable delay before the loss results in a cash saving by reducing or eliminating a tax bill. The loss in example 1 of the year to 31 December 1982 reduces the 1984/85 tax bill, which is payable in equal instalments on 1 January 1985 and 1 July 1985.

Loss set against other income (TA 1970, s 168)

Relief may be obtained more quickly by setting off the loss against any other income of the tax year in which the loss is incurred and/or the next tax year. This is, however, not permissible for losses incurred in 'hobby' trades as distinct from commercial activities. The set-off is also specificially prohibited for the sixth year of a consecutive run of farming and market gardening losses (reckoned before capital allowances) (TA 1970, s 180).

Strictly, a loss for set-off against other income should be calculated by reference to an income tax year, arrived at by splitting accounts, so that in example 1 the result for the income tax year 1981/82 would be:

$\frac{3}{4} \times £10,000$	7,500
$\frac{1}{4} \times (£7,000)$	(1,750)
Profit	£5,750

and for the income tax year 1982/83:

$\frac{3}{4} \times (£7,000)$	(5,250)
$\frac{1}{4} \times £8,000$	2,000
Loss	£(3,250)

Since the accounting loss incurred was £7,000 and only £3,250 would be relieved by reference to the loss actually incurred in the income tax year 1982/83, the balance of the loss, i.e. £3,750, would be carried forward. However, the Revenue will in practice usually accept that the loss of an income tax year may be treated as being the loss of the accounting year ended within it, so that the loss of £7,000 in the accounting year ended 31 December 1982 may be regarded as the loss of the income tax year 1982/83. As well as being more straightforward than splitting accounts, the Revenue concession usually operates in the taxpayer's favour, giving an immediate loss claim of £7,000 in example 1 rather than £3,250 now and £3,750 carried forward. The Revenue will not follow this practice in the first three years of assessment of a new business, nor in the last year of assessment. In those cases, the loss of the income tax year itself must be calculated by splitting results. But otherwise their practice is normally followed.

Having ascertained the loss, relief is available against assessable income of the tax year of the loss, or of the following income tax year (providing the trade is still carried on in that year), or, if the loss is large enough, of both years. Claims may thus be made in example 1 for 1982/83 (the tax year of loss) and/or for 1983/84.

The assessable income against which relief is given is all income from whatever source and not just the income from the trade. (Indeed, there will usually be no income from the trade itself in the second year of claim because of the loss in the basis period.) It is in fact not permissible to restrict the set-off to just part of the income, and as with the carry forward loss claim, the loss set-off must be made *before* deducting personal reliefs, so that in some cases personal reliefs may be wasted.

If the trade is the only source of income the effect of the claim will be to carry back the loss against the previous year's assessable profits. Thus, using the figures in example 1 and assuming no other sources of income, the assessments will be:

1982/83 (based on profit of year to 31 December 1981)	10,000	
Less Section 168 loss claim	(7,000)	
		£3,000
1983/84 (based on result of year to 31 December 1982)		Nil
1984/85 (based on profit of year to 31 December 1983)		£8,000

A loss claim would not be possible in 1983/84 because there is no income for that tax year.

For married couples who both have income the choice of how to claim relief is much wider, because it is open to the lossmaker, in either or both of the two relevant years (the year of loss and the following year) either to include the spouse's income in the claim or to exclude it. The loss will thus be set either against the lossmaker's income, earned before unearned, followed by the spouse's income in the same order, or just against the lossmaker's income. This gives added flexibility and a better chance of avoiding loss of personal reliefs. See example 2.

Example 2

Trader's results are:

Year ended 30 June	1981	Profit	£4,000
	1982	Loss	(£12,000)
	1983	Profit	£8,000

He has unearned income of £5,000 per annum. His wife earns £3,000 per annum and has unearned income of £2,000 per annum. Income before loss claims is:

		1982/83	1983/84	1984/85
		£	£	£
Husband—Earned		4,000	—	9,000
	Unearned	5,000	5,000	5,000
Wife	—Earned	3,000	3,000	3,000
	Unearned	2,000	2,000	2,000
		£14,000	£10,000	£19,000

	1982/83	1983/84	1984/85
Available personal allowances:	£	£	£
Married allowance	2,445	2,795	?
Wife's earned income relief	1,565	1,785	?
	£4,010	£4,580	£ ?

The best loss claim to make is against the husband's income only, firstly of 1982/83 then of 1983/84. This leaves the wife's income to cover the personal reliefs and also saves investment income surcharge in 1982/83 (on excess of unearned income over £6,250).

New trades—carry back of losses (FA 1978, s 30)

Where a loss occurs in any of the first four years of assessment of a new trade, relief is permitted against the general income of the three previous tax years, earliest first. See example 3.

Where a loss is large enough a combination of Section 168 and Section 30 claims may be made. The set-off rules as regards earned and unearned income and lossmaker and spouse are the same under Section 30 as under Section 168.

Capital allowances and stock relief (TA 1970, s 169; FA 1981, Schs 8 and 9)

Where there are losses or where capital allowances and stock relief exceed

Example 3

Trade started 1 August 1982.
Year ended 31 July 1983   Loss   (£10,800)
Year ended 31 July 1984   Profit   £2,400
There will be Nil assessments for 1982/83, 1983/84 and 1984/85 (see chapter 21), so unless there are other sources of income there would be no loss claims under Sections 168 and 171 until 1985/86.

For the first three years of assessment, loss claims must be calculated on the basis of the loss in the tax year itself, not on the accounting year ended within it.

The losses are:

	1982/83	1983/84
8/12 × (£10,800)	(£7,200)	—
4/12 × (£10,800)		(3,600)
8/12 × £2,400		1,600
		(£2,000)

Relief is available by carry back against general income of:

First	1979/80	1980/81
Then	1980/81	1981/82
Then	1981/82	1982/83

If there were also losses in 1984/85 and 1985/86 (making with 1982/83 and 1983/84 the first four years of assessment) relief would be available as follows:

For losses incurred in	1984/85	1985/86
Relief would be available by carry back against general income of: First	1981/82	1982/83
Then	1982/83	1983/84
Then	1983/84	1984/85

profits, unused capital allowances and stock relief relating to the loss period may be carried forward to set against later trading profits or used to increase Section 168 and/or Section 30 loss claims. Stock relief need not be included in a loss claim as well as capital allowances, but it is not possible to include stock relief without including capital allowances. The choice of including or excluding capital allowances and stock relief again gives flexibility in arriving at the best loss claim bearing in mind available personal reliefs.

Pre-trading expenditure (FA 1980, s 39)

Where expenditure is incurred within three years before a trade commences and it would have been allowable as a trading expense if incurred afterwards (see chapter 20 for allowable and non-allowable expenses), it may be treated as a loss of the first tax year and relief claimed under TA 1970, s 168 or 171 or FA 1978, s 30. This would cover, for example, rent paid on business premises before starting to trade.

Loss on cessation of trade (terminal loss) (TA 1970, s 174)

Losses arising when a trade ceases clearly cannot be carried forward against future profits of the same trade. A Section 168 claim may be made to set such a loss against current general income, if there is any. Alternatively, or if the loss is large enough, additionally, a claim may be made to set the loss of the last twelve months of trading (called a terminal loss) against the

---

Example 4

Trade ceases 30 September 1983.
Previous accounts have been to 31 December, recent results and assessments thereon (see chapter 21) being:
Period to 30 September 1983 Loss (£9,000) 1983/84 assessment Nil
Year to 31 December 1982   Profit £2,400 Escapes assessment
Year to 31 December 1981   Profit £1,000 Assessed in 1982/83
Year to 31 December 1980   Profit £5,000 Assessed in 1981/82
Year to 31 December 1979   Profit £7,000 Assessed in 1980/81

Terminal loss:
1 October 1982 to 5 April 1983
    First three months   Profit   600
    Next three months   Loss   (3,000)
                                    ───────   (2,400)
6 April 1983 to 30 September 1983   (6,000)
                                             ───────
                                             (£8,400)
                                             ───────

This may be carried back against assessments for:
1982/83   £1,000
1981/82   £5,000
1980/81   £7,000, reducing it to
                                 £4,600

Alternatively a Section 168 claim may be made to set the 1983/84 loss of £6,000 against any income of that year—which could arise through balancing charges and stock relief clawback in addition to any regular sources. If loss relief were obtained in that way, only the balance of the terminal loss of £2,400 would be the subject of a terminal loss claim. It may, however, be preferable to leave other income to cover personal allowances and claim terminal loss relief on the full amount.

trading income (after capital allowances and stock relief) of the three tax years prior to that in which the trade ceases, *latest* first. If there are unrelieved capital allowances for that twelve months they may be included in the claim. (It is more likely, however, that there will be a balancing charge to claw back excess allowances given. There will also probably be a stock relief clawback in the last tax year in respect of stock relief claimed in the six years up to cessation (see chapter 21).) See example 4.

Time limits for claims

TA 1970, s 168	Set-off against income of same tax year or following year	Within two years after the end of the year of assessment to which the claim relates
FA 1978, s 30	Set-off new business losses against income for three previous tax years, taking earlier before later years	Within two years after the end of the year of assessment in which the loss is sustained
TA 1970, s 171	Carry forward against future profits of same trade	Within six years after the end of the year of assessment to which the claim relates
TA 1970, s 174	Carry back of terminal losses	Normal six year time limit since no other time limit specified

Formal claims for relief must be made within these time limits, except for TA 1970, s 171, where the Inland Revenue will accept a computation indicating that the loss is being carried forward.

Repayment supplement (FA (No 2) 1975, s 47)

A loss claim will either prevent tax being payable or cause tax already paid to be repaid. A tax-free repayment supplement is paid to individuals receiving a repayment of at least £25 more than one year after the end of the tax year to which it relates. The supplement runs from the end of the tax year following that for which the repayment is made (or from the end of the tax year in which the tax was paid, if later). The rate of interest changes from time to time and is currently 8%. The supplement applies to all loss claims but is particularly beneficial in relation to carry back claims on new business losses.

Tax points

- The earliest relief is not always the best. The key question is how much tax do you save. Watch the effect of changes in tax rates and allowances in the various years.

- Claiming carry-back relief under FA 1978, s 30, instead of relief under TA 1970, s 168, for a first year loss leaves other income of that year available for a possible claim under FA 1978, s 30 for a loss in the fourth year.

- The tax-free repayment supplement on loss claims under FA 1978, s 30 can substantially boost the repayment. The supplement on claims under TA 1970, s 168 is likely to be much less.

- If married, leave a spouse's income to cover personal allowances if possible.

- For complex interactions of different loss reliefs, get expert advice.

26
Trading losses: companies

Loss reliefs available

As in the case of losses of individuals and partnerships (see chapter 25), trading losses of companies are calculated in the same way as profits, and have the immediate effect of reducing the assessment on the company under Schedule D, Case I to Nil.

The following alternatives are then available for relief of the loss:

Set-off against current profits (TA 1970, s 177(2)).
Carry-back against earlier profits (TA 1970, s 177(3)(3A)).
Carry-forward against future trading profits (TA 1970, s 177(1)).
When a loss occurs on ceasing to trade, carry-back against earlier trading profits (TA 1970, s 178).
Set-off against franked investment income (TA 1970, s 254).
Group relief (TA 1970, ss 258–264).

Set-off against current profits (TA 1970, s 177(2))

A trading loss of a company can be set against any profits of the same chargeable accounting period, thus reducing or eliminating the corporation tax thereon. Capital allowances and stock relief will have been deducted in arriving at the trading loss.

Profits for a company include all sources of income (other than UK dividends) plus chargeable gains, 15/26ths of the gains for the chargeable accounting period being included in the profit chargeable to corporation tax. With corporation tax at 52% the effective tax rate on the chargeable gains is 30%, which equates with the rate payable by an individual. (The small companies rate of corporation tax never applies to chargeable gains.)

Losses are set against income before gains, but where they are sufficient to reduce chargeable gains, losses of £3,000 will thus eliminate gains of £5,200.

Carry-back against previous profits and carry-forward (TA 1970, s 177(1)(3)(3A))

When a trading loss has been set against the profits of the current period, any balance may be carried back and set against any profits of previous accounts for a time period equal to the accounting period of loss. They can only be carried back to an accounting period during which the trade was carried on, but relief is not limited to set-off against profits of that trade.

Any loss not relieved against other profits may be carried forward for set-off against future trading profits of the same trade, without time limit.

Claims to set off losses against current and previous profits of any description are only permitted if the company carries on business on a commercial basis with a view to the realisation of profit. There is no commercial basis restriction for carrying losses forward, since the permitted set-off is only against trading profits of that trade.

Example 1

In its year to 31 October 1983 a company made a trading loss of £70,000. Its other results and loss claims arising are:

	Year ended 30.4.82	6 months to 31.10.82	Year ended 31.10.83	Loss and Loss claims
Trading profits	16,000	12,000	—	(70,000)
Investment income	7,000	11,000	6,000	
15/26ths chargeable gains	5,000	—	1,500	
Total profits	28,000	23,000	7,500	
Loss set-off:				
Against profits of same period			(7,500)	7,500
Against previous profits for up to 12 months				
6 months account		(23,000)		23,000
6/12 × 12 month account	(14,000)			14,000
Loss carried forward				£25,500
Profits remaining in charge (being income £9,000 and gains £5,000)	£14,000	—	—	

The loss may not be set against the remaining profit of the year to 30 April 1982 since the carry-back period cannot exceed the loss period, i.e. twelve months.

Where any part of a trading loss is attributable to first-year allowances on plant, that part of the loss may be carried back for three full years from the beginning of the loss period. See example 2.

Example 2

If the loss in example 1 had included first-year allowances of £16,000, they could have eliminated the remaining profit of £14,000 for the year to 30 April 1982. The balance of £2,000 could then have been set against the profits of the year to 30 April 1981 (and if those profits were insufficient, against 6/12ths of the profits of the year to 30 April 1980), reducing the loss to be carried forward to £9,500.

Charges on income (TA 1970, s 177(8))

A company pays charges such as loan interest, patent royalties and charity covenants net of basic-rate income tax, and accounts to the Revenue for the income tax deducted. (Bank interest on the other hand is paid gross and is a normal trading expense.)

Charges are deductible not from trading profits but from total profits, including chargeable gains. Trading losses, however, are set off in priority to charges (except for terminal losses, see below).

If trade charges exceed available profits the excess may be carried forward as a trading loss. Excess charges may never be carried back except in a terminal loss claim (see below).

If there are unrelieved charges that were *not* paid wholly and exclusively for the purposes of the trade, such as charity covenants, no relief is available. Non-trade charges are only relieved to the extent that profits of the period in which they are paid are available to cover them.

Terminal losses (TA 1970, s 178)

It is clearly not possible to carry losses forward when a trade ceases, so a company is permitted to carry terminal losses back for up to three years. Any available current set-off and carry-back loss claims under TA 1970, s 177 must be claimed first. There will not usually be any first-year allowances for the last twelve months, because first-year allowances are not given in the accounting period in which the trade ceases.

After all other possible loss claims have been made, any remaining losses of the last twelve months may be carried back, against trading profits only, for the three years immediately before the last year, being set against profits of later periods before earlier periods. Any unrelieved trade charges of the last twelve months are included in the terminal loss.

Terminal loss relief does not supersede relief for trade charges, so if the trading profits of the period to which losses are carried back have been used to cover trade charges, terminal loss relief is given on the balance of trading profit remaining.

Effect of carry-back of losses on tax paid and ACT set-off (F(No 2)A 1975, s 48)

Carry-back loss claims will result in corporation tax already paid being repaid, or in tax otherwise due not having to be paid. Relief may be obtained at one of three possible corporation tax rates: at 38% or 40% if the loss set-off is against income charged at the small companies rate; at 52% if the set-off is against profits in excess of the upper limit for marginal small companies relief or against chargeable gains; and at a rate between $55\frac{1}{2}$% and 66% if profits are between the small companies rate marginal relief upper and lower limits. See chapter 4 for detailed figures.

The carry-back will also reduce the income element of the profits which determines what advance corporation tax set-off may be made, so that if ACT has either been paid in that period or carried back or forward to it, the loss claim may require the ACT set-off to be adjusted, and surplus ACT may arise as a result. See example 3.

Example 3

A company produces the following results.

Year ended 31 August	1982	1983
	£	£
Trading profit (loss)	20,000	(10,000)
Investment income	3,000	3,000
15/26ths chargeable gains	4,000	2,000
Total profits	27,000	5,000
ACT maximum set-off before loss relief:		
30% × income of £23,000/£3,000	6,900	900
If loss relief under TA 1970, s 177 is claimed:		
Profits	27,000	5,000
Less loss	(5,000)	(5,000)
Total profits	22,000	—
ACT maximum set-off following loss relief:		
30% × income of £18,000/Nil	5,400	—

If the tax repaid amounts to £100 or more it attracts a tax-free repayment supplement, usually from twelve months after the due date of original payment. The rate of supplement was 12% from 6 January 1980, reduced to 8% from 6 December 1982.

Loss relief against franked investment income (TA 1970, s 254)

Although franked investment income (i.e. dividends from United Kingdom companies, including the attached tax credits) is not chargeable to corporation tax (hence the word 'franked'), it nonetheless forms part of the fund of corporate profit. When all other loss reliefs are exhausted, it is possible to set any remaining losses against such franked investment income (unless it has been used to frank a dividend payment), thus obtaining a refund of the basic-rate tax within it, rather than carry forward the loss to set against future trading profits. The relief obtained is, however, only at the tax credit rate of 30% rather than the corporation tax rate.

Such a claim is subject to adjustment in a later year if the company pays dividends in excess of its franked investment income. The adjustment is rather complex, but it effectively means that the company gives back to the Revenue the tax credit originally refunded and obtains relief for the trading loss at the corporation tax rate then applicable to its trading profits.

Group relief for losses (TA 1970, ss 258–264)

In a group consisting of a holding company and its 75% subsidiaries, trading losses may be surrendered from one company to one or more other companies within the group, provided that all the companies are resident in the UK. The accounting period of the loss-making company must correspond with that of the claimant company. This will not pose any difficulty when accounts within the group are prepared to the same date, but only a fraction of one company's loss will be available against the same fraction of another's profits where accounts are prepared to different dates. Relief is also proportionately restricted if the parent/subsidiary relationship does not subsist throughout the accounting period.

The set-off rules are quite flexible, and broadly the loss-making company may surrender any part of its loss, up to a maximum of the available profits of the claimant company or companies for the corresponding period. The profits of the claimant company available for relief are profits from all sources, including chargeable gains, but *after* deducting charges on income. The charges are not displaced by the group loss relief as they would be in the case of relief for a company's own losses.

Relief for surrendered losses is not, however, available against the franked investment income of a claimant company.

The major factor in deciding the optimum loss claim is the rate of tax saving, which for financial year 1982 will be at 38% or 52%, or at $55\frac{1}{2}$% if profits lie between the marginal small companies rate limits. The small companies rate limits are reduced proportionately according to the number of associated companies. Other things being equal, it will be best to surrender the loss against profits being charged at the small companies marginal rate (or indeed not to surrender it at all if the company's own profits are charged at that rate). The rules enable the loss to be divided among several group companies in order to obtain the maximum loss relief. See example 4.

Example 4

Company A is the wholly owned subsidiary of company B. (Small companies rate marginal relief limits for financial year 1982 are therefore reduced to £50,000 and £250,000.) Both companies prepare accounts to 31 March, and for the year to 31 March 1983, results are as follows:

Company A has a trading loss of	£80,000
and other profits (all income)	£20,000
Company B has total profits (all income) of	£120,000

Company A may claim its own available loss reliefs first and surrender the balance; or it may surrender the full £80,000 and pay tax on its own profits of £20,000; or it may surrender any other amount up to £80,000, as the companies wish.

Rates of tax relief available:	On Company A's profits	On Company B's profits
	38%	$55\frac{1}{2}$% on £70,000
		38% on £50,000

Company A should thus surrender at least £70,000 of the loss to company B. The relief on the remaining £10,000 will be at 38% in either company.

The group relief provisions are also available in certain circumstances to a consortium of five or fewer companies that owns all the share capital of a trading company or of a holding company with 90% trading subsidiaries. Losses can be surrendered both from the trading companies to the consortium companies and from the consortium companies to the trading companies.

Time limits for claims

TA 1970, s 177(2)(3)(3A)	Set off against profits of same accounting period and previous accounting periods of equal length (first-year allowances, previous three years)	Within two years after the end of the accounting period of loss

TA 1970, s 177(1)	Carry forward against later trading profits from same trade	Within six years after the end of the accounting period of loss
TA 1970, s 254	Set trading loss against surplus franked investment income	Within two years after the end of the accounting period of loss
TA 1970, s 264	Group loss relief	Within two years after the end of the accounting period of loss
TA 1970, s 178	Carry terminal loss back three years	Within six years of cessation of trade

Anti-avoidance provisions

There are provisions to inhibit the purchase of tax-loss companies, which prevent losses incurred before a change of ownership being carried forward if either:

(a) within a period of three years there is both a major change in the nature or conduct of a trade carried on by a company and a change in its ownership; or

(b) after the scale of activities in a trade carried on by a company has become negligible and before any considerable revival there is a change in ownership.

(TA 1970, s 483)

The 75% link for group relief purposes (see above) is defined very much more restrictively than simply 75% of ordinary share capital, to prevent companies taking advantage of the provisions by means of an artificial group relationship (FA 1973, s 28 and Sch 12).

Group relief is not available if arrangements are in existence whereby the loss-making company could cease to be a member of the group (FA 1973, s 29).

Tax points

- When considering loss claims, always look at the amount of tax saved. Set-off of losses may save tax at 52%, $55\frac{1}{2}$% where the set-off is within the marginal small companies tranche of profits for financial year 1982, or only 38%.

- Plan expenditure qualifying for first-year allowance with the three year carry back of resulting losses in mind. Remember that initial allowances on industrial buildings are not first-year allowances, and can only be carried back for an equivalent length of time to the loss period.

- Interest paid to a bank is a trading expense and can thus form part of a loss for carry-back. Interest paid to other lenders is a charge on income, and unrelieved charges can only be carried forward (except in a terminal loss claim). Bear this in mind if you have a choice between borrowing from a bank and borrowing elsewhere on equivalent terms.

- Remember that group relief for losses is not available if there is less than a 75% link holding/subsidiary relationship.

- If two or more companies are controlled by the same individual(s), group relief is not available.

- Watch the anti-avoidance provisions on group relief. An arrangement made partway through an accounting period to sell a loss-making subsidiary will prevent group relief being claimed for that account even though the parent/subsidiary relationship exists throughout.

27
Transfer of business to limited company

Choice of date

When the trade of an individual or partnership is transferred to a company the trade is treated as having ceased for income tax purposes, so that the closing year rules dealt with on page 157 will apply. The Revenue will have the option of taxing the profits of the two years before the last on an actual rather than a preceding year basis, but some profits will still escape assessment, provided that the trade has been carried on long enough for the early profits to have been assessed more than once.

The transfer date will determine what profits escape assessment, so it is important to make an appropriate choice. If profits are rising it will generally be better to transfer after the end of a tax-year rather than before.

Capital allowances and stock relief (FA 1971, Sch 8(13); FA 1981, Sch 9(20))

Normally a cessation of trade would involve a clawback of the stock relief claimed in the previous six years and a balancing charge on the disposal of the plant and equipment.

The sole trader or partners and the company may usually, however, jointly elect for the plant and equipment to be transferred at written-down value, and, provided that the trader or partners take an initial 75% shareholding in the new company, a stock relief clawback can also be avoided if a joint election is made within two years of the end of the company's first account.

Unused trading losses (TA 1970, s 172)

If there are unused trading losses these cannot be carried forward to a company as such, but they may be relieved against income received by the trader or partners from the company, either in the form of directors' fees or dividends, so long as the business is exchanged for shares and the shares are still retained at the time of the loss set-off. Other available loss claims may be made first, e.g. under TA 1970, s 168 against income of the year of loss, or terminal loss relief for a loss of the last year against the trading income of the previous three years (see chapter 25), and the relief against

Example 1

The net assets of a trader at the time of incorporation of his business were:

	£
Freehold premises at market valuation	51,000
Goodwill at valuation	30,000
Plant and equipment (cost £80,000)	35,000
Net current assets other than cash	64,000
Cash and bank balances	20,000
	200,000

The premises had been acquired for £30,000 and the trade newly commenced after 6 April 1965. Assume indexation allowance to date of transfer is 5%.

The potential chargeable gains on incorporation are:

			£
Freehold premises—market value		51,000	
Less: Cost	30,000		
Indexation allowance 5%	1,500	31,500	19,500
Goodwill (cost and indexation allowance Nil)			30,000
			£49,500

The gain on the premises can be avoided by the trader retaining ownership, but that on the goodwill cannot.

income from the company would then be available on the balance.

Capital gains tax (CGTA 1979, ss 29A, 62, 63)

When the transfer takes place, the general rule is that chargeable assets will be deemed to have been disposed of to the company at their open market value. Current assets are not chargeable assets, and plant and machinery, although chargeable, will not normally be valued at more than cost, so the most likely assets on which a liability may arise are freehold or leasehold premises and goodwill.

An obvious way of avoiding the charge on premises is for the proprietor or partners to retain ownership and to allow the company to use them either at a rent or free of charge. This will also save the stamp duty that would have been incurred on the transfer.

There is no way of not transferring the goodwill, since if the trade is transferred the goodwill must automatically follow. The valuation of goodwill depends not only on the size of the profits but also on the extent to which the profits depend on the skills of the proprietor or partners, the nature of the trade and many other factors. Any gain arising may be covered by reliefs, such as the annual exemption or possibly retirement relief if the sole trader or partners are over 60. Otherwise the capital gains tax effect must be considered. See example 1 above.

Capital gains rollover relief on transfer (CGTA 1979, s 123)

Relief is available where a business is transferred to a company, but not in respect of the transfer of individual assets. The relief may be claimed only where all the assets (other than cash) are transferred in exchange for shares in the company. In example 1 above this would require everything other than the £20,000 cash to be transferred, so that the premises could not be retained in personal ownership. This may of course influence the decision.

The relief is given by calculating the chargeable gains arising on the disposal of the business and treating the capital gains tax cost of the shares as being reduced by those gains. The lower base cost will of course increase the potential capital gains tax liability in the future, but further reliefs may be available at the time the shares are disposed of, for example retirement or gifts relief, or total exemption if the shares are still held at death. See example 2.

Example 2

In consideration of the transfer of the trade in example 1, the trader receives 100,000 shares of £1 each, fully paid, in the new company, transferring all assets except the cash of £20,000.

The base cost of the shares will be:

100,000 shares	180,000
Less gains otherwise arising on premises and goodwill	49,500
Cost of 100,000 shares for capital gains tax purposes	£130,500

The difference between the £100,000 par value of the shares and the £180,000 assets value in example 2 represents a share premium. It is almost inevitable that the par value will not correspond with the asset values since those values cannot be precisely determined before the transfer date.

If the transfer is made only partly for shares, and partly for cash or credit to a director's loan account, then only proportionate relief is given. See example 3.

Example 3

Suppose the consideration of £180,000 in example 2 was satisfied as to £120,000 shares and £60,000 cash. Only two-thirds of the chargeable gains can be deducted from the base cost of the shares.

		Shares	Cash
Consideration		120,000	60,000
Gains	£49,500	33,000	£16,500

Cost of shares for capital gains tax purposes £87,000

The £16,500 is assessed in the normal way.

Obtaining the maximum deferral of gains under CGTA 1979, s 123 therefore requires the consideration for the shares to be locked in as share capital, rather than provided on director's loan account, whereas if assets are not transferred and funding is provided through directors' loans money can be withdrawn much more easily and at no tax cost.

Gifts of business assets (CGTA 1979, s 126)

An individual can transfer a chargeable business asset to a company at its capital gains tax base value to him by using the business gifts relief outlined on page 42.

The company would have to be formed and a small number of shares taken by the persons concerned before transferring the assets. The consideration for the assets need not be shares and a credit may be made to a director's loan account or cash taken instead. This relief is available not only when a business is incorporated but also at any later stage if an asset owned by an individual and used in the trade of his family company is transferred to the company.

Using this gifts rollover to defer the gain on goodwill instead of the CGTA 1979, s 123 rollover dealt with in the previous section allows the premises to be retained in personal ownership, and further stamp duty may be saved if the transferors collect the debts of the business instead of transferring them.

The disadvantage is that the transferor is only credited in the accounts of the company with the original cost of the chargeable business assets to him (or 6 April 1965 value) plus any indexation allowance, not with the market value at the time of the transfer, and that lower value will also form the basis of future indexation allowance to the company when the assets are disposed of.

Stamp and capital duties

Stamp duty is a fixed or ad valorem charge on instruments, and if there is no instrument no duty is normally payable.

Stock and plant can be transferred to the company by delivery, so no stamp duty will be payable, and the company can either pay cash or credit the director's loan account.

Stamp duty will arise on the agreement for the transfer of the trade to the company according to the amount of the consideration. As has already been said, the stamp duty can be reduced by not transferring premises to the company and by the sole trader or partners collecting the debts instead of assigning them. Capital duty will be payable at 1% on the value of all shares issued (their full value, not the par value), whether the assets in respect of which the shares are issued are transferred by written agreement or otherwise.

Value added tax (VATA 1983, s 33; SI 1980/1536, para 4)

On the transfer of a business to a company VAT will not normally arise on the assets transferred and the company will take over the VAT position of the transferor as regards deductible input tax and liability to account for output tax. A claim may be made by the trader or partners and the company for the existing VAT registration number to be transferred to the company. It is advisable to contact the appropriate VAT office in good time to obtain the necessary forms and ensure that the various requirements are complied with.

Development land tax (DLTA 1976, Sch 8(52))

If land with development value is transferred to the company, a development land tax liability will arise on the excess of the transfer consideration over the relevant base value and any available exemption (and a partnership only has a single exemption of £50,000 in respect of partnership land). See chapter 6. If the conditions for relief under CGTA 1979, s 123 (see above) are satisfied, i.e. all assets other than cash are transferred, such tax as is just and reasonable may be deferred for up to eight years, proportionate tax being payable in that period if there is a disposal of part of the shares or of the land, and the balance paid at the end of the eight years.

Capital transfer tax

There will rarely be any direct capital transfer tax implications on the incorporation of a business, but the effect on the rate of business property relief available where partners form a company should be borne in mind. The 50% relief available in respect of partnership interests is reduced to 30% for any partner whose share allocation represents a minority interest in the company, although this may be compensated for by a lower valuation of the minority holding. Shares of husband and wife are related property and the available rate of relief is determined by their joint holdings.

As regards assets such as premises used in the company but owned personally, business property relief is only available to a controlling shareholder, the rate being 30%, and no relief is available at all for such assets owned by minority shareholders.

See also chapter 7.

Tax points

- Choose the transfer date with care to maximise the profits that escape income tax. With steadily rising profits this means after 5 April rather than before.

- Remember that stock relief clawback cannot be avoided unless the former owners hold 75% of the share capital in the new company. The holdings of associates cannot be taken into account.

- Where you want to claim relief under CGTA 1979, s 123 on the transfer of a business, minimise the amount locked up in share capital by not transferring cash and by making drawings prior to the transfer to reduce the net current assets, introducing the withdrawn cash to the company on loan account.

- Where premises are retained in personal ownership, this does not stop capital gains tax rollover relief being claimed if they are replaced, provided that the company is the owner's family company, which means a company in which he owns at least 25% of the voting rights, or that he and his family own 51%, with his own share at least 5%.

- You cannot get the best of all worlds on incorporation of a business. Maximising the capital gains and development gains deferral can only be done at extra cost in terms of stamp and capital duties and with the disadvantage of locking funds into share capital. Retaining some assets and using gifts relief on those that are transferred saves stamp duty and enables funding to be done through loans, but you only get credited with the cost or 6 April 1965 value of the gifted assets and the company will only get indexation allowance on that cost or 6 April 1965 value when it disposes of the assets.

28
Selling the family company

Background

There are two ways in which the family company may be sold—selling the shares or selling the assets and liquidating the company, and the most difficult aspect of the sale negotiations is usually reconciling the interests of the vendors and the purchasers.

The vendors will usually prefer to sell the shares rather than the assets to avoid the double capital gains tax charge which will arise on the assets sale and on the distribution to the shareholders when the company is wound up. The purchaser may prefer to buy assets in order to be able to claim plant first-year allowances (unless he is connected with the vendor) and because buying assets is frequently more straightforward and involves less legal formalities than a share purchase, and consequently lower costs.

If the purchaser acquires shares he will assume any latent liabilities and obligations of the company. He will clearly require indemnities and warranties from the vendors, but the vendors will want to limit these as much as possible, and in any event the purchaser would have the inconvenience of enforcing them or perhaps be unable to do so if he could not trace the vendor or if the vendor had insufficient funds.

The outcome will depend on the relative bargaining strength of each party and the adjustments each agrees to in order to resolve points of difference.

Selling shares or assets

Part of the sale consideration may relate not to tangible assets but to the growth prospects or the entrepreneurial flair of those involved with the company, and where goodwill is a substantial factor the valuation placed on it will be an important part of the negotiations.

The tax cost of selling the shares can be significantly less than that of selling the assets followed by a liquidation. See example 1. Knowing the tax advantage to the vendor of the share sale, the purchaser may well seek a reduction in price if this route is to be followed.

Other factors

The disadvantages of selling assets may be mitigated if the company has

Example 1

Company was formed in 1968 and 1,000 £1 shares were issued at par. Balance sheet of company immediately prior to intended sale was:

	£		£
Share capital	1,000	Net current assets	5,000
Accumulated profits	9,000	Premises and goodwill at cost	5,000
	£10,000		£10,000

A sale is proposed on the basis of the goodwill and premises being worth £105,000.

If the shares are sold:

Assets per balance sheet	10,000
Increase in value of premises and goodwill (105,000 − 5,000)	100,000
Sale proceeds for shares	110,000
Cost	1,000
Chargeable gain (ignoring indexation)	£109,000
Capital gains tax @ 30% (ignoring any set-offs and exemptions)	£32,700

If assets are sold and company is liquidated:

Assets per balance sheet		10,000
Increase in value of premises and goodwill	100,000	
Less provision for corporation tax on sale (ignoring indexation) Gain £100,000 × 15/26 @ 52%	30,000	70,000
Amount distributed to shareholders on liquidation (ignoring liquidation costs)		80,000
Cost of shares		1,000
Chargeable gain (ignoring indexation)		£79,000
Capital gains tax @ 30% (ignoring any set-offs and exemptions)		£23,700

example 1 continued overleaf

example 1 continued

Comparison of amounts received by shareholders:

	Proceeds	Capital gains tax	Net
On sale of shares	110,000	32,700	77,300
On liquidation	80,000	23,700	56,300
Extra cost of liquidation route			£21,000
Being: Corporation tax on sale of goodwill and premises			30,000
Less reduction in capital gains tax because of lower return to shareholders (£30,000 @ 30%)			9,000
			£21,000

current (as distinct from brought-forward) trading losses which may be set off against the gains on the assets.

If it is intended that the company shall continue trading in some new venture rather than be wound up, it may be possible to roll over or hold over the gains by the purchase of new assets. Alternatively, if the new trade commences before the old trade ceases, it may be possible to create current losses against which the gains may be set, through first-year allowance claims on new plant.

Capital gains tax retirement relief

Vending shareholders over age 60 will be entitled to claim retirement relief (currently a maximum of £50,000 but to be increased to £100,000 retrospectively from 6 April 1983—see page 41). The gain on which relief is given is restricted to the business assets proportion of the gain on the shares, and is thus restricted to the extent that the company's assets include shares in other companies or other investments. Even so the gain on the business assets may be sufficient to absorb the available relief.

There is in practice no difference in the treatment of a sale of business assets by the company followed by liquidation and a sale of shares. Retirement relief is available in both cases on the business assets proportion of the gain.

If the controlling shareholders personally own the premises from which the company's business is carried on, strictly retirement relief should not be given on any gain arising, but it is given by Revenue concession where the premises are disposed of in conjunction with a share disposal. The relief is, however, restricted if the company pays rent, and if the rent is the full market rent no relief is available.

Payments in compensation for loss of office

Compensation and ex gratia payments are dealt with in detail in chapter 16.

They may be challenged by the Revenue as not being 'wholly and exclusively for the purposes of the trade', and the company must be able to demonstrate that any payments are wholly unassociated with a sale of the shares and moreover are not a distribution to a shareholder. If that can be proved to the Revenue's satisfaction, a termination payment will not only reduce the corporation taxable profits prior to sale of the shares, but also the value of the net assets supporting the consideration for the shares, and thus the share sale proceeds.

Payments into a pension scheme

It is possible to deplete the cash resources of the company prior to selling the shares, and thus to reduce the sale proceeds, by an appropriate pension scheme contribution, the benefits of which may be taken partly as a tax-free lump sum and partly as a pension taxable as earned income. This is acceptable subject to the levels of contributions and benefits payable being within the stipulated limits. Company pension schemes are dealt with in chapter 17.

Stamp duty

Stamp duty at the rate of 2% will normally be payable on the consideration whether the sale is of assets or shares.

Stamp duty on the sale of assets can only be reduced to the extent that assets may pass by delivery, such as plant and machinery, or where the vendor company does not assign the debts but appoints the purchaser as its agent to collect them.

On a sale of shares, 2% duty applies when shares are transferred by a normal stock transfer form, but not where they are transferred on renounceable letters of allotment. It is thus possible to reduce stamp duty by allotting new ordinary shares out of reserves prior to the share sale and converting the existing ordinary shares to minimal value preference shares. The major part of the consideration will then be for the shares transferred on renounceable allotment letters, which are not subject to duty, and the minimal remainder for the old ordinary shares which have become new preference shares.

Value added tax (VATA 1983, s 47 and Sch 6 Group 5; SI 1980/1536 reg 25; SI 1981/1741)

Where the family company is sold by means of a share sale, the sale does not attract value added tax because it is an exempt supply, and furthermore a partially exempt business can ignore the share proceeds in its partial exemption calculations.

The sale of assets does not present any problem where all or part of the business is sold as a going concern by one taxable person to another. No value added tax is charged by the vendor and the purchaser has no input tax to reclaim on the amount paid. This only applies, however, where the assets acquired are such that they represent a business which is capable of independent operation.

Where the 'going concern' concept does not apply, value added tax must be charged on all taxable supplies. The disposal of book debts is an exempt supply and does not attract value added tax, but the vendor may ignore it in his partial exemption calculations where applicable. Taxable supplies will include goodwill, stock, plant and machinery, and motor vehicles (except that cars will only be chargeable to the extent if any that the disposal proceeds exceed original cost). It is important to ensure that the purchase agreement provides for the addition of value added tax and that the purchase consideration is allocated over the various assets acquired. If value added tax is not mentioned in the purchase agreement the price is deemed to be VAT inclusive.

Tax points

- When a company ceases to trade, this denotes the end of a chargeable accounting period, and if there are current trading losses these cannot be relieved against chargeable gains arising after the cessation. But gains are deemed to be made on the contract date, not on completion, so if the company enters into the contract and then continues to trade pending completion, the right to set off current losses will be preserved.

- Compensation for loss of office and ex gratia payments upon cessation of employment can only be expected to escape Revenue challenge if they are genuine payments for breach of contract or reasonable ex gratia amounts bearing in mind years of service etc.

- A close company (i.e. one controlled by its directors or by five or fewer people) has to pay out as dividends any investment income arising following a sale of its assets if it is to avoid an apportionment (see page 30). Since it no longer has any trading income, the permitted abatement of investment income cannot apply (abatement being £3,000 or 10% of trading income if less) and there is no de minimis £1,000 that escapes apportionment for a non-trading company.

- When selling shares in a family company with significant distributable reserves, you can get caught by the anti-avoidance provisions of TA 1970, s 460, which concerns stripping income from securities. You should ensure that Revenue clearance is obtained for the proposed sale (including clearance for any stamp duty saving scheme).

- When buying the shares in a company, you should look particularly for any capital gains tax liabilities you will inherit, such as the crystallisation after ten years of gains held over on depreciating business assets, or, if the company you are purchasing is leaving a group, the crystallisation of gains on assets acquired from another group company within the previous six years.

- If you buy a company with unused trading losses or surplus advance corporation tax, you will not be able to use them when you restore the company to profitability if the change of ownership takes place within a period of three years during which there is also a major change in the nature or conduct of the business.

29
Recent government measures

Background

The Government places high hopes on the small business as a factor in economic recovery and has introduced various measures in recent years to encourage investment in new and expanding companies and to enable companies that have become unwieldy to split into smaller units without adverse tax consequences. Provisions have also been introduced to enable a company to purchase its own shares, which makes it possible to resolve conflicts within a company by buying out disaffected shareholders, and also makes investment under the government schemes more attractive through enabling the investor to withdraw his funds after the appropriate period.

Although the aims are reasonable, the provisions that have been introduced are for the most part extremely complex and possibly unnecessarily restrictive. This has been recognised to some extent in the FA 1983 by the replacement of the business start-up scheme with the more generous business expansion scheme.

Business start-up scheme

The business start-up scheme introduced in 1981/82 enabled non-working investors in corporate trades to obtain tax relief on a subscription of equity share capital up to a specified limit in each tax-year. The legislation was, however, restrictive and hedged with anti-avoidance measures, and was confined to new businesses. No help was given to established companies requiring new capital. The scheme was originally due to operate until 5 April 1984, but it has now been replaced by the business expansion scheme, and the start-up scheme ceased on 5 April 1983.

Business expansion scheme (FA 1983, s 26 and Sch 5; F (No 2) A 1983, s 5 and Sch 1)

The business expansion scheme is wider in scope and does not apply only to new trades. Those who are attracted to this form of investment are unlikely to require income by way of dividends, and the hope is that the company can by this means both curtail the cost of funding through reduced bank or loan interest and also draw on the experience of successful business people.

For investment between 6 April 1983 and 5 April 1987, relief will be given for investment by a 'qualifying individual' in 'eligible shares' in a 'qualifying company' carrying on or intending to carry on a 'qualifying trade'.

The relief will not be allowed unless and until the company has traded for four months (except where there is a bona fide winding-up in that period). If the company is not carrying on the trade when the shares are issued, it must begin to do so within two years after the issue of the shares, otherwise again no relief is allowed.

The relief must be claimed within two years after the end of the year of assessment in which the shares are issued, or, if later, within two years after the end of the first four months trading. No claim may be made before 1 January 1984 nor before the company has been carrying on a qualifying trade for four months. Claims must be accompanied by a certificate from the company, issued on the authority of an inspector of taxes, stating that the relevant conditions have been satisfied.

If any of the requirements for a 'qualifying individual' or 'qualifying company' are breached during a 'relevant period' (broadly, in the five or three years respectively after the issue of the shares), the relief will be withdrawn.

Borrowing the money to subscribe for the new shares

Relief for interest on a loan to buy the shares is available so long as the investor acquires 5% or more of the issued ordinary share capital, and the company is a close company (broadly, it must be owned by five or fewer people or by its directors).

Amount of relief

The maximum relief for an individual in any year is £40,000, this being a joint limit for husband and wife. The minimum subscription by an individual to one company is £500 except where the investment is made through an approved investment fund. The relief is a charge on income at the payer's highest tax rate, including investment income surcharge, and, unlike the business start-up scheme relief, may be given through the PAYE system.

Eligible shares

New ordinary shares carrying no present or future preferential right to dividends or assets or redemption for five years from the date of issue are eligible for relief. The 50% restriction on the proportion of shares in a company on which relief may be given, which applied under the start-up scheme, has been removed.

Qualifying individual

The individual must be resident and ordinarily resident in the UK when the shares are issued and must not be 'connected with' the company (as specifically defined) at any time in the period beginning on the date of incorporation of the company (or if later two years before the shares were issued) and ending five years after the shares were issued.

Broadly, an individual is connected if he or an associate is an employee or paid director of the company or of a partner of the company, or is a partner of the company; if he has or is entitled to acquire more than 30% of the capital, including loan capital (but excluding bank overdrafts), or voting power; if he would be entitled to more than 30% of the assets in a winding-up; or if he has effective control of the company.

The intention of the legislation is to attract investors not dependent on the business. Although they cannot be paid as above, they may be involved in an advisory capacity, or receive professional fees in appropriate cases, and reasonable expenses may also be paid. After the five-year period has elapsed the investor may become a working director or employee.

Qualifying company

The company must be incorporated in the UK and must satisfy the following conditions throughout the three years following the date of issue of the shares qualifying for relief, or the three years from the start of trading if later:

  It must not be quoted on the stock exchange or unlisted securities market
  It must be UK-resident
  It must be a UK trading company and/or the holding company of a group of wholly-owned UK trading subsidiaries. It may not be an investment company, but there is nothing to stop a trading company owning land and buildings for use in its trade.
  All issued shares must be fully paid, but all shares need not be of the same class.
  It must not be a subsidiary, or have subsidiaries other than wholly-owned UK subsidiaries carrying on a 'qualifying trade'.

Relief will not be withdrawn as a result of a bona fide winding-up during the relevant period.

Qualifying trade

A qualifying trade is one conducted on a commercial basis with a view to the realisation of profits, but excluding finance, leasing, legal and accountancy services.

Withdrawal of relief

The shares must be held for a minimum of five years, otherwise the relief is withdrawn completely if the disposal is not at arm's length and is reduced by the consideration received for an arm's length bargain. Relief is also withdrawn if the individual receives value from the company within that time. 'Value' is exhaustively defined and includes the repayment of loans, provision of benefits, and purchase of assets for a consideration less than market value.

Capital gains tax

Even though the cost to the investor has been substantially reduced by income tax relief, the base cost of the shares for capital gains tax is the full price paid, except where a loss would result, in which case the relief is taken into account to determine the allowable loss. The relief thus provides a useful source of finance to companies and a highly efficient means of investment for shareholders. See example 1.

Example 1

For top rate taxpayers, an investment under the business expansion scheme can show a 300% growth over the five-year minimum period of ownership even if the value of the shares does not increase by the end of the period, viz:

	£
Cost of shares say	10,000
Tax relief at 75%	7,500
Net cost	2,500
Sale (or redemption by company) after five years	10,000
Surplus on £2,500 net cost	£7,500

Where not all shares of the same class have qualified for relief, disposals are identified first with shares on which business start-up relief was given, then with shares on which business expansion relief was given, then with any other shares.

Anti-avoidance provisions

A company is not a qualifying company if an individual (including his associates) acquires a controlling interest after 5 April 1983, and within the period commencing two years before and ending three years after the date on which the shares were issued (or the date the trade commenced if later) that individual (including his associates) has had a controlling interest in another trade and the services provided, or markets serviced etc. by the new company and the other trade are substantially the same.

The company must not during the period commencing with its incorporation (or two years before the shares are issued if later) and ending five years after the shares are issued repay or redeem any of its share capital which belongs to other members.

There are 'replacement capital' provisions to deny the relief to people who set up a new company to take over their existing business or company, the provisions applying where those who control the new company owned more than half of the old trade or controlled the old company.

Withdrawal of investment after relevant period

Potential investors may see a disadvantage in their being locked in as minority shareholders, but in fact they may arrange at the outset for their shares to be acquired after the five year period. Two separate pieces of legislation have facilitated the making of such an arrangement—the ability of a close trading company to retain trading income, and thus build up reserves within the company, and the ability of a company to purchase its own shares. The rules for the retention of close company income are dealt with in chapter 4 at page 30.

Purchase by company of its own shares (FA 1982, s 53 and Sch 9)

Where an unquoted trading company or the unquoted holding company of a trading group buys back its own shares (or redeems them or makes a payment for them in a reduction of capital) in order to benefit a trade, the transaction is not treated as a distribution, and thus liable to income tax, but as a disposal for capital gains tax. This does not apply if there is an arrangement whose main purpose is to get undistributed profits into the hands of the shareholders without incurring the tax liabilities on a distribution.

The main requirements are that the shareholder must be UK-resident, he must normally have owned the shares for at least five years, and he must either dispose of his entire holding or the holding must be 'substantially reduced'.

A company may apply to the Revenue for a clearance that the proposed purchase will not be treated as a distribution.

Demergers (FA 1980, s 117 and Sch 18)

The aim of the 1980 demerger legislation, according to the then Chancellor, was to enable businesses grouped inefficiently under a single company umbrella to be run more dynamically and effectively by being demerged and allowed to pursue their separate ways under independent management. Various tax obstacles to such a course were accordingly removed. The detailed provisions are very complex and the following is only an outline.

A company is not treated as having made a distribution for corporation tax purposes (and the members are not treated as having received income) where the company transfers to its members the shares of a 75% subsidiary, or transfers a trade to a new company in exchange for that new company issuing shares to some or all of the transferor company's shareholders.

In order for these provisions to apply, all companies concerned must be UK-resident trading companies, the transfer must be made to benefit some or all of the trading activities, and the transfer must not be made for tax avoidance reasons.

The distribution by the holding company of shares in subsidiaries to its members is also not treated as a capital distribution for capital gains tax purposes, and the capital gains tax and development land tax rules charging tax when a company leaves a group on assets acquired within the previous six years from other group companies do not apply.

Documents executing transfers that are not treated as distributions are exempt from stamp duty.

There are detailed anti-avoidance provisions, and there is also provision to apply for Revenue clearance of proposed transactions.

Tax points

- The anti-avoidance rules in relation to the provisions dealt with in this chapter are too extensive to deal with in detail, but should be looked at carefully by interested companies and investors.

- Relief may be denied in circumstances where there seems to be no valid reason for doing so, for example if while arrangements for the issue of share capital are being made an investor temporarily lends money to the company, he will be regarded as having 'received value' when it is repaid, thus denying him relief on the shares.

30
Your family home

General

The tax system encourages ownership of your family home by exempting any capital gain on its disposal and by giving relief for interest paid on loans, up to a maximum of £30,000, to buy or improve it, including a loan replacing an earlier qualifying loan. Where there is more than one loan, relief is given on the earliest loans first, and when the total qualifying loans exceed £30,000 no relief is given on the excess. Qualifying improvements are capital items such as home extensions, central heating, and double glazing. Repair expenditure does not qualify. If the borrowing is not used for a qualifying purpose, then even if the loan is from a building society and secured on the dwelling house, it will not qualify for relief. It is not possible to circumvent this rule by making a sale to your spouse and the spouse claiming relief on the borrowing.

Relief is extended in some cases to properties intended to be occupied in the future, and for those occupied by dependent relatives or by a former or separated spouse, but the £30,000 interest relief limit is an umbrella figure that must cover all qualifying loans to one borrower.

Dwelling occupied by a dependent relative (CGTA 1979, s 105; FA 1974, Sch 1(4))

One dwelling occupied rent-free and without other consideration by a dependent relative is exempt from capital gains tax on disposal. Any interest on borrowing is also relieved against income so long as your total qualifying loans are within the £30,000 borrowing ceiling, and unlike the capital gains tax relief, interest relief is not restricted to one house. Relief for both capital gains tax and interest is lost if rent is charged or any other consideration is received.

'Dependent relative' is defined as your own or your spouse's widowed mother, or any other relative incapacitated by old age or infirmity. There is no income restriction.

Dwelling occupied by a former or separated spouse

Both interest relief and capital gains exemption can be claimed in certain circumstances. The detailed provisions are in chapter 37.

If part of your home is let

The income from letting is chargeable to income tax after setting off appropriate expenses. Where no services are provided the income is charged as investment income. Even where services are included it is difficult to establish that the letting constitutes a trade, which would enable wife's earned income relief to be claimed if the wife is responsible for the letting.

As far as the capital gains exemption is concerned, there is no loss of relief if the letting takes the form of boarders who effectively live as part of the family. Where, however, the letting extends beyond this, the appropriate fraction of the gain on disposal is chargeable but there is an exemption of the smaller of £10,000 and an amount equal to the exempt gain on the owner-occupied part (FA 1980, s 80). See example 1.

Example 1

The gain on the sale of a dwelling is £20,000. The agreed proportion applicable to the let part is £12,000, the exempt gain being £8,000.

The £12,000 gain on the let part is reduced by the lower of

(a) £10,000 and
(b) an amount equal to the exempt gain, i.e. £8,000.

Therefore a further £8,000 is exempt and £4,000 is chargeable.

How relief is given for allowable interest

If the loan falls within the Mortgage Interest Relief at Source (MIRAS) scheme, you deduct basic rate income tax at source, and relief at rates above basic rate, where applicable, is given by a coding adjustment or in an assessment.

For loans outside the MIRAS scheme, either because of the identity of the lender or because the loan exceeds £30,000 and deduction at source has not been applied to the first £30,000, relief at both basic and excess rates has to be claimed, and is given by a coding adjustment or in an assessment.

The MIRAS scheme gives non-taxpayers the benefit of mortgage interest relief, because they are allowed to retain the basic rate tax deducted.

More than one house (CGTA 1979, s 101; FA 1974, Sch 1(4))

Two considerations apply here.

(i) Which is to be treated as your principal residence for capital gains tax purposes?

(ii) What is the position on interest paid?

You may elect within two years of acquiring a second home which of the two is to be the exempt dwelling for capital gains tax purposes. If you do not do so, the Revenue have the power of nomination, but you have a right of appeal. Provided that both houses have been your main residence for capital gains tax at some time, the last two years of ownership of both will in any event be exempt.

For mortgage interest relief it is a question of fact which is your main residence. In the event of a dispute between you and the Revenue it would be decided on appeal by the Appeal Commissioners.

The qualifying residence for interest relief need not be the one to which the capital gains exemption applies. In both cases, however, it is necessary for the house to be or have been your residence, and a pure investment property could not qualify.

Job related accommodation (FA 1974, Sch 1(4A); CGTA 1979, s 101(8))

If you live in accommodation related to your employment, for example as a hotel manager or minister of religion, you may wish to acquire a residence for your future occupation. Interest paid on borrowing for its acquisition is allowable (up to the statutory limit), and the house qualifies for capital gains tax exemption, although you do not live there.

Periods of absence (CGTA 1979, s 102)

Provided that a house has at some time after 5 April 1965 been your only or main residence, the last two years of ownership are always exempt from capital gains tax, whether you are living there or not. Other periods of absence similarly qualify for exemption provided that the house was your only or main residence at some time both before and after the period of absence, and that no other residence qualifies for relief during the absence. Those periods are any or all of the following:

(a) three years for any reason whatsoever (not necessarily a consecutive period of three years);
(b) up to four years where the duties of a United Kingdom employment require residence elsewhere; and
(c) any period of absence abroad where the duties of employment require residence abroad.

If those periods are exceeded, only the excess is counted as a period of non-residence. If you have to move to another place of employment, so that it is not possible to have a period of residence immediately after an absence, that condition is waived.

You can thus have long periods of absence without losing any part of the capital gains tax exemption. See example 2.

Example 2

Taxpayer purchases a house on 6 April 1960. It is let until 1963 and then owner-occupied until 5 October 1970. He then takes up employment abroad, returning to the house on 5 April 1975 until 5 October 1978. He then takes up employment in another part of the United Kingdom, returning to the house on 5 April 1981 until 5 October 1982, when he moves to a new principal private residence. He is unable to sell the old house until 31 December 1983, letting it from 1 January 1983 to 31 December 1983 in order to reduce the cost of having two houses.

Despite the periods of letting and absence, the house remains exempt throughout.

6.4.1960–5.4.1965	Periods before 6.4.1965 are ignored.
6.4.1965–5.10.1970	Owner occupied—exempt.
6.10.1970–4.4.1975	Employment abroad. Exempt since sandwiched between periods of occupation.
5.4.1975–5.10.1978	Owner occupied—exempt.
6.10.1978–5.4.1981	Employment in United Kingdom. Exempt since sandwiched between periods of occupation.
5.4.1981–5.10.1982	Owner occupied—exempt.
6.10.1982–31.12.1983	Part of last two years of ownership. Exempt when there has been a period of occupation since 6 April 1965.

For interest relief purposes, the Revenue, by concession, similarly disregard temporary absences of up to one year, or four years where required by your employment.

Bridging loans (CGTA 1979, s 102; FA 1974, Sch 1(4))

Owning two houses at the same time is covered for capital gains tax purposes by the exemption of the last two years of ownership. For interest relief purposes, a separate £30,000 limit applies to a bridging loan for a statutory period of one year, generally extended to two years by Revenue concession.

Part use for business purposes (CGTA 1979, s 103)

Interest on that part of any borrowing attributable to the business use of your home is allowed as a business expense, and the £30,000 limit then applies to the remainder of the loan.

Part of the capital gains exemption for the principal private residence will be lost, an apportionment being made for this purpose. The chargeable proportion will usually be the same as the business proportion of expenses such as rates, although there is no hard and fast rule.

When a claim for Schedule E expenses has included part of the expenses of the residence

Expenses are sometimes allowed concessionally within a Schedule E claim where there is some use of the residence in connection with your employment. Where such an allowance is not based on any specific proportion of the house being so used, the Inspector may well not assess any part of any gain on eventual sale of the house. The position is not, however, free from doubt, and where a Schedule E expenses claim is being made, the possible effect on the dwelling house exemption should be carefully considered.

Selling off part of the garden

The capital gains exemption for dwellings extends to grounds not exceeding one acre, or such larger area as is appropriate to the size and character of the house. It is therefore possible for the exemption to extend to the separate sale of building plots so long as they are sold before the house and immediately surrounding grounds. It is as well to remember, however, that the sale may involve development land tax if the realised development value exceeds £50,000 (see chapter 6), and that in certain circumstances the sale of the building plots may be challenged as trading.

Frequent purchases and sales

The capital gains tax exemption for a principal private residence does not apply if the dwelling was acquired with the intention of reselling at a profit (CGTA 1979, s 103). Where a series of dwellings have been purchased and substantially improved, the Revenue may assert that the frequency of moves coupled with the improvements amounts to a trade, resulting not only in the loss of the capital gains tax exemption but also in the taxation of the profits at income tax rates.

The circumstances may have to be exceptional, but it is worth remembering that, like the sale of part of the garden as building plots, the exemption is capable of challenge on the grounds of trading.

Tax points

- Show a new residence in the capital gains tax section of the tax return, but annotated 'exempt residence'. Otherwise the Revenue could maintain that the return is not complete since an initially exempt asset may not remain so if, for example, there is change of use.
  It also helps to show that the motive for purchase was for use as a dwelling.

- If you acquire a second house, consider carefully which is your main residence for mortgage interest purposes and which you wish to treat as your capital gains tax exempt residence, remembering that the last two years of ownership of a house which at some time has been your main residence for capital gains tax are exempt anyway.

- When considering the business proportion of mixed premises for the purpose of claiming relief for expenses, bear in mind the possibility of capital gains tax when the premises are sold.

31
A country life: farms and woodlands

Farming and market gardening profits

The profits of farmers and market gardeners are calculated in the same way as are those of other businesses, but some special rules apply as indicated below.

It is common in farming for members of the family to be employed on the farm. As with all businesses, expenses must be 'wholly and exclusively for the purposes of the trade', and it was held in a recent tax case that a farmer's wages to his young children were pocket money and thus not allowable as an expense (and consequently they were not to be treated as the children's income to enable their personal allowances to be used). The fact that the children were below legal employment age was taken into account, although it was not conclusive.

Farming as a single trade (TA 1970, s 110)

All farming carried on by one farmer is treated as a single trade, so that several holdings are treated as a single business and a move from one farm to another will not be treated as the cessation of one business and the commencement of another.

Loss relief (TA 1970, ss 168–171, 174, 180; FA 1978, s 30)

The usual reliefs for losses in early and later years and on cessation of trading are available to farming businesses (see chapter 25), but a loss in the sixth year of a consecutive run of farming and market gardening losses (calculated before stock relief and capital allowances) cannot be relieved other than by carry-forward against later profits of the same trade. This does not apply if a competent farmer or market gardener could not have expected a profit until after the six-year loss period. If losses are required to be carried forward, any related capital allowances are similarly treated.

Averaging (FA 1978, s 28)

The results of an individual farmer or market gardener or of a farming or market gardening partnership may be averaged over two tax-years if the profit of one year (before capital allowances and stock relief) is less than 7/10ths of the profit of the other year, with marginal relief if it is more than

7/10ths but less than 3/4. A claim for averaging must be made within two years after the end of the second tax-year. Averaging may not be claimed by farming, etc. companies.

If profits are averaged, the average figure is then used as the result of the second year and it may again be averaged with the result of the third year and so on. Losses are counted as nil profits in the averaging calculation, and relief for the loss is available in the normal way.

An averaging claim cannot be made in the first or last year of trading.

Averaging enables farmers to lessen the impact on their marginal tax rates of a successful year preceded or followed by a bad year. See example 1.

Example 1

Farmer's profits for years ended 31 December 1982 and 1983 are £40,000 and £10,000 respectively, and in the year to 31 December 1984 he makes a loss of £5,000.

Assessments may variously be as follows:

	No averaging	Averaging 1983/84 and 1984/85 only	All three years averaged
	£	£	£
1983/84	40,000	25,000	25,000
1984/85	10,000	25,000	12,500
1985/86	—	—	12,500

The loss of £5,000 is available for relief whether or not averaging is claimed.

Since the figures are averaged before capital allowances and stock relief, the benefit is sometimes reduced after capital allowances and stock relief are taken into account, but this may be offset by disclaiming capital allowances. The disclaimed amount will attract writing-down allowances in later years.

Herd basis (TA 1970, Sch 6)

Farm animals and other livestock are normally treated as trading stock on which stock relief is available. A production herd may, however, effectively be treated as a capital asset if an election is made for the herd basis. The election must be made within two years from the end of the first relevant year of assessment and is irrevocable, but a change in the constitution of a farming partnership may enable the election to be made even where the farming business has been carried on for several years.

A production herd is a group of living animals or other livestock kept for obtaining products such as milk, wool etc. or their young.

The effect of the election is that the initial purchase of the herd and any subsequent purchases that increase the herd attract no tax relief, but a renewals basis effectively applies where animals are replaced, so that the cost of the replacement is charged as an expense and the sale proceeds are brought in as a trading receipt. If the whole or a substantial part of the herd is sold and not replaced, no part of the proceeds is charged to income tax since it represents the sale of a capital asset, and capital gains tax does not arise since wasting assets on which capital allowances are not available are exempt (see chapter 5).

Compensation for compulsory slaughter

By concession, where compensation is paid for compulsorily-slaughtered stock to which the herd basis does not apply, the compensation may be left out of account in the year of receipt and brought in over the next three years in equal instalments.

Farm plant and machinery

Capital allowances on farm plant and machinery are available in the usual way (see chapter 22).

Agricultural buildings allowances (CAA 1968, ss 68, 69)

The owners or tenants of agricultural land may claim agricultural buildings allowances on the cost of construction of buildings, fences, roads and on the installation of services, including up to one-third of the cost of a farmhouse (see below). Any grants received are deducted from the allowable cost.

The allowances available are an initial allowance of 20% and writing down allowances of 10% of cost per annum, commencing in the first year, so that a maximum of 30% is available in that year with 10% available for each of the next seven years. All or part of the initial allowance may, however, be disclaimed, so that the maximum writing down period is ten years.

The allowances for individuals normally commence in the tax-year following the year ended 31 March in which the expenditure is incurred, but a farmer may arrange with the Revenue to use his normal basis period instead. The allowances for a company commence in the accounting period in which the expenditure is incurred.

There is no clawback of agricultural buildings allowances when an agricultural building changes hands, nor any balancing allowance if sold for less than written-down value. The purchaser continues the vendor's computation of allowances due and received, and the price he pays is irrelevant. He will not get any initial allowance and indeed will get no allowances at all if the cost has already been fully relieved to the vendor.

Agricultural landlords (CAA 1968, s 68; TA 1970, s 110)

The basis of taxation of income from letting agricultural land is as for any investment property (see chapter 33). Agricultural buildings allowances are given against the rents, and any excess may be set against any other income of the same year or against the total income of the following year. If any balance still remains it will be carried forward against agricultural income. If a farming tenant vacates his holding and does not receive any consideration for his unrelieved agricultural buildings expenditure from the incoming tenant, the landlord is entitled to relief for the residue.

Where an agricultural landlord lets grazing land this is regarded as a trade. The land therefore qualifies as a business asset on which rollover relief for capital gains tax is available if the land is sold and the proceeds reinvested in qualifying replacement land within one year before and three years after the sale (see chapter 5).

Small agricultural holdings

The profits of a commercial smallholding are assessed as trading profits under Schedule D, Case I, but if losses arise the Revenue may contend that the trade is not conducted on a commercial basis with a view to profit, so that the losses may only be carried forward against future income from the smallholding and not set against any other income. This is quite separate from their right to disallow farming losses from the sixth year onwards.

Problems may also arise in relation to VAT registration. The smallholder may seek voluntary registration even though his taxable supplies are less than £18,000, because he will then be able to reclaim input tax on his expenditure and he will have no liability on his supplies, which are zero-rated. Customs and Excise may not be prepared to register him if the commerciality of the venture is questionable.

The farmhouse (CGTA 1979, ss 101–103)

The restriction of agricultural buildings allowances on a farmhouse to a maximum of one-third of the expenditure recognises that the domestic and business activities overlap. In arriving at the farm profits some of the establishment charges of the farmhouse are usually charged. This will not jeopardise the capital gains tax private residence exemption provided that no part of the farmhouse has been used exclusively for business purposes. Where part is so used and a chargeable gain arises, rollover relief may be claimed if the farmhouse is replaced. If the farmhouse is disposed of on retirement over age 60, the gain may be reduced by retirement relief.

The capital gains tax exemption usually extends to grounds up to one acre, but for a farmhouse a larger area may be allowed because of the situation and character of the farmhouse and immediately surrounding grounds.

The capital gains tax exemptions and reliefs are dealt with in chapter 5.

Land let by partners to farming partnership, or by directors to farming company (CGTA 1979, ss 115–121, 124)

Where land is owned personally by a partner or director, and let to the farming business, any rent paid is allowed as an expense to the business and the rent is unearned income in the partner's or director's hands. If interest is paid on a loan to buy the land, it may be deducted from the rent (or any other rent) so long as the letting is on a commercial basis (see chapter 33 for the detailed treatment of let property).

Capital gains tax rollover relief may be claimed if the land is disposed of and replaced within one year before and three years after the sale.

The charging of a commercial rent will, however, prevent retirement relief being given when the land is disposed of by an individual aged over 60. If land is let rent-free, then retirement relief is available provided that the land is disposed of in conjunction with the disposal of the interest in the partnership or shares in the company. Proportionate relief will be given where a rent below the market rent is charged.

Capital transfer tax (FA 1976, Sch 10; FA 1982, Sch 14)

When agricultural property is transferred in lifetime or on death, agricultural property relief is given on the agricultural value, and where the property is also business property, business property relief is given on the non-agricultural value. The detailed rules for each relief are in chapter 7.

The rate of relief for tenanted agricultural property is 30% as against 50% for owner-occupied land, so a farmer who grants a lease to his farming partnership or to a farm company will on a subsequent disposal only get relief at the 30% rate. But the very act of granting the lease will usually reduce the value of the land, and the grant is specifically exempt from capital transfer tax so long as it is made for full consideration.

Woodlands (TA 1970, ss 91, 92, 111; FA 1975, Sch 9)

Commercially managed woodlands are charged to income tax under Schedule B unless an election is made within two years after the end of the year of assessment for the profits or losses to be dealt with as those of a trade under Schedule D, Case I. The advantage of Schedule B is that, whatever the profit, the assessment is made on one-third of the gross annual value. The disadvantage is that no relief is available for losses or capital allowances.

An election for Schedule D to apply will usually be appropriate where losses and/or heavy expenditure on plant and equipment are being incurred, but once the election is made it cannot be revoked so long as the woodlands remain in the same occupation.

The election for Schedule D must normally extend to all woodlands on the same estate, except that woodlands planted or replanted within the previous ten years can be treated as a separate estate. This enables the election to be made in respect of newly planted woodlands which are unlikely to be profitable for some years, leaving the mature, profitable parts of the holding charged under Schedule B.

An election under Schedule D enables loss relief to be claimed either against the total income of the same tax-year or the next tax-year under TA 1970, s 168, or against subsequent income from the woodlands under TA 1970, s 171, but it does not enable losses of the first four tax-years to be carried back against the income of the previous three tax-years under FA 1978, s 30. (See chapter 25 for details of loss reliefs available.) In the case of a company, loss relief is available against the total profits of the same year or the previous year, or by carry-forward against later profits from the woodlands. (See chapter 26.)

Capital transfer tax on woodlands (FA 1975, Sch 9; FA 1980, Sch 15)

Where an estate on death includes growing timber, an election may be made to leave the timber (but not the land on which it stands) out of account in valuing the estate at death. The election must be made within two years of the date of death and is only available if the deceased either had been beneficially entitled to the land throughout the previous five years or had become entitled to it without consideration (for example by gift or inheritance).

The election may not be made if the occupation of the woodlands is ancillary to the occupation of agricultural land, but agricultural relief would be given if the necessary conditions were fulfilled.

Following the election, the subsequent disposal by sale or gift of the timber gives rise to a charge to capital transfer tax on the sale price or, if the disposal is for less than full consideration, the market value, less allowable expenses in both cases. Allowable expenses are the costs of sale and expenses of replanting within three years of disposal, or such longer time as the Board allows (but excluding expenses that are allowable for income tax).

The net disposal proceeds or value are treated as value transferred at the date of death, forming the top slice of the property passing on death and thus attracting the highest rates of tax, but using the death scale rates current at the time of disposal. The tax is due six months after the end of the month in which the disposal takes place, with interest on overdue tax at the death rate. The person entitled to the sale proceeds is liable for the tax. Where there are no proceeds because the disposal is by way of gift, the additional tax arising out of this later transfer may be paid by instalments over ten years.

A lifetime gift of woodlands attracts capital transfer tax in the normal way, but where the disposal is one on which tax is payable following its being left out of account on an earlier death, the value transferred by the lifetime transfer is reduced by the tax charge arising out of the previous death.

If the person who inherits woodlands on which an election has been made dies before the timber is disposed of, no capital transfer tax charge can arise in respect of the first death. Furthermore, a new election may then be made on the second death.

Where woodlands constitute 'relevant business property' they qualify for 50% business property relief. Tax may be paid by instalments in the case of a lifetime transfer where the donee is to pay the tax and in the case of a death transfer where the value has not been left out of account. If an election is made to leave the timber out of account on a death, business property relief is given on the net sale proceeds when it is disposed of.

Tax Points

- If you have a smallholding which is likely to show consistent losses, you are unlikely to be able to relieve them against other income, and treating the smallholding as a trade may prejudice your capital gains tax private residence exemption. It may be preferable to show the holding in the capital acquisitions section of your tax return with a yearly note that the working of the holding is not by way of trade but only for the maintenance of the holding and that no profits arise.

- Where a smallholding or market garden is clearly a trade, make sure if possible that no part of the dwelling house is used exclusively for business so that there is no possible loss of the private residence exemption.

- When purchasing a holding with agricultural buildings, remember that what you pay for them does not entitle you to any relief. You can only get relief on any of the vendor's expenditure for which relief has not yet been given.

- If you are an agricultural landlord and have incurred expenditure on agricultural buildings, you can set the available allowances against any income to the extent that your agricultural income is insufficient. Relief can be given in the tax-year itself or the following year.

- Owning agricultural land personally and letting it to your partnership or company at a rent will not stop you getting rollover relief if the land is sold and replaced, but it will affect your entitlement to retirement relief.

32
Industrial buildings

Definition (CAA 1968, s 7; FA 1983, s 30)

An industrial building is broadly one in use for the purpose of a qualifying trade, the most common of which consist in the manufacture of goods or materials or the subjection of goods or materials to any process. Included are ancillary buildings, such as buildings for the storage of goods before and after the manufacture or process. Offices, shops and wholesale warehouses are excluded from the definition, but where part of a building does not qualify, for example because it is used as offices, the industrial buildings allowances on the whole building are not restricted if expenditure on the non-qualifying part does not exceed 25% of the total cost of the building (10% for expenditure incurred before 16 March 1983). This only applies where the offices are housed within the same building, not where they are a separate entity.

Who may claim industrial buildings allowances?

The allowances are given to both traders and investors.

Allowances for new buildings (CAA 1968, ss 1, 2; FA 1980, ss 74, 75 and Sch 13; FA 1982, s 73)

Relief is given on the cost of construction and no relief is available for the cost of the land, although site preparation works qualify. Where new capital expenditure is incurred on an existing building, the expenditure qualifies for relief as if it were a separate building.

An initial allowance is available for the basis period in which the construction expenditure is incurred, and an annual writing-down allowance for any basis period at the end of which the building is in qualifying use.

The basis period is that forming the basis of assessment to income tax for a sole trader or trading partnership (see p 154), the chargeable accounting period in the case of a limited company (see p 153), and the income tax year for an investor.

The rate of initial allowance has varied from time to time, but the maximum amount which may be claimed currently is as follows.

Very small workshops (see p 238 below)   100%

Industrial building in an enterprise zone	100%
Other industrial buildings	75%

Since the initial allowance is only given at the time of construction, or at the time of purchasing a newly constructed building from the builder, it is not available to a purchaser of a used building.

Only so much of the initial allowance as is required need be taken, and since annual allowances are at a flat rate, this has the effect of extending the period over which the annual allowances may be given. The annual writing-down allowance is currently 4% of the construction cost (25% for small workshops and buildings in enterprise zones) and is given until such time as that cost has been fully written off. See example 1.

Example 1

An engineering partnership acquired land costing £10,000 and in its year to 31 July 1982 spent £20,000 on construction costs of a workshop measuring 4,000 sq. ft. The work was completed in the next year to 31 July 1983, the balance of the cost being £60,000, and upon completion the building was immediately brought into use. The maximum initial allowance is claimed. The reliefs are:

Basis period	Year ended 31.7.82	Year ended 31.7.83
Year of assessment	1983/84	1984/85
	£	£
Land cost £10,000.		
No relief.	—	—
Construction costs	£20,000	£60,000
Initial allowance 75%	£15,000	£45,000
Annual allowance		
Not in use at 31.7.82	—	
In use at 31.7.83		
4% × £80,000		£3,200

Annual allowances continue until the expenditure is completely relieved, so that they would be given at £3,200 per annum for the five years 1985/86 to 1989/90 inclusive, with £800 in the year 1990/91.

Income or profits against which relief is allowable

The allowances in example 1 would be available against the trading profits for the relevant tax years, enabling loss relief to be claimed if they turned what would otherwise be a profit into a loss.

Allowances for a corporate trader are deducted in computing trading profit, and as with the unincorporated trader, might turn a profit into a loss, for which the usual relief for company trading losses could be claimed (see chapter 26), but the extended three-year loss carry back period is not available for industrial building initial allowances.

Allowances claimed by individual or corporate investors are given first against rent income, any excess being set against other income in the case of the individual, or against other profits in the case of a company.

Relief for the individual investor is available against any rent income of the same tax year (not just the rent of the building itself) and then any other income of that tax year or of the following tax year. See example 2.

Example 2

In 1983/84 an individual purchased from a developer for £30,000 (including land £6,000) a 1,000 sq. ft. workshop for letting to a trader carrying on a qualifying trade. His rent income was £4,000 in 1983/84 and he had other income of £15,000. His total income in 1984/85 was £50,000. He claims £24,000 industrial building allowance in 1983/84, which he can utilise as follows.

	£	Allowance £
		24,000
Rent income	4,000	
Set off	(4,000)	(4,000)
		20,000
Other income	15,000	
Set off	(15,000)	(15,000)
Relief remaining for 1984/85		£5,000

But he may instead claim the balance of £20,000 against the £50,000 total income for 1984/85, thus obtaining relief at the higher tax rates prevailing in that year and avoiding wasting his 1983/84 personal reliefs.

A corporate investor is allowed relief against the total profits (including capital gains) first of the same accounting period and then of the previous accounting period.

For both individuals and companies, allowances not given by set-off against other income can be carried forward, against future trading income of traders, and against future rent income of investors.

Consequence of new building purchased for investment not subsequently being let for a qualifying purpose (CAA 1968, s 1)

The initial allowance is given in the year of purchase, whether the building has been let or not. Writing-down allowances are not available until letting takes place. Should the letting prove to be for a non-qualifying purpose, the initial allowance already given will be clawed back by an assessment under Schedule D, Case VI.

Sale of the building (CAA 1968, ss 2, 3)

This will involve consideration of the need for a balancing adjustment on the vendor and for a claim for relief by the purchaser.

Whilst there are rules to deal with periods of non-industrial use, the basic adjustment is to amend the vendor's relief to the cost of having owned the building, a balancing charge normally being made to claw back excess allowances or a balancing allowance being given to make up any shortfall.

The purchaser cannot claim an initial allowance. He gets relief by way of equal annual allowances over the remainder of the 'tax life' of the building. Furthermore, the maximum amount on which he can claim relief is the original building cost, which may have been incurred many years earlier and bear little relation to current prices. The tax life of industrial buildings is normally twenty-five years, although certain older buildings (those used before 6 November 1962) have a tax life of fifty years. See example 3.

Assessment of income where building is let (TA 1970, ss 67 to 90)

Assessments are made under Schedule A based on the rent receivable in the basis period less the expenses arising. If rent is received late it is still included in the period when it was due, but if it later proves irrecoverable it can be deducted as a bad debt.

The assessment for individuals is on the income less expenses of the income tax year itself, and since the tax is payable on 1 January before the end of the tax year a provisional assessment based on the finally agreed figure for the previous tax year is made in time for the tax to be paid on 1 January. This assessment is then subsequently amended to reflect the actual income less expenses of the tax year.

The income of a corporate investor is included in the company profits for the chargeable accounting period.

Interest on the purchase monies (TA 1970, s 130; FA 1974, Sch 1(4)(7))

Where the building is purchased for trading purposes, interest paid on a loan to finance the purchase will be allowed as a trading expense or as a charge against corporate profits.

Example 3

The construction costs of an industrial building in 1974 were £45,000. The land had been purchased for £2,000 in 1966. Initial and annual allowances totalling £40,500 have been claimed.

The building (including £6,000 for the land) is sold in 1984 for

  (a) £10,000   (b) £30,000   (c) £60,000

The vendor's position is

	(a) £	(b) £	(c) £
Sale proceeds	10,000	30,000	60,000
Land included	6,000	6,000	6,000
Building proceeds	4,000	24,000	54,000
Building cost	45,000	45,000	45,000
Cost of owning building	41,000	21,000	Nil
Allowances already given	40,500	40,500	40,500
Balancing allowance/(charge)	£ 500	£(19,500)	£(40,500)

In the case of (c) there would also be a chargeable gain.

Proceeds (land and buildings)	60,000
Cost (land and buildings)	47,000
Chargeable gain (subject to indexation allowance)	£13,000

The purchaser would get reliefs as follows.

	(a) £	(b) £	(c) £
Cost to him (building only)	£4,000	£24,000	£54,000
Restrict to original cost if less than purchase price			£45,000
Annual allowance 1/15th	£267	£1,600	£3,000

(15 years of 25-year life remaining, ignoring fractions of year for illustration.)

Where interest is paid on borrowings for buildings acquired for letting the interest is not tax deductible unless the building has been let for a continuous period of twenty-six weeks out of fifty-two, and unless, when not let, it was available for letting or not so available only because of works of repair or improvement. Where those letting conditions are met, the interest is deductible from the rent on *any* let properties.

Very small workshops

Expenditure incurred before 27 March 1985 on the construction of 'very small workshops' (i.e. those having gross internal floor space of 1,250 sq. ft. or less) attracts an initial allowance of 100%. Annual allowances of 25% of cost are given to write off any expenditure for which an initial allowance is not taken.

The same reliefs are available for expenditure incurred after 15 March 1983 and before 27 March 1985 on the conversion of existing larger buildings into workshops whose average gross internal floor space does not exceed 1,250 sq. ft. The relief is not available on the conversion of *unused* larger buildings.

Tax points

• The availability of industrial buildings relief to lessors makes new industrial buildings an attractive investment. However, the requirement that the building must be unused in order to obtain the initial allowance will usually have an effect on the resale price if early realisation is required, and there will also be a clawback of relief on realisation.

• There is a choice of two tax years in which an individual investor can get relief against his total income. Watch the operative tax rates and personal reliefs to ensure maximisation of relief.

• Ensure that the expenditure on any non-qualifying parts of an industrial building (for example offices) does not exceed the allowable 25%.

• Since the purchase of land does not qualify for relief, more tax efficient use of capital expenditure can be achieved by constructing on lease-hold land.

• An intending investor who considers the cost is too high for him may participate on a co-ownership basis, sharing the reliefs in proportion to the cost borne.

33
Investment properties

Income from land

Income from UK land and buildings is usually charged to income tax as investment income under Schedule A. There are some exceptions, such as the letting of grazing land, which is specifically treated as a trade, or where one of the privileges of an office or employment is the entitlement to rent from a particular property, in which case although the rent is charged under Schedule A it is treated as earned income. The normal treatment of rental income, however, is as investment income, liable to investment income surcharge if your income is high enough.

Calculation of rent (TA 1970, ss 67, 87)

Rent is brought in for tax purposes when due and payable, the actual date of receipt not being relevant and no apportionment being made over the period which it covers. Relief is given for rent not received where it proves to be irrecoverable after appropriate action, or where it is waived without consideration in order to avoid hardship. See example 1.

Example 1

Rent of £1,000 is due on the usual quarter days under a seven-year lease commencing on 29 September 1983.

The rent to be brought in for 1983/84 is:

29 September 1983	1,000
25 December 1983	1,000
25 March 1984	1,000
	£3,000

even though on an accruals basis only a little over £2,000 relates to 1983/84, and whether or not rent is in fact paid on those dates.

Allowable expenses (TA 1970, s 72)

Allowable expenses include rates, rent payable to a superior landlord, maintenance, repairs and redecorations, insurance and management expenses, including advertising for tenants, and any other expenses which under the terms of the lease are to be met out of the rent. Improvement expenditure, on for example building extensions or installing central heating or double glazing, is not allowable.

Normally expenses incurred when a property is not let would not be allowed, but, for leases at a full rent, periods when a property is empty between the time of acquisition and being let at a full rent, and between full-rent leases, are regarded as part of a continuing lease, enabling expenses during the void periods to be deducted against rents as if the property had been let continuously. This does not apply, however, to expenditure on newly acquired property to rectify dilapidations arising before you bought it. Such expenditure is deemed to form part of the capital cost and is not allowable for income tax.

A full-rent lease is one under which the rent is sufficient taking one year with another to meet the landlord's outgoings.

Several properties (TA 1970, s 72)

Where you have several let properties, whether the expenses of each have to be isolated against the rent of each depends on the type of lease.

Where a full-rent lease is one under which the landlord pays for the whole or substantially the whole of the repairs, known as a 'landlord's repairing lease', the rents and expenses of all properties let on such leases are aggregated in a profit and loss account and one figure of profit or loss ascertained. A profit is included in the total Schedule A assessment. If a loss arises it must be carried forward against future profits on landlord's repairing lease property.

Where a full-rent lease is one under which the tenant bears the whole or substantially the whole of the cost of repairs, known as a 'tenant's repairing lease', a profit is likewise included in the total Schedule A assessment. A loss should not normally arise on this type of letting because of the obligation of the tenant to defray the cost of repairs. If a loss does arise it will often be because of the tenant falling down on his obligations and thus shifting the burden of cost to the landlord. The loss may be set against profits on the pool of landlord's repairing leases. Alternatively it may be carried forward against a future profit on the same property, and indeed this may be the only way of getting relief if it is the only property involved.

Where properties are let below a full rent, for example to a relative or friend for an insignificant return, losses arising may only be carried forward against any future profit not only on that particular property but also while it is let to the same tenant under the same lease.

Relief for interest (FA 1974, Sch 1(4))

Interest on borrowing for the purchase or improvement of let property is allowable, provided that the property has been let at a commercial rent for at least twenty-six weeks out of fifty-two and, when not so let, was available for letting or was being repaired or improved or was used as the only or main residence of the borrower. Relief is given against income from any let property, not just that to which the borrowing relates.

Payment of income tax (TA 1970, s 68)

Tax under Schedule A is payable on 1 January in the tax-year. Since the assessment is based on the net rents less allowable interest of the tax-year, which still has three months to run, an adjustment of the tax payable is required after each 5 April. A provisional assessment is raised in time for payment on the due date, based on the finally agreed assessment for the previous tax year. This is then amended to the actual net rents less interest after the end of the tax-year.

If one or more of the properties has been disposed of since the beginning of the previous year, the taxpayer can apply to have the provisional assessment for the current year adjusted to take account of any estimated reduction in the final assessment.

Where a premium is charged (TA 1970, ss 80, 85 and Sch 3; CGTA 1979, Sch 3(5))

There are two sorts of premium, one where an existing leasehold interest is assigned, the other where a lease or sublease is granted. The first is wholly a capital gains tax matter, being the disposal of a chargeable asset.

The second gives rise to both capital and income aspects if the lease is a short lease, i.e. of 50 years duration or less, in that the premium is partly assessed to income tax and partly to capital gains tax. The income proportion is the amount of the premium reduced by 2% for each complete year of the lease except the first, the reduced amount being treated as additional rent. The amount by which the premium is reduced is treated as the proceeds of a part disposal for capital gains tax, the cost of the part disposed of being the proportion of the total cost that the capital element of the premium bears to the full premium plus the value of the reversion. See example 2.

Since the income part of the premium is treated as additional rent, any extraordinary expenses incurred can be relieved against it. The premium might in fact have been charged to recover such extraordinary expenses, perhaps necessitated by a previous defaulting tenant.

The income tax portion of a premium on a short lease is wholly assessed in the year the lease is granted, although the lease may run for anything up to fifty years. Top-slicing relief is available to reduce the tax rate on the premium to what it would be if only one year's proportion were charged. See example 2.

Example 2

Lease is granted for 21 years commencing 25 March 1984 at a rent of £5,000 per annum, payable quarterly in advance, together with a premium of £8,000. The cost of the freehold was £15,000 in 1970. The value of the freehold reversion after the grant of the lease was £24,000.

The rent for 1983/84 is:		£
25 March 1984 1 quarter's rent due		1,250
Premium	8,000	
Less Treated as part disposal for capital gains (21–1) or 20 years at 2% = 40%	3,200	
Amount treated as additional rent		4,800
Rent for 1983/84		£6,050

The chargeable gain is:

Capital proportion of premium	3,200
Less Allowable proportion of cost	
$15,000 \times \dfrac{3,200}{(8,000 + 24,000)}$	1,500
	£1,700

The landlord has taxable income in 1983/84 (including the rent of £1,250 but excluding the additional rent of £4,800) of £8,000 earned and £6,000 unearned, totalling £14,000.

Tax rates on an extra £4,800 unearned income would normally be:

$$600 \text{ @ } 30\%$$
$$2,600 \text{ @ } 40\%$$
$$1,600 \text{ @ } 45\%$$
$$£4,800$$

Investment income surcharge on (10,800 − 7,100)

$$£3,700 \text{ @ } 15\%$$

Tax rate on $\dfrac{4,800}{21}$ or £229 extra unearned income would be only 30%.

Therefore the tax rate on the whole £4,800 is reduced to 30%.

Furnished lettings (TA 1970, s 67)

Since Schedule A is concerned with letting of land, it does not cover situations where furnishings and services are included. Furnished lettings are assessed under Schedule D, Case VI, but the taxpayer may elect for the property rent element to be included under Schedule A, leaving the payment in respect of the furnishings and/or services to be charged under Schedule D, Case VI. The advantage of separating the furnishings rent and the property rent is that the property rent may enable relief to be given for losses on unfurnished properties that would otherwise be carried forward.

The expenses of furnished lettings are, as with Schedule A, allowed broadly on a common-sense basis. Additionally relief is given for wear and tear on furnishings, as distinct from normal repairs, the Revenue usually accepting a figure of 10% of the rent less rates for this purpose.

Tax under Schedule D, Case VI on the full amount of the net income of the current year, or on the furnishings element as the case may be, is due on 1 January within the year of assessment. As with Schedule A an estimated assessment is raised to enable a payment on 1 January, an adjustment being made after 5 April when the actual position is known.

Unless a trade is clearly carried on the Revenue are reluctant to accept that a furnished letting amounts to a trade, particularly where the letting is by a married woman, since to do so would give an entitlement to wife's earned income relief. Legislation is, however, proposed (backdated to 6 April 1983), deeming income from furnished holiday lettings to be earned income and according capital gains tax reliefs (see below) to property used for such lettings.

Capital gains on sale of investment properties (CGTA 1979, ss 111A and 111B)

The usual capital gains tax principles apply (see chapter 5), including the relief dealt with in chapter 30 where part of the property is owner-occupied. Apart from the disposal of land let as grazing land, there is no rollover relief on disposal of investment properties except where the disposal is occasioned by compulsory purchase. In this case the legislation takes the view that the person disposing should not be deprived of part of his proceeds through taxation if he wishes to maintain his investment by reinvesting in another property, provided that the reinvestment is made within the period beginning one year before and ending three years after the disposal. The replacement property cannot, however, be a capital gains tax-exempt dwelling-house.

Interaction with development land tax

Where the proceeds of sale include realised development value, a development land tax computation will have to be made (see chapter 6). Development land tax may not be payable, either because of the size of the allowable base value or because of the exemption for the first £50,000 of realised development value, but where development land tax does arise, the amount subject to development land tax is deducted from the chargeable gain.

Property dealing

Although the income from letting is assessed under Schedule A or Schedule D, Case VI as the case may be, any surplus on disposal of a property may even so be liable to income tax as a trading transaction instead of as a chargeable gain. Whether or not a trade may be inferred is dealt with in chapter 20, but at least the letting will help to resist a trading assessment by indicating an investment motive.

Stamp duty on buying

When property is purchased stamp duty arises on the following scale:

Amount of consideration	Rate %
£25,000 or under	Nil
£25,001 to £30,000	$\frac{1}{2}$
£30,001 to £35,000	1
£35,001 to £40,000	$1\frac{1}{2}$
over £40,000	2

The stamp duty paid forms part of the cost for capital gains tax purposes on a subsequent disposal.

VAT on renovation

VAT on property repairs will be an added cost since there will not be any possibility of reclaiming it, but in the case of new building work the supply will be zero-rated.

Assured tenancy scheme (FA 1982, s 76 and Sch 12)

Capital allowances are available for expenditure on dwellings for letting under the assured tenancy scheme. The scheme was introduced by the Housing Act 1980 to enable bodies approved by the Secretary of State for the Environment to let dwellings at freely negotiated rents that are not subject to the Rent Acts.

The allowances are available for an experimental period of five years, in respect of expenditure incurred after 9 March 1982 and before 1 April 1987, and broadly follow the industrial buildings allowances rules. An initial allowance of 75% of the expenditure on the building (excluding the amount paid for the land) is available in respect of expenditure incurred in the basis period, and writing-down allowances at 4% of cost p.a. allowed provided that the dwelling is let under an assured tenancy at the end of the basis period. There is no provision for disclaiming either initial or writing-down allowances. There is a limit on the amount which qualifies for relief in respect of each dwelling, being £60,000 if the dwelling is in Greater London and £40,000 if it is elsewhere. Where a dwelling forms only part of the building (for example a flat or maisonette) the expenditure is apportioned appropriately, with expenditure on any common parts of the building also being appropriately apportioned.

Balancing adjustments are made if the dwelling is disposed of within twenty-five years and a second-hand purchaser gets writing-down allowances based on the residue of expenditure after the sale, split over the remainder of the twenty-five years.

There are provisions for dwellings not to qualify for the allowances in certain circumstances, for example where landlord and tenant are connected persons.

The allowances are given by discharge or repayment of tax, primarily against Schedule A income from qualifying dwelling houses or balancing charges relating to qualifying dwelling houses, but then against income generally.

Tax points

- Since losses on leases not at full rent can only be relieved by carry-forward and not by set-off, there is no point in charging a nominal rent to a dependent relative. To do so destroys the capital gains tax exemption for dependent relative occupation and also the relief for interest on money borrowed to purchase the property.

- Although you can get relief against *any* rent income for allowable interest on borrowing to purchase property for letting at a commercial rent, the interest is not allowable unless the property is actually let for the appropriate period. This is particularly important for industrial buildings, which may be difficult to let because of the present glut (see chapter 32 for industrial buildings in particular).

- Even though property is being let it does not prevent an income tax assessment instead of a chargeable gain arising on a disposal if the circumstances indicate trading, so every effort should be made to demonstrate the investment motive.

34
Interest received from banks, building societies etc.

General provisions

Interest may either be received gross or after deduction of basic rate tax. Building society interest is strictly neither, because it is subject to a special arrangement between the building societies and the Revenue (see below).

INTEREST RECEIVED GROSS	INTEREST TAXED AT SOURCE
Bank interest, including National Savings Bank interest Interest on $3\frac{1}{2}$% War Loan Interest on Government Stocks held on the National Savings Stock Register and acquired through the Post Office or Trustee Savings Bank Interest on loans to individuals	Interest on Government stocks, except $3\frac{1}{2}$% War Loan and stocks acquired through Post Office or Trustee Savings Bank Interest on local authority loans Company debenture interest

Where interest is received gross it is charged to tax under Schedule D, Case III, normally on a previous year basis but with special rules for new and discontinued sources as explained below. You are exempt from tax on the first £70 of interest received on ordinary accounts with the National Savings Bank. If you are married you get an exemption of £70 each, but it cannot be transferred from one to the other.

Interest that is received net of basic rate income tax is treated as income of the year of receipt. The gross amount must be entered on your tax return, but if you are a basic rate taxpayer you will have no further tax to pay. If you are liable at rates above the basic rate you will be charged the extra tax. If you are not liable to tax, for example because of available personal allowances, all or the appropriate part of the tax deducted at source will be refunded to you following a repayment claim.

Date on which interest arises

Interest arises when it is received or when it is credited to your account. There is no apportionment for tax purposes over the period when it accrues. The first interest on a loan or bank deposit account therefore arises on the date of receipt or crediting, not by apportionment from the date when the account was opened.

There is no assessment if interest is not received and hence no relief is required for bad debts. But this lack of bad debts relief extends to the capital if that is lost, except where the loss relates to a 'debt on a security', which means loan stock or similar, or where the loss is on a loan or guarantee made to a UK-resident trader for use in his trade. In these circumstances an allowable capital loss arises (subject to certain anti-avoidance provisions).

Basis of assessment for interest received gross

The normal basis of assessment is the interest arising in the previous income tax year. In the first and second tax-years in which interest arises, however, the assessment is based on the interest arising in the tax-year, and it is also open to the taxpayer (but not to the Revenue) to elect for the assessment for the third tax-year to be based on the interest arising in the third year itself. The choice for the taxpayer is thus whether the second or the third year's interest forms the basis for two years of assessment. See example 1, in which such an election by the taxpayer would be unfavourable, as it would cause £130 to be taxed twice (in 1983/84 and 1984/85) rather than £80 (in 1982/83 and 1983/84).

Example 1

A deposit account was opened in November 1981 and is closed in September 1986. Interest credited and related assessments are as follows:

Interest credited		Assessments	
December 1981	£10	1981/82	£10
June 1982	£30	1982/83	£80
December 1982	£50	1983/84	£80
June 1983	£70		
December 1983	£60	1984/85	£130
June 1984	£80		
December 1984	£95	1985/86	£175
June 1985	£70		
December 1985	£65		
June 1986	£70		
September 1986	£25	1986/87	£95

Since there can be no assessment for a period after a source of interest ceases, the assessment for the tax-year in which a source ceases is based on the interest arising in that year. It is open to the Revenue to base the assessment for the last year but one on the interest arising in that year, if it is greater than that arising in the preceding year. In example 1 the Revenue would not do so, as the assessment for 1984/85 would be reduced from £175 to £135. In any event, one year's interest will escape assessment, thus compensating for one year's interest in the opening years being taxed more than once.

Where there are several accounts

Technically each deposit account or interest-bearing loan is a separate source of income, requiring the opening and closing years' rules to be applied as necessary. The Revenue tend, however, to deal with all deposit accounts as one source and to ignore the movement on individual accounts unless a substantial tax advantage is being obtained by the movement of funds into and out of an account, in which case the strict rules will be applied.

Funds on special deposit

Most banks will arrange for substantial funds to be placed on special deposit with their Treasurer's Department—the name varies from bank to bank. Interest arising on such deposits is included for assessment in the year in which it is received, the preceding year basis never applying.

Date of payment of tax (TA 1970, s 4)

Where interest is taxed at source, any higher-rate tax and investment income surcharge arising is payable on 1 December following the tax-year.

Where interest is received gross, the due date of payment is 1 January within the year of assessment. The assessment on 1 January may cover tax at all rates, but sometimes the excess over the basic rate is included in the assessment on taxed income due on 1 December.

Death of account holder or spouse

When a single person dies, the final interest to the date of death is assessed in the tax-year of death, with the Revenue option applying to the penultimate year. The interest from the date of death is assessed on the personal representatives.

In the case of a joint account between husband and wife, if the husband dies the interest on the basis of the preceding year is divided in the tax-year of death between the husband to the date of death and the wife thereafter, future years' assessments being continued on the wife on the preceding year basis, subject to the rules for new and discontinued accounts. If the wife dies, assessments will continue on the husband.

If the account is in the sole name of the deceased but devolves on the surviving spouse by the terms of the will or on intestacy, the preceding year basis may still be continued, with apportionment between spouses in the year of death.

Where a husband dies and his wife has her own account, the normal preceding year basis will apply, the assessment for the year of death being divided between the deceased husband and the widow by reference to the date of death.

Partners and other joint owners

The assessment is not joint. Each partner or co-owner is assessed on his share. The rules for new and discontinued sources apply to each person's share.

Building society interest (TA 1970, s 343)

The building societies have made a special arrangement with the Revenue under which they account for tax on interest paid to their depositors at a composite rate which is less than the basic rate (25.25% for 1982/83). Not more than £20,000 may be deposited with any one society, but you can have up to that amount in any number of societies.

As a result of the special arrangement tax is not deducted from building society interest, but the interest is nonetheless effectively treated as if it were an amount net of basic-rate tax. The amount of building society interest received must be stated on your tax return.

No further tax is due from a basic-rate taxpayer, but those liable at rates above the basic rate must pay the extra, which is included in the assessment of higher-rate tax and surcharge due on 1 December following the tax-year.

If, however, you are not liable to tax you cannot recover any tax on building society interest since none was actually deducted. See example 2.

Disposal of Government stocks (CGTA 1979, ss 67–70, 84 and Sch 2)

Unless British Government stocks are disposed of within twelve months of acquisition they are not chargeable assets for capital gains tax, so no chargeable gains or allowable losses will arise. Gains and losses on disposals within the twelve-month period are calculated in the normal way. No indexation allowance can arise since the indexation allowance is not available on assets held for less than twelve months.

There are anti-avoidance provisions to prevent stocks being sold to establish an allowable loss within the twelve-month period and then bought back.

If you receive Government stock in exchange for shares on nationalisation, the gain or loss arising at that time on the shares is held over until you sell

Example 2

Two single pensioners aged 70 each receive a state pension of £1,730 in 1983/84. One has interest from a local authority loan of £600 gross, £420 net, and the other receives building society interest of £420. The tax position of each is as follows.

	1st pensioner	2nd pensioner
Pension	1,730	1,730
Loan interest	600	
Building society interest (treated as gross equivalent)		600
	2,330	2,330
Age allowance	2,360	2,360
Taxable income	Nil	Nil
Tax repayable	£ 180	Nil

the Government stock, at which time the nationalisation gain or loss crystallises, even though you may then have held the replacement Government stock for more than twelve months.

Tax points

- When you close your bank account, try to time it so that you maximise the saving from one year's interest escaping tax.

- If your income is less than your available allowances, building society accounts are not a tax-effective investment because you cannot get back the tax that is deemed to be deducted.

- If you buy Government stocks on the National Savings Stock Register you will receive the interest gross and pay tax later, rather than receiving the interest net if you acquire the stocks on the Stock Exchange. The end result will be the same but your cash flow will be improved.

35
Holding shares in a limited company

Dividends received

When a company pays a dividend it pays advance corporation tax to the Revenue. Although the advance corporation tax is relievable against the company's tax liability, it is passed on as a tax credit to the shareholder, covering his liability to tax at the basic rate. A basic-rate taxpayer thus has no further tax to pay, a shareholder not liable to tax can claim repayment of the tax credit, and a taxpayer liable at rates above the basic rate will pay only the excess. Dividends and tax credits received are shown on the tax return as income of the tax-year in which they are paid. Where tax is due at excess rates it is charged in an assessment covering all other sources of taxed income as well as dividends. The tax is due for payment on 1 December following the relevant tax-year.

The effective rate of corporation tax on distributed profits

Since the basic-rate credit in the hands of the shareholder is imputed from the company's corporation tax liability, it follows that the true rate of corporation tax on distributed profits is reduced accordingly. See example 1.

Capital gains tax when shares are disposed of (F(No 2)A 1975, s 58; FA 1982, ss 86–89 and Sch 13)

The disposal of shares gives rise to the need for a capital gains tax computation, and because of the special problems associated with shares— bonus and rights issues, takeovers, mergers, etc.—and because of the need to deal with shares already on hand on 6 April 1965 when capital gains tax started, there are inevitable complications for shareholders with a portfolio of any size. Those complications were considerably increased by the introduction in Finance Act 1982 of an 'indexation allowance' which applies after assets have been held for twelve months, and the complexities have now been further magnified by the introduction of 'parallel pooling' for companies in Finance Act 1983.

The indexation allowance is calculated by applying to the cost of the asset the increase in the Retail Prices Index from March 1982, or from the twelfth

251

Example 1

	Small Company Rate	Normal Rate	Marginal Rate
Rate of corporation tax paid by company	38%	52%	$55\frac{1}{2}\%$
Less advance corporation tax deductible from company liability	30%	30%	30%
True rate on distributed profits	8%	22%	$25\frac{1}{2}\%$

month after acquisition if later, to the month of disposal. It is only available to reduce a gain and cannot create or increase a loss.

Shares acquired prior to commencement of indexation

The position prior to the introduction of indexation on 6 April 1982 (1 April 1982 for companies) was that shares of the same class in the same company, whether quoted or unquoted, were treated as a single asset, growing with purchases and diminishing with sales, so that an average price was used as the cost of disposals. Unquoted securities already owned on 6 April 1965 were excluded from this pooling treatment. Quoted securities owned on that date were also excluded from pooling unless the taxpayer made a pooling election, the effect of which is to pool pre-6 April 1965 quoted securities at their quoted price on that date with other later acquisitions of shares of the same class in the same company.

Identification rules

Following the introduction of indexation each acquisition is treated as a separate asset. The general rule for relating disposals to acquisitions where there have been various acquisitions at different times is to identify disposals in the following order:

(a) With acquisitions in the twelve months preceding the disposal on a first in, first out (FIFO) basis.
(b) With any other acquisitions on a last in, first out (LIFO) basis.

The general rule is subject to some special identification rules that take priority, relating mainly to stock exchange disposals and acquisitions within the same account or sometimes in two consecutive accounts. These provisions effectively make 'bed and breakfast' transactions (selling to establish a loss, or a gain within the annual exemption, and buying back shortly afterwards) more risky and also more costly. There are also anti-avoidance provisions to prevent most bed and breakfast transactions by companies and to stop manipulation of the indexation provisions by transfers between husband and wife and within a group of companies.

Share pools in existence at 6 April 1982 (1 April 1982 for companies) do not normally have to be disentangled and are treated as a single asset acquired one year before that date.

See example 2.

Example 2

Shares are held in one company as follows.

		Number	Cost
Held for more than one year at 6 April 1982		10,000	15,000
Purchases 1 July 1982		4,000	8,000
	1 November 1982	2,000	2,000
Sales	1 January 1983	5,000	15,000
	1 May 1984	5,000	20,000

Retail prices index March 1982 313.4, November 1983 say 335.0, May 1984 say 340.0

Sale of 5,000 shares for £15,000 on 1 January 1983:

Identified with acquisitions in previous twelve months on FIFO basis

Sale 4,000 shares $4/5 \times 15,000$	12,000		
Cost 1 July 1982	8,000	Gain	4,000
Sale 1,000 shares $1/5 \times 15,000$	3,000		
Cost 1 November 1982 $\frac{1}{2} \times 2,000$	1,000	Gain	2,000
	Total gain		6,000

Sale of 5,000 shares for £20,000 on 1 May 1984:

No acquisitions in previous 12 months.
Identified with earlier acquisitions on LIFO basis

Sale 1,000 shares $1/5 \times 20,000$			4,000		
Cost 1 November 1982 $\frac{1}{2} \times 2,000$	1,000				
Indexation allowance					
$1,000 \times \dfrac{340.0 - 335.0}{335.0}$		15	1,015	Gain	2,985
Sale 4,000 shares $4/5 \times 20,000$			16,000		
Cost 6 April 1982 $4/10 \times 15,000$	6,000				
Indexation allowance					
$6,000 \times \dfrac{340.0 - 313.4}{313.4}$		509	6,509	Gain	9,491
		Total gain			12,476

'Pooled' shares acquired in twelve months prior to indexation

To prevent indexation allowance being given from March 1982 on shares owned for less than twelve months at that date, some special rules apply to the pool as at April 1982, but they are not relevant if the cost at 5 April (31 March for companies) 1982 is equal to or lower than the cost at 5 April (31 March) 1981, or if, although the 1982 cost is greater, the number of shares at the 1982 date is equal to or less than the number of shares at the 1981 date.

If both the 1982 cost and the 1982 number of shares are greater than those at 1981, the holding has to be divided into a 'reduced holding' and 'excluded holding(s)'. The reduced holding is the number of shares held at 5 April (31 March) 1981 and the excluded holdings represent the acquisitions less disposals between 1981 and 1982, disposals being identified with acquisitions in that period on a last in, first out basis regardless of whether the acquisition occurred before or after the disposal. The total cost at the 1982 date is then split between the reduced and excluded holdings pro rata to the numbers of shares, the actual costs of the respective holdings being ignored. The reduced holding and each of the excluded holdings are treated as separate assets, with the reduced holding treated as having been acquired twelve months before 6 April (1 April) 1982 and indexation allowance applying from April 1982. Indexation on the excluded holdings applies from twelve months after acquisition.

Shares held on 6 April 1965 (CGTA 1979, Sch 5, Parts I and III)

The general identification rule means that shares held on 6 April 1965 will not be treated as having been disposed of until after all later acquisitions and will then themselves be subject to a last in, first out rule (except where quoted securities are included in the post-April 1965 share pool following an election).

For unquoted securities the sale proceeds are compared with the cost to compute the overall gain or loss, the indexation allowance being applied to reduce a gain but not to create or increase a loss. The overall gain or loss is then time apportioned over the total period of ownership (excluding any period before 6 April 1945) and the chargeable gain or allowable loss is the post-6 April 1965 proportion. The taxpayer may, however, make an irrevocable election to have the gain or loss computed by reference to the value of the asset on 6 April 1965, but if the election would substitute a loss for a gain the result is treated as neither gain nor loss, and the election cannot establish an allowable loss greater than the total loss over the whole period of ownership. In general, allowable losses are unlikely to arise, because pre-April 1965 cost figures are being compared with current sale proceeds. See example 3.

For quoted securities, the sale proceeds are compared with either the cost or the 6 April 1965 value, whichever shows the lower gain or lower loss, and if one method shows a gain and the other a loss the transaction is treated as giving rise to neither gain nor loss. Indexation allowance will apply to reduce a gain but not to create or increase a loss. See example 4.

Example 3

Unquoted shares acquired:
   6 April 1940   1,000 for £1 per share
   6 April 1963   2,000 for £2 per share
Market value at 6 April 1965 considered to be £4 per share.
2,500 shares sold 6 April 1983 for £10 per share.
Increase in retail prices index from March 1982 to April 1983 say 5%.

Sale identified on LIFO basis:

Using time apportionment			Using 6 April 1965 market value		
Sale 2,000 shares @ £10		20,000	Sale		20,000
Cost 6.4.63 @ £2	4,000		6.4.65 MV		
Indexation			2,000 @ £4	8,000	
allowance 5%	200	4,200	Indexation		
			allowance 5%	400	8,400
Overall gain		15,800			
			Gain		£11,600

Post-6 April 1965 proportion:

$$\frac{6.4.65 - 6.4.83}{6.4.63 - 6.4.83} = \frac{18}{20}$$

Gain   £14,220

Gain on election to use 6 April 1965 market value   £11,600

Sale 500 shares @ £10		5,000	Sale		5,000
Cost 6.4.40 @ £1	500		6.4.65 MV		
Indexation			500 @ £4	2,000	
allowance 5%	25	525	Indexation		
			allowance 5%	100	2,100
Overall gain		4,475			
			Gain		2,900

Post-6 April 1965 proportion
(excluding before 6 April 1945):

$$\frac{6.4.65 - 6.4.83}{6.4.45 - 6.4.83} = \frac{18}{38}$$

Gain   2,120

Gain using time apportionment (election for 6 April 1965
value not beneficial)   £2,120

Example 4

Quoted securities acquired:	Number	Cost
1.1.1959	2,000	6,000
10.9.1964	3,000	15,000
Between 6.4.65 and 5.4.81	14,000	84,000
Sales:	Number	Consideration
6.4.83	12,000	68,000
10.11.83	6,000	45,000

6 April 1965 market value £4 per share.

No election made to pool pre-6 April 1965 acquisitions.

Increase in retail prices index from March 1982, say 5% to April 1983 and 7% to November 1983.

No acquisitions in previous twelve months, so sales identified on LIFO basis.

Sale 12,000 shares   68,000

$$\text{Cost} \frac{12,000}{14,000} \times 84,000 \qquad\qquad 72,000$$

Loss (indexation allowance not available to increase loss) 4,000

example continued opposite

Parallel pooling (FA 1983, s 34 and Sch 6)

Because of the vast quantity of records needed to keep track of disposals and acquisitions following the introduction of the indexation allowance, some modified pooling is permitted for companies only, not for individuals. Companies must make a formal election not later than two years from the end of the accounting period in which they make their first disposal after 31 March 1982, such election being irrevocable, and the parallel pooling provisions then apply to all disposals of securities after 31 March 1982, both quoted and unquoted, except that where a company owns quoted securities acquired before 6 April 1965 in respect of which no election had been made to pool them with later acquisitions, those securities are excluded from the parallel pooling provisions. Gilt-edged securities are also excluded.

The parallel pooling provisions do not come into operation until the shares have been held for twelve months, so they do not avoid any of the identification complications arising in those twelve months. They require two separate pools of expenditure to be maintained for each shareholding, one unindexed and the other indexed. Whenever shares are to be added to the two pools after the expiry of twelve months from acquisition (the shares not having been identified with any disposals within that twelve months)

example 4 continued

Sale 6,000 shares deemed to be:				
Sale 2,000 shares				15,000
Cost $\dfrac{2,000}{14,000} \times 84,000$			12,000	
Indexation allowance 7%			840	12,840
Gain				£2,160
Sale 3,000 shares		22,500		22,500
Cost 10.9.1964	15,000			
6.4.65 market value			12,000	
Indexation				
allowance 7%	1,050	16,050	840	12,840
	Gain	6,450	Gain	9,660
Chargeable gain (the lower of the two)				£6,450
Sale 1,000 shares		7,500		7,500
Cost 1.1.1959	3,000			
6.4.65 market value			4,000	
Indexation				
allowance 7%	210	3,210	280	4,280
	Gain	4,290	Gain	3,220
Chargeable gain (the lower of the two)				£3,220
Total chargeable gain (£2,160 + £6,450 + £3,220)			£11,830	

the indexed pool is first uplifted by the index increase since the last increase (or since March 1982 if the pool was in existence at that date and no index increase has been applied in the meantime). An index uplift is also made prior to dealing with a disposal of shares. The indexation allowance on a disposal is the difference between the proportion of the indexed pool relating to the shares disposed of and the corresponding proportion of the unindexed pool, but the indexation allowance as always cannot create or increase a loss.

The parallel pooling provisions will probably only be relevant to the large institutional investors and to companies with computerised records.

Takeovers, mergers and reconstructions (CGTA 1979, ss 77–81 and Sch 5(14); FA 1982, Sch 13(5))

An exchange of new shares for old shares does not normally involve a chargeable gain, the new shares standing in the shoes of the old both as regards acquisition date and cost.

Where both cash and new shares are received a partial disposal arises, in the proportion that the cash itself bears to the cash and market value of the shares acquired in exchange. See example 5.

Example 5

Shares in company A, held for at least twelve months at 6 April 1982, number 10,000 at £5,000 cost.
Company A is taken over by company B on 6 September 1983.

(a) 12,000 shares in company B, valued at £15,000, received in exchange for the 10,000 shares in company A.
No chargeable gain on the £10,000 excess value of the shares received in company B over the cost of those in company A no longer held.
Instead the 12,000 shares in company B take over base value of £5,000 for the 10,000 shares in company A which they replace.

(b) 12,000 shares in company B, valued at £7,500, together with £7,500 in cash received in exchange for the 10,000 shares in company A.
The 12,000 shares in company B have a base value of:

$$\text{£5,000 cost of original Company A shares} \times \frac{\text{£7,500 value of shares acquired in company B}}{\text{(£7,500 shares acquired} + \text{£7,500 cash =) £15,000}} = \text{£2,500}$$

plus indexation allowance from 6 April 1982 to 6 September 1983.
The cost to set off against the £7,500 cash received for the part disposal is likewise £2,500, using the same formula, plus indexation allowance on £2,500 from 6 April 1982 to 6 September 1983.

In the case of the 12,000 company B shares taken in part-exchange, these do not have to be held for twelve months before indexation can again apply.

In the case of a disposal of unquoted shares acquired pre-6 April 1965 where there has been a reorganisation of the share capital prior to the disposal:

(a) If the reorganisation took place before 6 April 1965 the time apportion-ment method cannot be used on the subsequent disposal—the gain or loss has to be computed using the 6 April 1965 market value as the cost price.
(b) If the reorganisation took place after 5 April 1965 the calculation is in two stages:
  (i) The gain up to the date of the reorganisation is computed by time apportionment or by electing to use 6 April 1965 market value.
  (ii) The gain after the reorganisation is computed separately.
  The two are then aggregated to give the overall gain.

Scrip and rights issues (CGTA 1979, ss 77–81; FA 1982, Sch 13(4) (5))

Scrip and rights issues are identified with the shares out of which they arise, but the cost of rights does not attract indexation allowance until the rights shares have been held for twelve months.

If rights are sold nil paid the proceeds are treated as a part disposal of the holding, unless they do not exceed 5% of the pre-rights value of the holding, in which case they are deducted from the cost instead. To avoid loss of indexation allowance in these circumstances the allowance on a later disposal is first calculated on the full cost from twelve months after the date of acquisition (or March 1982 if later) then reduced by an indexation amount on the rights sale proceeds from twelve months after receipt.

Disposal by gift (FA 1980, s 79)

Where shares are disposed of by gift, the proceeds are deemed to be the open market value of the shares. If a gain arises the donor and donee may jointly elect for the donee to adopt the base cost of the donor for capital gains tax purposes, as increased by the indexation allowance to the date of the gift. The donee then has to retain the shares for another year before indexation can again apply.

If a loss arises on a transaction with a connected person (which broadly means close family of the donor and his spouse) the loss is not allowed against gains generally but only against a gain on a subsequent transaction with the same person.

Death (CGTA 1979, ss 5, 49 and Sch 1(4))

When a taxpayer dies his estate has no capital gains tax liability on any excess of the value at the date of death over acquisition cost. If assets are sold by the executors to raise funds for testamentary expenses, capital transfer tax or pecuniary legacies, there will be a liability on the difference between the disposal proceeds after costs and the value at death plus indexation allowance if the disposal is more than twelve months later. In the year of death and in the next two tax-years, the executors are entitled to the annual capital gains tax exemption, currently £5,300.

If shares are the subject of a specific legacy, or are distributed by the executors in specie as part of a residual bequest, the specific residuary legatee acquires the shares at market value at the date of death, and does not have to hold them for a further twelve months after death for the indexation allowance to apply.

Relief against income for losses on shares in unquoted companies (FA 1980, s 37)

Where shares are sold at a loss the loss is normally relievable, like any other capital loss, against gains on other assets. Where, however, the shares are in an unquoted UK trading company and were acquired by subscription as distinct from transfer, relief is available instead against any other *income* of the year of loss or of the following year, in the same way as an individual's or partner's trading loss.

This is not normally relevant to a loss on shares acquired under the business expansion scheme (see chapter 29), since the whole of the cost of the shares will usually have been relieved at the time of acquisition in that case, except where the amount subscribed has exceeded the available scheme limit.

Tax points

- Selling quoted shares is often a convenient way to realise capital gains to use the annual exemption, currently £5,300. 'Bed and breakfast' transactions should still be looked at prior to the end of the tax-year, but the increased costs following the introduction of indexation will make it too expensive in most cases.

- If you are a small investor, unit and investment trusts can be a useful way of getting the benefit of a wide spread of investments, with the added advantage of expert management. Such trusts are exempt from tax on their capital gains. You pay capital gains tax in the usual way when you dispose of your investment in the trust.

- If you propose to dispose of shares to make a gift to charity, it is usually better to give the charity the shares directly, because the gift will then be exempt from capital gains tax, whereas a sale of the shares followed by a cash gift would attract capital gains tax in the usual way.

- If there is some control over the time of payment of a dividend, as with a family or other small company, watch that the date of payment does not aggravate an already high marginal position where the income of the major recipient shareholders varies from year to year.

- When taking shares in an unquoted trading company which does not qualify for relief under the business expansion scheme, ensure that they are subscribed for and not taken up by transfer, so that if a loss arises on disposal it may be relieved against income rather than capital gains.

36
Miscellaneous income

Casual or irregular receipts (TA 1970, s 109)

To be chargeable to income tax, a receipt must come within the scope of one of the income tax Schedules or Cases described in chapter 3. Most receipts of an income nature clearly fall under a particular heading, but in order to deal with residual items that do not come within one of the specified headings but nonetheless have the quality of income rather than capital, a charge is made under Schedule D, Case VI on 'annual profits or gains not falling under any other Case of Schedule D and not charged by virtue of Schedule A, B, C or E'. The word 'annual' does not mean that the item has to be recurrent but indicates that the profits or gains are measured from year to year.

Income or capital

Schedule D, Case VI does not enable the Revenue to charge an item to income tax merely because it escapes capital gains tax. A profit on a chattel sold for less than £3,000, for example, will escape capital gains tax since it is specifically exempt (see chapter 42), but the Revenue cannot use Case VI to charge the profit to income tax. If they can prove that the sale of chattels is such that it amounts to a trade, it will be chargeable under Schedule D, Case I, but a charge cannot be raised under any other heading.

Some specific items

In some cases it is specifically prescribed by statute that income or deemed income from certain sources, or even a capital item, is to be taxed under Case VI. A capital profit on the sale of a patent, for example, is charged under Case VI over six instalments commencing with the year of receipt, unless the taxpayer elects to have the whole sum assessed in that year. (Patents are dealt with on p 168.) Income from furnished lettings (dealt with in chapter 33) is charged under Case VI, as are receipts from a trade or profession after the source has ceased (see chapter 21).

Case VI is also used to charge income from personal activities where the activities are insufficient to be regarded as those of a profession or vocation assessable under Schedule D, Case II, e.g. casual income from writing and occasional commissions.

In general, income charged under Case VI is classed as unearned income, and is subject to the 15% investment income surcharge where total investment income of a tax-year exceeds (for 1983/84) £7,100 (see chapter 3). Certain items, e.g. the post-cessation receipts referred to above, and receipts from the sale of know-how are, however, specifically charged under Case VI as earned income.

Basis of assessment (TA 1970, s 125)

The basis of assessment is the actual income arising in the tax-year, less appropriate expenses. The due date of payment is 1 January in the tax-year or 30 days after the issue of the assessment if later.

Losses (TA 1970, s 176)

If a loss arises on a Case VI source, it may be set against any Case VI profits of the same tax-year, and any remaining balance will be carried forward to set against later Case VI profits. It is not possible to set Case VI losses against income from any other source.

Tax points

- The Revenue will often argue that income from occasional writing falls within Case VI rather than being taxed as from a profession within Case II. This enables them to restrict loss relief to Case VI sources of income, and in most cases there will not be any, so that the losses would have to be carried forward.

- If you expect to make a profit on one source of Case VI income and a loss on another, try to ensure that they occur in the same tax-year, because Case VI losses cannot be carried back and if there is insufficient profit to cover them they must be carried forward.

- The Case VI charge on furnished lettings covers both the use of furniture and the use of property unless you have elected for the property rent to be charged under Schedule A instead (see chapter 33).

37
Husband and wife

General

The income and capital gains of husband and wife are aggregated for the purpose of calculating income tax and capital gains tax, except in the year of marriage, and subject to the right of husband and wife to elect that the wife is taxed separately on her earnings.

Either husband or wife may also make an election for separate assessment of income or chargeable gains, under which the liability on their aggregated incomes or gains is apportioned between them and charged on each separately, but the total tax remains the same.

Unless there has been a separate assessment election, the husband is responsible for completion of returns and for payment of the tax. Direct assessments on his wife's income will be made on him, although tax on a wife's income from employment is collected from her through the PAYE system.

For capital gains tax purposes, transfers between husband and wife who are living together are not chargeable, and any indexation allowance arising to the date of transfer effectively increases the allowable base cost in the acquiring spouse's hands. Only one period of twelve months' ownership by either spouse is required for indexation purposes. If, however, after an inter-spouse transfer qualifying for indexation allowance, the acquiring spouse later disposes of the asset at a loss, the allowable loss is reduced by the indexation allowance on that earlier transfer.

Whether or not separate assessment of capital gains has been applied for, an election may be made within three months after the end of the year of assessment for capital losses of one spouse not to be offset against gains of the other. This may enable them to make better use of the annual exemption of £5,300.

For capital transfer tax purposes, husband and wife are treated as separate persons, each having separate exemptions and a separate threshold. Transfers between the two are exempt unless one of them is not domiciled in the United Kingdom, in which case the transfers to the other spouse are exempt up to £55,000.

Disposals between husband and wife are chargeable to stamp duty in appropriate cases.

Year of marriage (TA 1970, s 37; FA 1976, s 36)

The income of husband and wife is not aggregated in the year of marriage. The wife gets a single person's allowance against her income for the whole year. She does not get the separate wife's earned income relief against her earnings from the date of marriage.

The higher personal relief is given to the husband, subject to a deduction for 1983/84 of £84.17 for each complete tax month (ended on the 5th) prior to the date of marriage, being 1/12th of the difference between the married and single person's relief. Thus if you marry on 29 October 1983 the allowance for 1983/84 is £2,290, i.e. £2,795 less six months @ £84.17.

The non-aggregation of income does not enable a claim to be made for additional personal relief in respect of a child born after the marriage (see page 17), although this relief can continue in the year of marriage for a child of either husband or wife before marriage. In the case of a child of the husband the proportion of the higher personal relief could not be claimed as well.

If the husband's income is too low to use his available allowances, the excess may be used against the wife's income, whether that income arose before or after the marriage. The wife on the other hand cannot transfer any unused allowances to her husband other than dependent relative relief, blind person's relief and relief for services of a son or daughter.

As far as interest is concerned, the wife can transfer unrelieved interest paid after the marriage and the husband can transfer any unrelieved interest. If the interest is mortgage interest paid under the MIRAS scheme, however, tax relief is retained at source whether there is any taxable income or not.

If the maximum life assurance relief (premiums of the greater of £1,500 or 1/6th of total income) is not used by either husband or wife, it is available to swell the premium limits of the other.

Later years (TA 1970, s 37)

The income of husband and wife is aggregated, thus aggravating the higher rates and investment income surcharge position if the incomes are sufficiently high. There is no separate personal relief for the wife against her share of the investment income.

Wife's earnings (TA 1970, s 8; FA 1971, s 23)

Wife's earned income relief, equivalent to the amount of her earnings up to a maximum of £1,785 (the same as the single person's relief), is given against her earned income.

Where the wife's earned income is significant and the joint income is high enough to attract higher rates, a joint election may be made by husband and wife for the wife's earnings to be taxed separately on her as though she were a single woman. The husband then gets the single personal allowance instead of the married allowance, and if the wife pays charges, for example mortgage interest, the charges must be set against her separate earnings instead of reducing the joint investment income, which remains assessable on the husband.

For the election to be beneficial you need to save enough higher-rate tax to offset the loss of the excess of married man's over single allowance.

Example 1

Income of married couple:		£	
Husband's earnings		14,000	
	unearned income	4,000	
Wife's	earnings	7,000	
	unearned income	6,000	
		£31,000	

	Without separate taxation of wife's earnings	With separate taxation of wife's earnings	
		Husband's earnings and joint unearned income	Wife's earnings
Total income	31,000	24,000	7,000
Personal relief	(2,795)	(1,785)	(1,785)
Wife's earned income relief	(1,785)		
Taxable income	26,420	22,215	5,215
Tax thereon	£9,800	7,698	1,564
		£9,262	
Tax saving with separate taxation election		£538	

The election does not affect the investment income surcharge. In either case £435 is payable (£10,000 − £7,100 @ 15%).

The level at which an election for separate taxation of wife's earnings will save tax depends on the total income and the level of the wife's earnings, but it will not be beneficial for 1983/84 unless the total income is at least £22,067 with the wife's earnings therein £5,682 or more. As the total income increases, the requisite level of wife's earnings reduces, but an election will never be beneficial if they drop below £3,805.

Husband and wife must make a joint written election within the period commencing six months before and ending one year after the tax-year for which it is first to apply, and the election may be jointly revoked within the same period. Once the election is made it continues in force until it is revoked. Since personal allowances and tax thresholds are being increased annually it is important to check the position every year.

The election does not affect the husband's liability to make a return of the joint incomes.

Separate assessment (TA 1970, s 38)

An election for separate assessment may be made by either husband or wife within the six months before 6 July in any tax-year, and the election then remains in force until revoked. The total tax liability remains the same, but husband and wife are each responsible for payment of the tax on their own income and each completes a separate tax return. Charges are deducted from the income of whoever pays them, and the tax saving from personal reliefs is apportioned in proportion to the respective incomes, except for dependent relative relief, which is given to whoever maintains the relative, and life assurance relief, which is retained at source by whoever pays the premium.

A husband may prefer separate assessment in order to make his wife responsible for paying the tax on her income. The wife may prefer separate assessment if she wants an independent status and does not want her husband to know her income, although if the Revenue's calculations of the respective liabilities are to be checked someone needs to have the details of both incomes.

Death of the wife

The husband is entitled to the full married personal relief for the tax-year in which his wife dies. For later years until remarriage he has a single allowance, but he may claim the additional personal allowance in respect of a qualifying resident child (see page 17). The wife's income to the date of her death will be aggregated with that of the husband (subject to any election for separate taxation of wife's earnings, see above). Investment income arising on her assets following death will be assessed through her estate and will form part of the husband's income to the extent that he is the ultimate beneficiary.

Death of the husband

The joint income of husband and wife is assessed on the husband to the date of his death, with a full year's married allowance being given in that tax-year and also full wife's earned income relief on any earnings of the wife before the husband dies (subject to any election for separate taxation of wife's earnings, see above). The wife gets a full year's single allowance for the remainder of the tax-year, together with the widow's bereavement allowance, and, if there is a dependent child, the additional personal relief. The widow's bereavement allowance continues for the next tax-year provided that she has not remarried before it commences, and the additional personal allowance continues for so long as there is a dependent child or children and she remains unmarried at the beginning of the tax-year.

Her income will include any she is entitled to from her husband's estate.

Separation

If husband and wife separate in such circumstances as are likely to be permanent, the husband is assessed on his own income for the whole of the year of separation and his wife's income to the date of separation, the wife being separately chargeable on her income from that date.

The date of separation is a question of fact. The husband is entitled to the married personal allowance for the tax-year of separation. He will not be entitled in later years unless he wholly maintains his separated wife by unenforceable payments, and the allowance will cease in any event in the tax-year following a divorce.

The wife is entitled to a single person's relief for the tax-year of separation and for each year thereafter until remarriage.

The wife is entitled to the additional personal allowance from the tax year of separation onwards if she has a qualifying child resident with her. The husband may also claim the additional relief if the conditions are satisfied, but not in any year when he is entitled to the married man's allowance. If they both claim in respect of the same child the allowance is apportioned between them, but if each has a different qualifying child resident with him or her for at least part of the year each can claim the allowance in full.

Where enforceable maintenance is paid by one spouse to the other (usually but not necessarily husband to wife) the payer is entitled to relief at all rates of tax including investment income surcharge. The recipient is assessable on the same amount, but it is not assessable to investment income surcharge.

The maintenance may be enforceable because of a formal agreement between husband and wife, or because of a court order, or because it is clear from correspondence etc. that if the payments were not made proceedings would be taken to enforce the right to support.

Unless the payments are by court order and are within the levels of small maintenance payments (see below) the payer of maintenance obtains basic rate tax relief by deduction of tax at source, the recipient being able to make an income tax repayment claim in appropriate cases. Relief at rates above basic rate is given by an adjustment to a PAYE coding or in an assessment.

Maintenance payments to or for children

Income tax relief can be obtained on payments of maintenance direct to children, but only if paid under an order of the court. In that event the income is treated as the child's income, against which the child's personal relief may be used.

If maintenance is paid to children by agreement between the parties, the income is regarded as arising under a parental settlement and remains that of the paying parent for tax purposes.

If instead of being paid direct to the child the maintenance is paid to the custodial parent for the child's benefit, it will be deemed to be that parent's income and the payer will be entitled to relief at his highest tax rate in the same way as if the maintenance had been for the benefit of the spouse.

The only way, therefore, to utilise the child's personal relief is for maintenance to be paid direct to the child under a court order, with a receipt being given by the custodial parent. See example 2.

Example 2

Husband is ordered by court to pay £10,000 per annum maintenance to his separated wife and children. The wife and children have no other income.

	Terms of Court Order: £10,000 to be paid to wife for herself and children	£4,000 to be paid to wife and £2,000 to each of three children	
	Wife	Wife	Each child
Total income	10,000	4,000	2,000
Personal relief	(1,785)	(1,785)	(1,785)
Additional personal relief	(1,010)	(1,010)	—
	7,205	1,205	215
Tax at 30%	2,162	362	65

× 3 children = 195

557

Therefore saving by appropriate Court Orders is £2,162 − £557 = £1,605, being 30% on £1,785 personal relief for each of three children.

Since the payer obtains tax relief at his highest tax rate on all enforceable maintenance payments (except where they are paid direct to his children by agreement rather than by court order) it is clearly more tax efficient to make such payments rather than retain the married personal allowance through wholly supporting the wife by non-enforceable payments.

Small maintenance payments (TA 1970, s 65)

Maintenance payments both to the spouse and to children are paid net of basic rate tax unless they are 'small maintenance payments'. Small maintenance payments are payments under a court order that do not exceed the following limits:

(a) £33 a week or £143 a month where paid to the spouse for his or her maintenance or directly to a child under 21 years of age for his own benefit, maintenance or education
(b) £18 a week or £78 a month where paid to the spouse or any other person for the benefit, maintenance or education of a child under 21 years of age.

Small maintenance payments are paid gross and relief at all rates of tax is given by means of a PAYE coding adjustment or in an assessment.

In the hands of the receiver, they are subject to direct assessment under Schedule D, Case III, subject to a set-off for available reliefs, the tax being due on 1 January in the tax-year. In many cases where the recipient is working, however, tax is collected by means of an adjustment to the PAYE coding.

Divorce

The tax position of divorced couples is the same as that of separated couples, except that the higher personal relief is not available in any circumstances in tax-years after that in which the divorce occurs. In most cases it will already have ceased following separation because of the greater tax savings to be made through paying enforceable maintenance.

A divorced wife continues to be entitled to life assurance relief on a policy on her husband's life taken out before the divorce, but not on one taken out afterwards. If she wishes to protect herself against the loss of maintenance on her husband's death this can be done with her husband's cooperation if he takes out a policy on his own life in trust for her.

Income in year of separation or death

There is no problem in deciding how much of a husband's income is assessable on him, since he is liable on his own income for the whole of each tax-year up to the date of his death.

The wife's income, however, has generally to be split in the year of

269

separation or in the year of her husband's death, the income up to the relevant date being charged on her husband and the income for the remainder of the year being assessed on her as a single woman. The split is arrived at as follows:

According to the date of receipt	Split on a time basis

Wages, salaries, pensions
Dividends and interest from
    which tax is deducted at
    source
Building society interest
	Rent
	Business profits*
	Bank interest*
	
	* Preceding year basis still
	    applies where appropriate

Separation and divorce—the matrimonial home (FA 1974 Sch 1(4); CGTA 1979, ss 101, 102)

Two aspects are important—relief for mortgage interest paid and the capital gains tax position.

The £30,000 umbrella for mortgage interest relief (see chapter 3) has to cover the borrowing on your own home and on a home provided for a divorced or separated spouse. You are, however, entitled to relief on £30,000 each following separation or divorce, so if the £30,000 limit is likely to be exceeded because one of you is funding two properties, the position could be improved by paying a larger amount of maintenance to enable each to fund a separate mortgage.

For capital gains tax the matrimonial home will cease to be the principal private residence of the spouse who leaves it. That part of any gain on a subsequent sale relating to the period of non-residence will therefore be chargeable except to the extent that it is covered by exemptions or reliefs. The last two years of ownership always count as a period of residence, even if a new qualifying residence has been acquired. If the property is disposed of more than two years after a spouse leaves it, part of the gain will be assessable, but only to the extent of the excess period over two years as a proportion of the total period of ownership. Even then the gain may be covered by the annual exemption of £5,300. There is a Revenue concession covering absences outside the two-year period, but only where the property is eventually transferred to the spouse remaining in it as part of the financial settlement, and relief has not been claimed on a new qualifying residence in the meantime.

Capital gains tax—other chargeable assets (CGTA 1979, s 44; FA 1980, s 79)

The inter-spouse exemption only applies to assets transferred in a tax-year when you are living together. In later tax-years capital gains tax is chargeable in the normal way, and this must be remembered when considering a matrimonial settlement following separation. But if both agree, any gains arising may be rolled over under the gifts relief provisions. See chapter 5.

Capital transfer tax (FA 1975, Sch 6(1))

The spouse exemption for capital transfer tax is not lost on separation but continues until the time of divorce. Even then there is an exemption for transfers to former spouses for the maintenance of themselves and the children. See chapter 7.

Living together without being married

There is no aggregation of the income or gains of an unmarried couple. Each is entitled to a single person's relief and the full lower tax rate bands against any income, and to have investment income of £7,100 before paying surcharge. Where the relevant conditions are satisfied, it is open to each to claim the additional personal relief for a different child if there is more than one, so that they get total reliefs equal to two married personal allowances. It is only when two people claim the relief for the same child that the relief is apportioned, the split being made according to how long the child resides with each claimant in the tax-year, unless they have agreed some other split.

Following divorce or separation, where each party takes another partner without remarrying, it is possible for all four to claim the additional personal relief provided that the relevant conditions are satisfied, and if there are four children each could get the full relief if he/she claimed for a different child. Claimants other than the child's own parent are not entitled to the relief unless they maintain the child.

Each of an unmarried couple is entitled to the £5,300 capital gains tax annual exemption.

Tax points

- The big tax savings available in the year of marriage ceased some years ago. The only minor point to remember now is that every 5th of the month that goes by before the wedding loses you about £25 of the available tax saving (i.e. £84.17 @ 30%).

- If you have elected for separate taxation of wife's earnings, make sure that mortgage interest is paid by whoever will save the most tax, remembering that any charges paid by the wife will only reduce her earnings and not her investment income, which is assessed on the husband.

271

- If your joint wealth is substantial, you can save capital transfer tax by equalising your estates. See chapter 39 for details.

- A court order for maintenance to a child may sometimes include a provision for part to be paid direct to a school to cover school fees, with an official of the school being empowered to give a receipt. This is only effective where the contract for payment of the fees is between the school and the child, otherwise the Revenue will argue that the payment discharges an obligation of the parent, not the child, and that the child's personal relief is consequently not available against the payment. To be on the safe side the payment should be made direct to the child, and the school fees can then be paid out of it.

- If you are arranging an amicable separation and the wife has earnings, try to ensure that she earns enough before the separation to cover the wife's earned income relief of £1,785. She can then get a single personal allowance of £1,785 on her income for the remainder of the year.

- If you are single, divorced or separated and there are qualifying children for whom additional personal relief could be claimed but one of you has insufficient income to make use of the allowance, it is always possible for the other to covenant income to them. (But the covenant is a binding obligation for, usually, a seven-year period, although the covenantee does not necessarily have to enforce it.)

38
Especially for the senior citizen

Age allowance

If you are married and either of you is 65 years of age or over in the tax-year, the normal married personal relief of £2,795 is replaced by an age allowance of £3,755, so long as your joint income does not exceed £7,600. If you are single, the age allowance is £2,360 instead of the single personal allowance of £1,785 and the income limit remains at £7,600. Although single women get the state pension at age 60 they do not get age allowance until they are 65.

The extra allowance is not wholly lost if the income slightly exceeds £7,600. The allowance is reduced by £2 for every £3 of income over the limit. Since the income is itself taxed at 30% and the loss of relief is effectively 20% (2/3rds × loss of relief at 30%) the extra tax payable where income marginally exceeds £7,600 is 50%. See example 1.

Example 1

	(a)	(b)
Single person aged 67 has income of:	7,600	7,900
Age allowance		
Unrestricted	2,360	
Restricted by 2/3rds of £300		2,160
Taxable income	5,240	5,740
Tax thereon @ 30%	£1,572	£1,722

Additional tax payable on extra £300 is £150, i.e. 50%.

Building society interest

The grossed-up equivalent of building society interest is included in income for tax purposes, but the basic-rate tax cannot be recovered by an individual taxpayer. It is not therefore a tax-effective investment compared with an equivalent amount of gross interest from another source for a person who has unused personal allowances. For an illustration see the example at page 249. Where income exceeds the age allowance limit of £7,600, the amount charged at the marginal 50% rate will include the grossed-up building society interest and not the actual amount received.

Covenanted income from adult children

If your income falls short of your allowances and there is no possibility of increasing it by reinvestment or casual earnings etc., a deed of covenant in your favour by a child or children, or indeed by anyone else, will enable them to help you with an extra benefit in the form of a tax repayment. See example 2.

Example 2

Age relief (widow)	2,360
State pension and investment income	1,960
Unused relief	400

A £400 covenant in favour of the widow would cost the covenantor £280 after £120 basic rate tax relief.
The widow would receive £280 from the covenantor, plus £120 tax refund from the Revenue.

You have to watch the effect of the covenant on other benefits such as rate rebate. Further details on covenanting are in chapter 40.

Settling a capital sum

As an alternative to your relatives providing you with income by way of covenant, they may settle a capital sum on you, from which you will then derive the income, and there are no capital transfer tax disadvantages when the capital reverts to them in their lifetime (see chapter 45). The advantage of this method over a covenant for the relative making the settlement is that he effectively gets tax relief at his highest rate, since the income produced is no longer his, whereas he can get only basic-rate relief on a covenant.

Maximising investment income

People with high incomes often seek capital growth instead of income. With investment income surcharge not starting until £7,100 of net investment income, and the basic rate threshold going up to £14,600 after personal reliefs, it may be sensible for you to reappraise your investments following retirement with a view to maximising income instead of concentrating on capital growth.

Making the most of the dwelling-house

The dwelling-house is often the most significant asset of the senior citizen, and yet it can be the biggest liability in the sense of having to maintain it, and it also represents non-income producing wealth.

You can turn it to effective use by letting part of it or by using it as security for a loan to buy a life annuity (see below). Letting will not cause you to lose your capital gains tax private residence exemption (see chapter 5) on disposal of the property provided that the gain on the let part does not exceed that on the exempt part, subject to a maximum exempt gain on the let part of £10,000. Taking in boarders who live as part of the family does not affect your capital gains tax exemption at all.

Purchased life annuities

A purchased life annuity is the receipt of an annual sum for your lifetime in exchange for a capital payment. The characteristic of a purchased life annuity is that part of it is regarded as a return of capital and thus escapes tax; the older you are the greater the tax-free capital element. You do, of course, sacrifice the capital required to buy the annuity, and this loss of capital must be weighed against the greater income arising. You may think the loss of capital is worthwhile to enable you to improve your standard of living, particularly if you have no dependants or others you want to leave your capital to.

If you are over 65 it is possible to boost your income by means of a purchased life annuity, using your house as security for a loan to buy it, and the interest on the loan being allowable for tax purposes. See example 3.

Helping the family

You may be in a position to give financial help to your family rather than requiring help from them.

If you make gifts out of your income as part of your normal, habitual expenditure, and you still have enough income to maintain your usual standard of living, there are no capital transfer tax consequences for you, and the person receiving the gift will have no tax liability on it since it is theirs as a gift and not as of right. On the other hand you will not be entitled to any tax relief on the gift.

If on the other hand you make income gifts by way of deed of covenant, then unless they are to your own unmarried children under 18, they are tax-effective and you save the basic-rate tax thereon. This is a useful way of giving, say, to grandchildren, no matter how young they are, because it enables them to make use of their income tax personal allowance. Their parents can make a tax repayment claim on their behalf.

Example 3

	Tax calculation	Cash available
Annual income of a single taxpayer over 65 is	3,000	3,000
Age allowance	2,360	
Tax at 30% on	640	192
Net spendable income		£2,808

A purchased life annuity is acquired for £15,000, this amount having been raised by a loan on the taxpayer's house. The mortgage interest is £1,500 p.a. The annuity produces £2,250 of which the capital element is determined at £1,300.

The effect on the net spendable income is:

Income as before	3,000	3,000
Income element of annuity	950	950
Capital element of annuity	—	1,300
	3,950	5,250
Mortgage interest payable	1,500	1,500
	2,450	3,750
Age allowance	2,360	
Tax at 30% on	90	27
Net spendable income		£3,723

The net spendable income has been increased by £915 (£3,723 − £2,808) at a cost of reducing the equity in the house by the £15,000 borrowing to purchase the annuity.

If gifts are not covenanted and are not normal expenditure out of income, they will be covered to the extent of the annual capital transfer tax exemption of £3,000, and any excess will not attract capital transfer tax until you have made cumulative gifts up to the tax-exempt threshold, currently £60,000. Any gifts made more than ten years previously are excluded from the cumulative total.

Husband and wife are treated separately for capital transfer tax, and each is entitled to the annual exemption and tax-free threshold.

Tax position on your death

When you die your wealth at death and the capital transfers you have made in the previous ten years will determine whether any, and if so how much, capital transfer tax is payable. There is no capital transfer tax on assets passing to your husband or wife. There is no liability to capital gains tax on your estate, and those who acquire your assets are deemed to have bought them at their market value at the date of your death. Further details on the position at death are in chapter 39.

If you have made gains before the date of death, they will be chargeable, subject to the usual annual exemption of the first £5,300. Any losses in the year of death may be carried back to set against gains chargeable to tax in the three previous years, and tax will be repayable accordingly.

As far as income tax is concerned, the income of a single person to the date of death is charged to tax in the usual way, with a full personal allowance against it. In the case of a married couple, when the husband dies the joint income to the date of his death is assessable on him, with a full year's personal allowance and full wife's earned income relief available where appropriate. The widow is then taxed as a single woman on her income for the remainder of the year, with a full single person's allowance. Where any of the wife's income is charged by direct assessment, for example rents, bank interest or self-employed earnings, the assessment is split according to the period before and after the husband's death, that assessment having been made on the normal preceding year basis where appropriate. Any of her income taxed at source is deemed to be income of the husband or widow according to the date it is received. A widow is also entitled to a widow's bereavement allowance of £1,010 in the year of her husband's death, and in the following year unless she has remarried before the beginning of it. On remarriage she cannot transfer any unused allowance to her new husband.

Where the wife dies first, the husband retains the full married man's allowance for the tax-year in which she dies but thereafter reverts to a single person's allowance.

Tax points

- The marginal tax rate for those over 65 with income over £7,600 is 50%, so that investments that produce tax-free income are preferable.

- Although the lower age limit for a purchased life annuity scheme secured on the home is 65, the annuity rates will not usually make it attractive unless the annuitant has reached the age of 70.

- Covenants from adult children to their dependent parents, and from grandparents to grandchildren, are tax-effective and can utilise available personal reliefs.

39
Tax considerations in making a will

General considerations

The prime objective in making a will is to ensure that those left behind are provided for in the way you wish, and although there are important tax implications, which it can be expensive to ignore, they should not be allowed to override the main aim. Some less than optimal arrangements from a tax point of view may be the most suitable taking all other factors into account.

Capital transfer tax: spouse exemption

Gifts between husband and wife are exempt from capital transfer tax for both lifetime and death transfers. Transfers between husband and wife in a tax-year when they are living together are also exempt from capital gains tax, so that the only charge on the transfer of assets will be stamp duty where appropriate (see chapter 8).

Since husband and wife are each entitled to the annual capital transfer tax exemption of £3,000 and to the tax exempt threshold of £60,000 before transfers become chargeable, it is clearly sensible for the joint wealth to be equalised if it exceeds £60,000. The tax advantage may, however, be lost on death if the estate is then left to the surviving spouse. If, say, each had £60,000 wealth and made no chargeable transfers in lifetime, no tax would arise if each left the wealth to the next generation, because it would be covered by the tax exempt threshold. But if the wealth were left to the surviving spouse, that spouse would then have £120,000 (ignoring any capital diminution in the meantime) which would attract a tax liability at current rates of £20,500.

Bypassing your spouse will not be practicable if he/she is left with inadequate assets to maintain his/her standard of living. If you want to give the surviving spouse the benefit of the joint capital during his/her lifetime at the extra tax cost this may entail, it is possible to preserve the family wealth for the next generation through the use of life assurance to cover the tax liability, as indicated later.

Jointly owned assets

There are two ways in which assets may be held jointly—as joint tenants or as tenants in common. If you have a share as a joint tenant, it cannot be given away in lifetime without first severing the joint tenancy, and on your death the share automatically passes to the other joint tenant(s). With a tenancy in common each has a separate share which can be disposed of in lifetime or on death as the person wishes. Husband and wife are presumed to own assets as joint tenants, and other people are presumed to own them as tenants in common, so if they want to vary the normal presumption this must be done explicitly.

Jointly held assets still form part of a person's estate for capital transfer tax whether they are held on a joint tenancy or as tenants in common, but where they are held jointly by husband and wife, any assets passing to the spouse are covered in any event by the surviving spouse exemption. Holding as joint tenants has the advantage in the case of a joint bank account that when your spouse dies, all that is needed to enable you to take over sole ownership of the account is production of the death certificate. You do not have to wait for grant of probate or administration.

The joint ownership principles must be borne in mind when planning the use of the tax-exempt threshold and lower-rate bands, and express action taken to vary the normal presumptions where necessary.

Legacies

The grossing-up principle where the donor pays the capital transfer tax on a gift is described in chapter 7 at page 55. It also applies on death, where, unless the will specifically provides otherwise, legacies are received in full and the tax comes out of the residue of the estate, so that the legacy has to be grossed up to ascertain the tax payable. This has to be looked at carefully, otherwise a surviving spouse for example may receive far less than was intended. See example 1.

It may be possible to enable the donee to pay the tax on legacies by providing the funds through appropriate insurance cover, and in example 1 this would reduce the tax to £20,500 and would leave the widow with an exempt residue of £80,000.

Where there are deaths in quick succession

Where a person's estate on death has been increased by a lifetime or death gift made to him within the previous five years the double tax charge is mitigated by quick succession relief. The tax payable is reduced by a percentage of the tax paid on the earlier transfer (see chapter 7 at page 62).

Quick succession relief is obviously not available on assets received by a surviving spouse, since the transfer on the first death was exempt. Even

Example 1

A has made no chargeable transfers in lifetime and leaves an estate of £200,000 as follows:

        £40,000 to each of B, C and D
        Residue to his wife E

The capital transfer tax position on A's death is as follows:

	Gross £	Tax £	Net £
Net legacies			120,000
Gross equivalent and tax thereon	155,454	35,454	

The estate will accordingly be divided as follows:

Gross estate	200,000
Legacies to B, C and D	(120,000)
Capital transfer tax payable out of residue	(35,454)
Remainder to widow E, covered by spouse exemption	£44,546

where the first transfer attracted tax, the relief is based on the tax charged on that transfer and not on the tax attracted by the gift in the donee's estate. While not losing sight of the overriding principle of family provision, there are cases where it is clearly not sensible to increase a person's estate by incoming transfers, such as when they are old and have adequate resources already. It will often be more tax-efficient, say, for people to leave to their grandchildren instead of their children. This gives the added advantage that the income arising is then that of the grandchildren in their own right against which income tax allowances and lower rate bands are available.

Simultaneous deaths and survivorship clauses

Where two closely related people die at the same time, or in circumstances in which it is impossible to decide who died first, each is in effect deemed to have survived the other for capital transfer tax purposes, so that neither estate has to be increased by any entitlement from the other. This provision does not apply if it is in fact clear who died first. It is therefore often advisable to include a survivorship clause in a will making a bequest conditional on the beneficiary outliving the deceased by a given period, and this is effective for capital transfer tax providing the period does not exceed six months. This is particularly useful to a husband and wife who wish to leave their estates to each other to make sure that there is adequate provision for the survivor's lifetime, because the aggregation of the estates would be of no benefit in the event of both deaths occurring in quick succession, and the tax on the second death would otherwise be correspondingly higher.

Deeds of family arrangement

It is possible for those entitled to a deceased's estate to vary the way in which it is distributed, or to disclaim their entitlement, provided that they do so within two years after the death and notify the Revenue within six months of the date of the variation or disclaimer. Capital transfer tax is then charged as if the revised distribution had operated from the date of death. Such a variation or disclaimer is also effective for capital gains tax purposes, and the ultimate beneficiary takes the asset at the market value at the date of death, with no charge arising on any increase in value in the meantime. As far as income derived from the assets is concerned, the personal representatives will have paid basic-rate tax thereon, but the income is deemed to have been received not by the ultimate beneficiary who actually receives it but by the original beneficiary, who will be liable for any tax arising in excess of the basic rate on the income up to the date of variation or disclaimer.

A deed of variation or disclaimer could be used to advantage where, for example, an estate has been left to the surviving spouse without the deceased's tax-free threshold and/or lower rates having been used. If the surviving spouse is already adequately provided for, part of the estate could be left to, say, the children. It could also be useful where, for example, children have sufficient assets of their own and would prefer legacies to go to their own children.

Deeds of variation and disclaimer can therefore be used to mitigate adverse tax consequences of the disposal of a deceased's estate, but it is necessary for all concerned to consent to the arrangement, and they should be regarded as something in reserve rather than a substitute for appropriate planning.

Insurance

There are various instances where life assurance may be useful in planning for capital transfer tax. Frequently it is not possible to reconcile making adequate provision for the family with mitigating the tax liability, and insurance may then be used to cover the anticipated liability.

There is no point in insuring your own life for the benefit of the estate, because the proceeds would then form part of the estate and attract tax, and furthermore they would not be available until grant of probate or administration is obtained. If, however, a policy on your life is arranged by someone with an insurable interest, say your children, or you take out a policy yourself and pay the premiums, with the proceeds in trust for someone else, again say your children, the funds will not be taxable in your estate. A trust policy has the added advantage that you will get income tax life assurance relief on the premiums, and the premiums themselves can probably be regarded as normal expenditure out of income, and thus exempt from capital transfer tax, or otherwise covered by the annual exemption of £3,000.

Life policies can also be a useful way of avoiding the tax cost of grossing-up of legacies. You can require the donee to pay the tax on the legacy but put him in funds to do so by means of the insurance proceeds receivable.

Tax points

- There is little to be gained from the tax point of view in equalising estates between husband and wife if they then attract a higher tax liability through being brought together again at the first death. But the needs of the surviving spouse must be paramount, and at least the equalisation will enable both to use annual exemptions.

- Where tax at death cannot be avoided, consider covering the liability through life assurance in favour of those who will have to bear the tax.

- If you have already used your tax-exempt threshold and plan to leave most of your estate to your spouse but to make some small legacies, consider leaving the entire estate to the spouse and letting the spouse make the gifts out of annual exemptions and/or the tax-exempt threshold. You will of course need to be sure that your spouse will carry out your wishes.

40
Covenanting

Characteristics of a covenant

A covenant is effectively a legally binding settlement of income on one person by another. It signifies an enforceable obligation to make the payment, thus distinguishing it from a voluntary payment.

Covenants are typically used to transfer income in a tax-efficient way to charities or to individuals who have insufficient income to use available tax reliefs. Such covenants have to be in the form of a deed, which means that the document must be signed, sealed and delivered in the presence of a witness. Whilst sealing is done by attaching an adhesive red disc, the Revenue will usually accept that a covenant is under seal if the deed states that this is so.

Covenants to your own unmarried children under the age of eighteen are ineffective for tax purposes.

Covenants to anyone else are effective if they are capable of exceeding six years. Charity covenants need only be capable of exceeding three years. The most popular terms for covenants are thus seven years and four years respectively. Provided that the term of the covenant is *capable* of exceeding the stipulated period it is immaterial whether it in fact does so.

The payer deducts basic-rate income tax when he makes the covenanted payments, the net amount being sufficient to discharge his legal obligation under the covenant. An annual certificate on form R185(AP) showing the tax deducted is given to the recipient.

Rate of tax relief

Relief is given to the payer at his top rate of tax (including investment income surcharge) if the covenant is in favour of a charity and to the extent that the total covenanted payments to charity by that taxpayer in the tax-year do not exceed £5,000 gross (£3,000 for 1982/83) (TA 1970, s 457). Since only basic-rate relief is retained at source out of the payment, relief for higher rates and surcharge has to be given by repayment or by reducing the tax payable under direct assessments.

Other payments under deed of covenant are relieved at the basic rate only, so that the available relief is obtained by the deduction at source.

Should the payer for some reason not have sufficient taxable income in a tax-year to cover his covenanted payments, then, having deducted basic-rate tax on making the payments, he will have to hand over the tax deducted to the Revenue, since to the extent that he is not a taxpayer he is not entitled to tax relief. The Revenue will raise an assessment under TA 1970, s 53 for this purpose.

Position of the recipient

The gross covenanted income is aggregated with any other income the recipient has to determine the tax liability, if any. If the recipient is not liable to pay tax, because of available reliefs or charitable status, the tax deducted at source will be recovered by the recipient by means of a repayment claim.

Covenants to charities

The ability to recover tax deducted from payments substantially boosts covenanted income to charities. Since 5 April 1981 relief has been available to the donor at his highest rate of tax on charity covenants, initially up to £3,000 a year, but now increased, for 1983/84 onwards, to £5,000 a year. The high tax rate donor may be persuaded to increase his gross covenanted sum, thus passing the higher-rate tax saving on to the charity.

Example 1

Taxpayer is prepared to contribute £70 per annum to a charity.

	Donor liable to tax at basic rate	Donor liable to tax at 75%
	£	£
Total income received by charity	100	280
less tax deducted and repaid to charity	30	84
Net payment by donor	70	196
Higher rate and surcharge relief to donor @ 45%	—	126
Net cost to donor	70	70

Charities usually have printed covenant forms available for intending donors.

Covenants to your own children

Covenants to your own children who are over eighteen or married are a useful way of helping to support them while they are students. You get relief at basic rate only, but the child can recover the tax deducted provided that he or she has available personal reliefs to cover the gross covenanted sum. Other sources of income may, however, have used some or all of the child's personal allowance, for example vacation earnings, and if you covenant to your married daughter, it is the couple's joint income which determines whether the married personal allowance has been used or not. She has no single allowance of her own.

The effect of the child having other income is to reduce or eliminate the availability of the tax repayment. It does not affect the validity of the covenant in any way.

The Inland Revenue issue a leaflet IR47 containing a suitable form for a parent's covenant to an adult student.

Covenants to children other than your own, for example grandchildren

Such covenants are not restricted by reference to the age of the child, so that they can be used to transfer to infant children free of tax an amount equal to the child's personal allowance (provided that the child has no other sources of income).

The parent can make the repayment claim on behalf of the child.

Covenants to dependent relatives

Those over 65 years of age get the higher personal age allowance (£3,755 for married couples and £2,360 for single people for 1983/84). They are therefore more likely to have an excess of available allowances over taxable income. A covenant from a relative, perhaps an adult child, may utilise these excess allowances. For an example, see p 274 above.

A covenant to your widowed mother could be worded as follows:

I (name of person making the covenant) of (address) covenant to pay my mother (name) (widow) of (mother's address) the sum of £_____ gross on (date) in each year for the period of seven years, or for the period of our joint lives, whichever is the shorter, the first payment to be made on

_____

Signed, sealed and delivered by _____

In the presence of _____

If payment is not made

A covenant is a legally binding obligation, non-payment of which entitles the covenantee to take appropriate action for recovery. But where a covenant was entered into to help the covenantee and the covenantor's circumstances change so that he has difficulty in meeting his obligations, the covenantee may be disinclined to pursue his right to payment, and is not obliged to do so.

If a covenanted payment is not made, the covenantor cannot be called upon to account for the tax he would have deducted if he had paid it, nor can the covenantee make a repayment claim.

Non-reciprocity

Covenants are not tax-effective where they are part of reciprocal arrangements. This prevents 'back to back' arrangements such as A covenanting to B's children and B covenanting to A's children, and also prevents the use of covenants as disguised annual subscriptions to clubs, etc. which provide substantial benefits in return.

For deeds of covenant other than to charities, the Revenue may ask for a certificate that the covenant is not in payment of an obligation.

Tax points

- If you have to support adult children or dependent parents who have unused personal reliefs, a covenant can reduce the amount you need to contribute, but watch the effect on entitlement to other benefits such as rate rebates.

- Where a charity requires substantial sums for immediate use, consider linking a four-year covenant with an interest-free loan. You will provide the total net covenanted sum in a single amount, and the annual loan repayments will be appropriated by the charity to satisfy the amounts due under the covenant.

- The tax advantage of covenanted income to a grandchild could be increased by the grandchild paying the amount received into a life assurance policy on his life, on which 15% life assurance relief is then available.

  If the grandchild is under twelve years of age, he is considered by the Revenue not to be old enough to appreciate the significance of the contract. The policy may still be entered into but life assurance relief is not given until the child reaches age twelve.

41
Tax-efficient investment

Introduction

This chapter is not concerned with 'loophole' schemes which may be subject to Revenue attack, but with those investments, available to the majority of taxpayers, that may have tax advantages.

Building society investment

Building society interest is in effect deemed to be net of basic-rate income tax, but the notional tax deducted is not refundable to individuals, so this form of investment should be avoided by those who have spare personal reliefs available. For details see page 249.

National savings bank accounts

The National Savings Bank operates both ordinary and investment accounts. Interest on both types of account is credited gross annually on 31 December.

The first £70 of interest on an ordinary account is exempt from tax (for husband and wife, £70 each). Although the rate of interest is low, a balance which produces interest of £70 may be attractive to higher-rate taxpayers.

The investment account usually pays interest at a competitive rate and may be more attractive than a building society account if you have spare personal reliefs—you need to compare the gross rate on the investment account with the 'net' rate offered by the building societies.

National savings certificates

These are particularly attractive to individuals paying income tax at higher rates, as the interest accumulates over the period of the investment, and when the certificates are cashed the capital appreciation is totally free from income tax and capital gains tax. A maximum holding of certificates is prescribed for each issue, that for the current 25th issue being £5,000. The certificates are repaid at their purchase price if encashed during the first year, but after that the tax-free yield rises from 6% at the end of the first year to 9.65% at the end of the fifth year. If you have a marginal income tax rate of 75% you would need to find an investment yielding 38.6% to leave sufficient income after tax to match the return in the fifth year. The compound tax-free annual interest rate over the full five years is 7.51%.

National savings index-linked certificates

Provided that these certificates have been held for at least one year their repayment value is equal to the original purchase price augmented by the increase in the retail prices index since the month of purchase. Supplements are added from time to time and, provided that the certificates have been held for a period of five years, a further bonus of 4% of the purchase price is payable on encashment. Any increase in the value when the certificates are cashed is free of income tax and capital gains tax.

Although there is a limit on the holding of certificates in each issue, a maximum of £10,000 being prescribed for the second issue, you do not have to cash the certificates of previous issues, which continue to attract a tax-free addition.

These certificates are suitable for taxpayers who are prepared to forgo immediate income to protect their capital in real terms, although with inflation falling this form of investment is less attractive.

Save As You Earn (SAYE)

The Government encourages regular savings contracts with building societies and the Department of National Savings, tax-free bonuses being added to the investment at the 5th and 7th anniversaries. The maximum monthly investment is £50.

The Government also operates an index-linked SAYE scheme which it guarantees. Each monthly contribution is indexed in line with the movement in the retail prices index between the month of investment and the end of the contract. The indexed aggregate value of all contributions can be claimed at the end of the contractual period or the savings can be left in the scheme, where they will continue to be indexed in line with the retail prices index and will also attract a bonus when finally repaid. If a contract is terminated in the first year, contributions are refunded without indexation, and in the event of a termination in the second year a tax-free interest payment is made instead of indexation.

Capital appreciation throughout the contract is tax-free, making this form of investment attractive if you wish to protect the real value of your capital. A SAYE contract may be linked to a share option scheme—see chapter 12.

Friendly societies

Although most friendly societies originated in Victorian times, several new societies emerged following the enactment of the Friendly Societies Act 1974. These societies pay no tax on their income or capital gains, so savers with them enjoy a tax 'holiday' on their money. Moreover, premiums into the society are eligible for 15% life assurance relief, and the policy proceeds payable at the end of ten years are tax-free.

The drawbacks of investing in friendly societies are:

(a) Life assurance is restricted to £2,000.
(b) Premiums cannot exceed £280 per annum.
(c) Only married men and women and single parents with dependent children are eligible.
(d) Early surrender values cannot exceed gross premiums paid.

Despite these restrictions the tax benefits are so worthwhile that most people who are eligible to save with a friendly society are well advised to take out a policy provided they can maintain contributions for the full ten years.

Premium savings bonds

Any person over 16 can buy these bonds. The current maximum holding is £10,000. They do not carry interest, but, once a bond has been held for three calendar months, it is included in a regular monthly draw for prizes of various amounts. All prizes are free of income tax and capital gains tax and the bond itself can be encashed at face value at any time. This gives you the chance to win a tax-free prize, but at the cost of not receiving any income or protection of the real value of your capital.

Yearling bonds

These are so called because they are used by local authorities to raise loans on an annual basis, being attractive as an investment because their interest rates are competitive and they can be quickly realised if necessary. Interest is paid half-yearly, after deduction of basic-rate income tax at source. Sale proceeds are subject to capital gains tax.

These bonds have an added attraction if you pay tax above the basic rate as they offer the opportunity of realising accrued interest as a capital gain by selling the bond on the stock market 'cum interest' and effectively receiving the interest as part of the sales proceeds. The selling costs involved have to be considered, and, more important, there are anti-avoidance provisions to enable the Revenue to calculate what income should have been received on an accrued basis and to tax it accordingly. Provided, however, that the use of this arrangement does not reduce your charge to excess liability by more than 10% of what it would have been had the interest actually been received, the Revenue would not normally require an adjustment.

Government dated stocks

These represent borrowings by the British Government or certain national-ised industries, and they vary considerably in terms of interest. With the exception of 3½% War Loan, basic-rate income tax is usually deducted at source. It is possible, however, to purchase stocks that are on the National Savings Stock Register through your local post office or trustee savings bank, and thereby to receive interest gross. Interest received is liable to tax at all rates, whether it is received gross or net.

Most of the stocks have a redemption date upon which the par value will be paid to the holder, so if you buy them below par you will have a guaranteed capital gain at a given date, which is exempt from capital gains tax if the stock has been held for more than 12 months. In the meantime, the value of the stock will fluctuate with market conditions, so that there may be opportunities to make capital gains before the redemption date, again free of capital gains tax if the stock has been held for more than 12 months. If, however, you make losses on holdings disposed of more than 12 months after acquisition they are not allowable for set-off against chargeable gains.

A purchase for capital growth may well be better for an investor with a marginal income tax rate in excess of the basic rate than an investment producing a greater income with no growth prospects. See example 1.

Example 1

Investor with marginal income tax rate of 75% has a capital sum of £8,000 for investment.

(a) £8,000 invested in local authority loan for five years at 10% would produce:

Capital at redemption		8,000
Interest for five years at 10%	4,000	
Less income tax at 75%	3,000	1,000
		£9,000

(b) £8,000 invested at £80 per £100 in a 3% Government Stock giving £10,000 nominal would produce:

Capital at redemption (full par value)		10,000
Interest for 5 years at 3% on £10,000	1,500	
Less income tax at 75%	1,125	375
		£10,375

As in the case of yearling bonds, it is possible to sell holdings 'cum interest' to avoid higher rates and investment income surcharge, but again the Revenue can counter this if the arrangements become systematic.

As well as being suitable for the higher-rate taxpayer Government stocks can be useful as a means of providing for future known commitments, such as school fees. They can also be attractive to people who have retired, in that they combine reasonably high yields with the opportunity of some capital growth.

Ordinary shares in quoted companies

Ordinary shares are 'risk capital' and investors have to be prepared to accept the risk element in return for rising income and capital appreciation.

Dividends attract a tax credit which satisfies basic-rate tax liability and is repayable to non-taxpayers. If you are liable to tax above the basic rate you must pay higher rates and investment income surcharge on the total of the dividends plus the tax credit. Gains on disposal are chargeable to capital gains tax in the usual way.

Taking a low income yield with a potential chargeable gain may be preferable to a high-income investment if you are liable at excess rates. On the other hand, although quoted shares are readily marketable, the price can fluctuate considerably, so they are not recommended if you may need to make an unplanned sale to meet unexpected commitments.

The detailed treatment of shares and government stocks is in chapters 34 and 35.

Purchased life annuities

If you pay a lump sum to a life assurance company to get a fixed annual sum in return, the annual sum is partly regarded as non-taxable return of capital, thus giving a comparatively high after-tax return on the cost of the annuity. You have, however, effectively spent your capital to secure the annual income and thus at the end of the annuity term the capital is exhausted.

It is therefore common for purchased life annuities to be acquired in conjunction with life assurance policies, part of the annual income being used to fund the life assurance premium so that at the end of the annuity period the life assurance policy proceeds can replace the purchase price of the annuity. There are numerous variations on this sort of arrangement.

Purchased annuities may be acquired by those over 65 by means of a loan secured on their home—see chapter 38.

Other investments

Other chapters deal in detail with investing in:

(a) Industrial buildings (chapter 32).
(b) Unquoted trading companies through the business expansion scheme (chapter 29).
(c) Single premium life assurance bonds (chapter 43).
(d) Chattels (chapter 42).

Tax points

- If you have spare personal reliefs building society accounts are not a good investment because you cannot recover the notional tax deducted.

- Many of the National Savings schemes on offer are particularly attractive to higher-rate taxpayers because of the tax-exempt receipts.

- If you are a small investor you can benefit from a wide range of investments through a unit or investment trust. The trust is exempt from tax on its gains. You pay tax on income and gains in the normal way.

- Premium bonds are a gamble not an investment!

- A Friendly Society policy is very worthwhile if you are eligible and can make contributions for ten years.

42
Chattels and valuables

What are chattels?

Chattels are tangible moveable property such as coins, furniture, works of art.

Income tax

Many people have turned to investing in valuable objects because money rates of interest have frequently barely kept up with inflation. This can be a tax-efficient exercise because the appreciation in value does not attract income tax, which cannot generally be charged on notional income. Conversely there can be no tax relief for any expenses of ownership such as insurance or charges for safe custody.

A succession of profitable sales may suggest to the Revenue that chattels and valuables are held for trading purposes. This will particularly be so where the scale and frequency of the sales, or the way in which they are carried out, or the need for supplementary work between purchase and sale, suggest a trading motive. Indeed, even a single purchase and sale has on occasion been held to be a trading transaction. However, an important indicator of trading is the lack of significant investment value or pride of ownership. Where chattels have those qualities, sales are more readily defended as not being by way of trade.

Capital Gains Tax (CGTA 1979, ss 127, 128)

Chattels that are wasting assets (i.e. with a predictable life not exceeding fifty years) are exempt from capital gains tax, unless they are business chattels on which capital allowances have been or could have been claimed. This restricts the capital gains tax charge to business assets and valuable objects of a durable nature (which would exclude items such as fur coats, greyhounds and yachts).

Non-wasting and business chattels sold for £3,000 or less are exempt from capital gains tax. This does not, however, apply to foreign currency. Where the proceeds exceed £3,000 the chargeable gain cannot exceed 5/3rds of the excess proceeds over £3,000.

Example 1

	£	£
Sale proceeds of chattels are		4,200
Cost in 1970 was	600	
Indexation allowance, say	30	630
Chargeable gain		£3,570
But limited to $5/3 \times (4,200 - 3,000)$		£2,000

Where a loss arises on the disposal, then if the proceeds are less than £3,000 they are deemed to be £3,000 in calculating the allowable loss.

Example 2

	£	£
Cost of chattel		3,500
Sale proceeds	1,500	
but deemed to be		3,000
Loss, although £2,000, is limited to		£ 500

Items comprising a set or collection are treated as separate assets unless they are sold to the same or connected persons (as defined in CGTA 1979, s 63—see p 42), in which case the sales are aggregated and treated as arising on the occasion of the last sale. Splitting up a set and selling it to different unconnected people would usually not be sensible because it would substantially reduce its value. See example 3.

Coins

Demonetised coins (for example pre-1838 sovereigns) are chargeable chattels but qualify for the £3,000 exemption. Krugerrands, on the other hand, being legal tender in South Africa, are foreign currency and thus do not qualify for the £3,000 exemption. Sterling currency (which includes post-1838 sovereigns) is wholly exempt from capital gains tax.

Gifts

A gift of a chargeable asset is deemed to be a disposal at open market value at the date of the gift. In order to arrive at an estimated valuation, some

Example 3

Purchase of silver tea service in 1980 for £2,200.
Part sold in 1982 for £2,000 and the remainder to the same person
in 1984 for £2,500.

			£
Proceeds	1982 sale		2,000
	1984 sale		2,500
			4,500
Cost		2,200	
Indexation allowance from 6 April 1982 to date of second sale, say		200	2,400
Chargeable gain			£2,100

This is less than $5/3 \times (4,500 - 3,000) = £2,500$, so that the chargeable gain is £2,100.

evidence of the transaction in the form of correspondence etc. is advisable.
If the value is below the £3,000 exempt level no tax charge will arise, but the
valuation will form the base cost of the asset to the donee and may thus
affect a later tax charge.

If the value of the gift exceeds the exempt level and a gain arises, tax need
not be paid on the gain immediately. The gain may instead be treated as
reducing the base cost of the asset to the donee (see p 42).

Tax points

- Include substantial chattel acquisitions in the capital gains acquisition
  section of the tax return. This helps to demonstrate a non-trading
  motive if the question is ever raised.

- Watch the trading trap. Don't engage in regular buying and selling.

43
Sensible use of life assurance

Background

The various life offices offer a number of arrangements designed to take advantage of the tax relief available for life assurance and also the tax provisions for non-qualifying policies. Except where you include term assurance in a personal pension plan and thus obtain relief at your marginal rate of tax on earned income (see chapter 18), the rate of relief available on a qualifying policy is 15% of the premiums paid, subject to maximum allowable premiums of either £1,500 or one-sixth of your total income whichever is higher. See chapter 3.

Qualifying policy (TA 1970, ss 19, 21 and Sch 1; FA 1975, Sch 2)

The definition of qualifying policy is complex, but broadly it must be on your own or your spouse's life, it must secure a capital sum on death, earlier disability or not earlier than ten years after the policy is taken out, the premiums must be reasonably even and paid at yearly or shorter intervals, and there are various requirements as to the amount of the sum assured and sometimes as to the surrender value.

Purchased life annuities (TA 1970, s 230)

A qualifying policy is particularly useful to higher-rate taxpayers in combination with a purchased life annuity (see chapter 41). Only part of the purchased annuity is liable to income tax, the remainder being regarded as a return of capital.

Instead of making a conventional investment and losing a substantial part of the income in tax, a higher-rate taxpayer could purchase a life annuity and use the net income arising to fund a qualifying life policy, the profits on maturity of the policy being tax-free. See example 1.

If you are an older taxpayer a variation is available under which only part of the net annual sum from the annuity is used to fund a qualifying policy to replace the initial cost of the annuity, the remainder being retained as spendable income. It is also possible to borrow the money to buy an annuity on the security of your house if you are over 65 (see chapter 38).

Example 1

Taxpayer aged 45 with a marginal tax rate of 70% uses £5,000 to fund the first premium of £700 gross, £595 after 15% life assurance relief, on a qualifying life policy and to purchase a 9 year annuity of £805 for £4,405

The position is:

	£	£
Capital element of annuity (say)		505
Income element (say)	300	
Less tax at 70%	210	90
Annual amount		595
When the policy matures after 10 years:		
Proceeds, say		9,500
Net cost: First premium	595	
Cost of annuity	4,405	5,000
Tax-free profit after 10 years		4,500

Compare this with investing £5,000 at say 10% to yield £500 gross, £150 net, per annum, to give total after tax income of £1,500.

Early surrender of qualifying policies (TA 1970, ss 394, 395, 399; FA 1975, s 7)

If a qualifying policy is surrendered within the first four years, all or part of the tax relief obtained is clawed back by a deduction from the surrender value. The deduction is made by the insurance company, who pay it over to the Revenue. The amount clawed back is as follows:

Time of surrender	Clawback of premiums	Maximum clawback
Within first 2 years	15%	Surrender value less 85% of premiums
In third year	10%	Surrender value less 90% of premiums
In fourth year	5%	Surrender value less 95% of premiums

If a qualifying policy is surrendered less than ten years after the policy is taken out (or, for endowment policies, before the expiry of three-quarters of the term if that amounts to less than ten years), any profit arising is charged to tax at the excess of the payer's marginal rate of tax over basic rate (but top-slicing relief is available—see below).

It is possible to surrender a qualifying policy after the four years have elapsed for an amount equal to the gross premiums paid, so that there is no clawback of relief, and although the surrender within ten years is a chargeable event, there is no tax liability because there is no profit as such, the benefit lying in the tax relief retained.

Non-qualifying policies (TA 1970, s 399)

If a policy is not a qualifying policy there is no life assurance relief and the proceeds are not wholly tax-free. They are free of capital gains tax, but the capital appreciation is chargeable to income tax at the excess of the payer's marginal tax rate over basic rate in the tax-year of surrender or assignment, subject to certain special provisions.

Investment bonds

A non-qualifying policy usually takes the form of a single premium investment bond. When invested by the life office the single premium should grow more rapidly than an equivalent amount in the hands of a higher-rate taxpayer reinvesting net income from a conventional investment. You are able to make withdrawals of not more than 5% of the initial investment in each policy year (ending on the anniversary of the policy) without attracting a tax liability at that time, such withdrawals being treated as partial surrenders which are only taken into account in calculating the final profit on the bond when it is cashed in. The 5% is a cumulative figure and amounts unused in any year swell the tax-free withdrawal available in a later year, which could be useful if you want to save the withdrawal facility for some particularly heavy item of expenditure. If you withdraw more than the permitted 5% figure you will be charged to tax on the excess, but only if your marginal rate of tax exceeds the basic rate, so that if the excess occurs in a year when you are a basic rate taxpayer no charge will arise. The same applies to the position when you finally cash in the bond, because if this can be arranged in a year when your income, even with the addition of the bond profit, will not attract higher rates, no tax will be payable (and see below as regards top-slicing relief). Thus it may be possible to surrender in a year when your income is low because of business losses, or following retirement. If the bond is cashed in on your death, the mortality element of the profit as distinct from the surplus on the underlying investments is not taxable, and since the income of the year of death will usually not cover a full tax-year, even on the taxable portion there may be little tax liability at rates above the basic rate.

Top slicing relief (TA 1970, s 400)

In the tax-year when you cash in the bond top-slicing relief is available to lessen the impact of the higher-rate charge. (Top-slicing relief is also available where a tax charge arises on early surrender of a qualifying policy.) The surplus on the bond is divided by the number of complete years it has been held, and the amount arrived at treated as the top slice of your income, to ascertain the tax rate, which is then applied to the full profit. The longer the bond has been held the smaller the annual equivalent on which the tax charge is based. See example 2.

Example 2

		£
Taxpayer purchases investment bond for		10,000
He takes annual withdrawals of £500 for six years		
(covered by 5% rule)	3,000	
He cashes in bond in 1983/84 for	11,800	14,800
Profit liable to tax in 1983/84		£4,800

His taxable income after all allowances and reliefs is £14,300, including £6,500 investment income.

Annual equivalent of bond profit (1/6th × £4,800)	800	
Tax thereon as extra unearned income: 300 @ 30%	90	
500 @ 40%	200	290
Remainder of surcharge exempt band (£7,100)	600	—
Balance of investment income @ 15%	200	30
		320
Less basic rate tax on £800 @ 30%		240
Tax at excess rates on £800		£80
Tax charge on full profit of £4,800 is £80 × 6, or		£480

If you are an astute investor you will usually want to switch your investments from time to time, say from equities to properties, then to gilts and so on. For a small administration charge a life office will let you switch the investments underlying your bond, and the switch has no tax effect, other than the tax charge on any extra profit that is eventually realised.

To give you added flexibility it is possible to take out a number of smaller bonds, so that you can arrange to cash them as and when necessary, and an element of double discounting arises in that the original investment is being cashed over a number of years and the amount liable to tax in any year is itself top-sliced in arriving at the tax payable. This type of arrangement may be used as an alternative to a purchased life annuity to fund a qualifying policy, and also to pay large items of recurrent expenditure such as school fees.

Use of trust funds

The principle of a trust is that where there is an interest in possession (which means that someone is entitled as of right to the income from the trust funds) the fund is deemed to belong to the life tenant for capital transfer tax purposes.

If you take out a policy on your own life in trust for, say, your children, the policy is thus deemed to belong to them, and, when the proceeds are received, there is no capital transfer tax charge because all that has happened is that the child no longer has an interest in a trust fund but has free estate (the cash proceeds) instead.

Example 3

Taxpayer takes out a qualifying policy on his own life assuring £100,000 on his death. The first annual premium is £5,000 gross, £4,250 after 15% life assurance relief.

The policy is gifted to trustees for the benefit of his son, but he continues to pay the premiums.

The effect is:

The taxpayer will continue to get life assurance relief because he is paying the premiums.
The gift of the net annual premiums will be covered by the capital transfer tax exemption for gifts out of income.
The son will receive the eventual proceeds without any tax charge whatsoever.

Tax points

- Life assurance relief at 15% is available on a qualifying policy on your own life or your spouse's life no matter how young you are, and whether or not you are a taxpayer, except that the Revenue consider that a child under 12 is not capable of understanding the nature of the transaction and cannot be said to have made the contract. A policy can still be taken out by a younger child but life assurance relief is not available until they reach age 12.

- There is no point in taking out a policy on your own life to cover any capital transfer tax arising on your death if the policy forms part of your estate. Although it will produce a capital sum, that sum will increase the taxable estate, and moreover will not be available until a grant of probate or administration has been obtained. A policy for the benefit of someone else will escape tax in your estate and the policy monies will be available to that person on production of the death certificate and appropriate claim form.

- A wide range of ways of investing through life assurance and purchased annuities is on offer by the various life offices, and an arrangement can often be tailored to your specific requirements. Specialist advice on what is available is essential.

- A single premium bond can be a simple and convenient way of investing without the need for any complex records such as those required when you invest on the Stock Exchange.

- Bonds are also a convenient way to get into and out of the property market by choice of appropriate funds, and you can give away one of a series of property fund supported bonds much more easily than giving land itself, with no capital transfer tax charge if the gift is kept within the annual exemption.

44
The overseas element

Background

There are two aspects to the overseas element: the tax treatment of UK citizens and UK-resident companies with income or assets abroad; and the tax treatment of foreign nationals or foreign-resident companies with income or assets in the UK. In all cases the tax liability may be affected by double taxation relief.

An individual's liability to UK tax depends on his country of residence, of ordinary residence and of domicile. For a company, ordinary residence and domicile are not normally significant, and the company's tax liability depends only on its residence. Within the scope of this book it is only possible to give a brief outline of the meaning of residence, ordinary residence and domicile. The Inland Revenue publishes a useful booklet IR 20, 'Residents and Non-residents, Liability to Tax in the United Kingdom', covering the provisions in more detail.

Residence and ordinary residence of individuals (TA 1970, ss 49–51, 153)

Residence is a question of fact and requires physical presence in a country. It is possible for an individual to be resident in more than one country for tax purposes. Ordinary residence is broadly equivalent to habitual residence.

You are regarded as remaining resident and ordinarily resident in the UK despite a temporary absence abroad unless the absence spans a complete tax-year. If you leave the UK to take up employment abroad for a period which will span a complete tax-year you are regarded as non-resident from the date you leave and as a new resident when you return. If you leave the UK for any other purpose you may be provisionally treated as non-resident if you can produce evidence of ceasing residence, e.g. selling your house here and buying one abroad, and the provisional ruling will be confirmed when your absence has spanned a complete tax-year. If evidence is not available at the start of the absence your residence status will be tested over three years, and if at the end of that time it is clear that you intend to remain out of the country the period of non-residence will be backdated to the time of leaving.

New permanent residents are regarded as resident and ordinarily resident from the date of arrival in the UK. A visitor who does not know how long he is going to stay will be regarded as ordinarily resident from the beginning of the tax-year in which the third anniversary of his arrival falls, or possibly earlier if it becomes clear before then that he intends to stay on a long-term basis.

Those who visit the UK without taking up permanent residence and who do not have accommodation available in the UK will be regarded as resident in any tax-year in which their visits add up to six months in total. If UK visits, while not amounting to six months a year, average three months a year for four consecutive years a visitor is then regarded as becoming both resident and ordinarily resident in the UK. If it was clear at the outset that he was going to make such regular, substantial visits he may be regarded as resident and ordinarily resident from the start.

If a person has accommodation available in the UK he is regarded as resident in any year when he visits the UK, no matter how short the visit, unless he works full-time in a business, profession or employment abroad, in which case the accommodation is disregarded in determining his status. Accommodation rented for use during a temporary stay is ignored if the rental period is less than two years for furnished accommodation or one year for unfurnished accommodation.

Where a business is carried on in partnership and the business is controlled and managed abroad, the partnership is deemed to reside abroad even though some of the partners are resident in the UK.

Residence of companies

A company resides where its central management and control are situated, and the place where the directors meet may be an important indicator. A company may have more than one country of residence, but this requires some substantial business operations in each place as well as part of the management and control.

Domicile

Domicile is different from nationality and residence and a person can only have one domicile at any one time. An individual's domicile is usually the country in which he has his permanent home. A domicile of origin is acquired at birth and under UK law this is the father's domicile for legitimate children and the mother's domicile for illegitimate children. A wife used to take her husband's domicile automatically, but since 1 January 1974 a wife's domicile is ascertained independently of her husband's. Women already married on 1 January 1974 retain the domicile they had on that date until action is taken to change it.

The domicile of origin may be abandoned and a domicile of choice acquired. This necessitates positive action, e.g. changing residence, making a will under the laws of the new country, obtaining citizenship of the new country. A high standard of proof is required to establish a change of domicile.

Domicile sometimes has an extended meaning for capital transfer tax—see chapter 7.

Effect of residence, ordinary residence and domicile on UK tax position for individuals

Income tax is charged broadly on the world income of UK residents, subject to certain deductions for earnings abroad and for individuals who are not ordinarily resident or not domiciled in the UK. Non-residents are liable to income tax only on income that arises in the UK.

Capital gains tax is charged on individuals who are resident *or* ordinarily resident in the UK—on world gains if domiciled in the UK, and on gains arising in or remitted to the UK if domiciled elsewhere.

Development land tax is charged, subject to certain exemptions, where development value is realised on the disposal of UK land, whether the person disposing of it is UK-resident and domiciled or not.

Residence has no bearing on capital transfer tax, which applies to an individual's world wide property if he is domiciled in the UK and to his UK property if he is domiciled elsewhere.

Basis of charge for foreign income (TA 1970, ss 93, 122–124, 181; FA 1974, ss 22, 23)

The basis of charge under Schedule E for income from employment is the earnings for the tax-year, no matter when they are received. Deductions are available as indicated below.

Other income from abroad may be charged under Schedule C, Schedule D, Case IV or Schedule D, Case V.

Schedule C relates to the income from government securities, both UK and foreign, that is paid through a UK paying agent such as a bank. The paying agent deducts and accounts for tax at the basic rate, so that a basic-rate taxpayer has no further liability, those liable at rates in excess of the basic rate are charged the excess and those not liable to tax can claim a refund. The withholding of basic-rate tax at source also applies to foreign dividends and interest chargeable under Schedule D where they are paid through a UK paying agent.

Schedule D, Case IV covers income from foreign securities, such as foreign debentures, and Schedule D, Case V charges income from foreign possessions, which covers all other income from abroad except that from employment. Except where tax is deducted at source as explained above, income under Schedule D, Cases IV and V is normally charged on the preceding year basis. For the first two years and the last year, however, tax is charged on the actual income of the tax-year. For the third year the taxpayer may choose the actual basis instead of the preceding year basis, and for the penultimate year the Revenue may do likewise. The effect of the taxpayer or Revenue electing for the actual basis is that a different year's income is charged twice or escapes assessment as the case may be. These provisions are the same as those for Schedule D, Case III, which are illustrated in chapter 34.

For individuals who are resident, ordinarily resident and domiciled in the UK, foreign business profits assessed under Case V are reduced by 25% and foreign pensions by 10% (or by 50% if the pension is paid as a result of Nazi persecution).

If you are resident but not ordinarily resident or not domiciled in the UK, you are not charged to tax on income from abroad unless you remit it to the UK. If you do remit it you are charged on the full amount remitted, with no percentage deduction.

Where the remittances basis applies, the assessment rules outlined above for Schedule D, Cases IV and V apply to remittances, rather than to the income arising. The first year of charge is the year in which income is first remitted to the UK.

UK citizens with earnings from employment abroad (TA 1970, s 181; FA 1977, s 31 and Sch 7)

If your employment abroad spans a complete tax-year and all your duties are performed abroad, you will be treated as non-resident from the date of leaving and as a new resident when you return. Otherwise you will remain UK-resident.

Notice that it is not the length of the absence but whether it spans a tax-year that is important, so that if you were working away from 1 April 1983 to 30 April 1984, a period of thirteen months spanning a tax-year, you would be non-resident for that period, but if you were working away from July 1983 to December 1984, a period of eighteen months that does not span a tax-year, you would remain resident throughout.

If you are non-resident you escape tax on all income other than that arising in the UK.

If you are resident, you are liable to tax on your earnings both in the UK and abroad, but a deduction of 25% is allowed for earnings during short or intermittent absences working abroad, and a deduction of 100%—which effectively makes the earnings exempt from UK tax—for earnings during a long absence. A day does not count as a day of absence unless you are absent at the end of it, i.e. midnight.

To qualify for the 25% deduction you must have thirty qualifying days of absence in the tax-year. A qualifying day is broadly a working day, but days when you are travelling in the performance of your duties abroad are included, and if an absence spans seven days or more it is looked at as a whole, so that normal days off, say on Saturday and Sunday, would count as qualifying days. The 25% deduction is given against the proportion of your earnings that the number of qualifying days abroad bears to 365, but a larger proportion may be given if it is shown to be reasonable, for example if there is an increased rate of pay for the overseas duties. The 25% deduction is usually operated through the PAYE system, either by a coding allowance or by an arrangement with the Revenue which allows the employer to charge tax on 75% of the overseas earnings.

If you have a separate employment abroad with a non-resident employer the 25% deduction is given whether you satisfy the 30 day rule or not.

The 100% deduction is given in respect of earnings abroad during a qualifying period of at least 365 days. A qualifying period is one consisting either wholly of days of absence or of days of absence linked by UK visits that do not overstep certain limits. The limits are that UK visits must not exceed 62 consecutive days and that the days spent in the UK must not exceed one-sixth of the total days in the period. This one-sixth rule cannot be calculated as a proportion of the total spell of employment abroad but must be considered at the end of each absence. See example 1.

Example 1

Two employees each spend fifteen months working abroad (not spanning a tax-year), the time abroad and in the UK being as follows:

	1st employee Days	2nd employee Days	1/6th limit exceeded 1st employee	2nd employee
Abroad	100	100		
UK	10	60		
Abroad	150	150	No (10/260)	Yes (60/310)
UK	60	10		
Abroad	130	130	No (70/450)	
	450	450		

A deduction of 100% is given to first employee.

Second employee will only get a deduction of 25% on each of the three separate periods of absence abroad, unless he can link the 2nd and 3rd absences to a further spell of overseas duty covering 365 days in all, with the UK visit limits not being breached.

If, although he satisfies the 365 day qualifying period rules, an employee has both overseas earnings and UK earnings, i.e. for work during his UK visits, the 100% deduction applies only to the overseas earnings.

The 100% deduction also applies to earnings in a period of paid leave at the end of the employment, but if the paid leave is spent in the UK it cannot be counted as part of the 365 day qualifying period. Thus a twelve-month contract abroad with the last month of it spent on leave in the UK would not qualify, whereas if the leave were spent abroad it would qualify (provided that the 62 day and 1/6th rules were satisfied).

As with the 25% deduction, the 100% deduction is given where possible through the PAYE system.

Travelling and board and lodging expenses (FA 1977, s 32)

For an employee resident and ordinarily resident in the UK, the costs of travelling from and to the UK when taking up and ceasing an employment wholly abroad are allowed, and also the costs of travelling between a UK employment and a foreign employment and between foreign employments. If the employer pays or reimburses the cost of board and lodging abroad the amount paid or reimbursed is offset by an expenses allowance, but no deduction is given for board and lodging payments that an employee bears himself.

If an absence lasts 60 days or more (not necessarily in one tax-year) an employee can claim a deduction for the travelling expenses of two journeys per person in each direction for his wife and children (under 18 at the start of the journey) to visit him, and/or for him to visit them, but only where the travelling expenses are paid or reimbursed by the employer and not where the employee bears them himself.

Earned income from self-employment abroad (FA 1978, s 27 and Sch 4)

If a business is controlled in the UK the profits are assessable under the rules of Schedule D, Case I even though some of the profits are earned abroad, but a 25% deduction is given on the proportion of the assessable profit that the number of qualifying days abroad in the tax-year bears to 365 (or, in the first or last year of the trade, to the number of days for which the trade was carried on). The assessable profits are profits after capital allowances and stock relief but before deducting losses. See example 2.

The definition of qualifying days is the same as for short or intermittent absences in an employment (see above), a qualifying day being either a working or travelling day or one of seven consecutive days which, taken as a whole, are substantially devoted to the activities of the trade, and no relief is available unless there are at least thirty qualifying days in the tax-year.

Because of the previous year basis of assessment, there is no matching of the 25% deduction against the profits actually earned abroad except in the opening and closing years, when profits are charged on an actual basis. A claim for the deduction must be made within two years from the end of the relevant tax year.

If a business is controlled abroad the profits are charged under Schedule D, Case V as income from a foreign possession.

Example 2

Sole trader spends 50 days abroad in connection with his business in 1983/84. His 1983/84 assessable profits, based on his accounts year to 31 December 1982, are £12,000 and he has claimed capital allowances and stock relief totalling £2,000.

	£
Relief for work abroad:	
Profits	12,000
Less capital allowances and stock relief	2,000
	10,000

$50/365 \times £10,000 = £1,370$.
25% thereof $= £343$, reducing assessment to £9,657.

A UK-resident sole trader would find it virtually impossible to establish that his business was controlled abroad, so it is generally only the profits of partnerships that may be assessed under Case V instead of Case I.

If a business is controlled and carried on wholly abroad but has some UK-resident partners, their profit shares are charged under Case V. If a foreign controlled partnership carries on some trading operations in the UK, the UK activities are assessed under Case I and the foreign activities under Case V.

Other sources of foreign income (TA 1970, s 418)

For UK citizens who are resident and ordinarily resident in the UK, other sources of foreign income, such as dividends and interest, are charged on the full amount arising, with no percentage deduction available. There are provisions to treat income that is locked into a foreign country, and not capable of being extracted, as not arising until it is free to be brought to the UK.

Where the income is not received through a paying agent and thus not subject to deduction of tax at source the preceding year basis normally applies as explained above.

Leaving and returning to the UK

In the tax-year when you leave the UK to take up permanent or long-term residence abroad, you are treated as non-resident from the date of departure and get a full year's personal allowances against your income for the part of the year prior to your departure. As a non-resident you will be exempt from UK tax on interest from certain government securities, and you will also, by extra-statutory concession, escape tax on bank interest for any complete tax-years of non-residence, unless the interest is taxed in the name of a UK agent or the UK tax is offset against relief due to you under a non-resident's claim for personal allowances. You do not escape liability to capital gains tax unless you are both not resident and not ordinarily resident in the UK.

If you are abroad for some time and then become UK-resident again, you are treated as resident for income tax from the date of arrival, with a full year's allowances on your income for the remainder of the year. If you have been away for at least thirty-six months, capital gains are subject to assessment only if they arise after your return. If you have been away for less than thirty-six months you will be charged on all gains in the tax-year you return, whether they arise before or after your arrival.

Capital transfer tax will continue to be chargeable so long as you remain UK-domiciled or are deemed UK-domiciled (see chapter 7). Development land tax will apply to development value realised on the sale of UK land whether you are resident or not.

Non-residents and personal allowances (TA 1970, s 27; FA 1972, s 87)

Non-residents cannot normally claim UK personal allowances. Non-resident British subjects and certain other categories of non-resident may do so if it is their advantage. A claim for allowances may also be provided for by the terms of a double tax agreement.

The relief, if any, is ascertained by calculating tax on the world income (after deducting personal allowances) as if it were liable to UK tax at all rates, including investment income surcharge where appropriate, and then taking the fraction of the tax arising that relates to the income liable to UK tax. In many instances this would give a higher tax liability than the tax withheld at source on UK income, particularly where there are UK dividends, because dividends have to be taken into account inclusive of the related tax credits for a non-resident's relief claim, whereas if no claim is made a non-resident is liable to UK tax only on the amount of the dividend excluding the credit and then only to the extent of the excess, if any, of higher rates and surcharge over the basic rate.

Husband and wife (TA 1970, s 42)

The residence and ordinary residence status of a husband and wife are determined independently, and if one is resident and the other not resident in the UK they are taxed as if they were permanently separated, except that this cannot have the effect of increasing the joint tax liability.

If for example a wife remains in the UK while her husband is abroad for a period which spans a tax-year, she will be taxed as a UK-resident on her UK and foreign income, with a single person's reliefs, and her husband will, as a non-resident, be exempt from UK tax on income arising outside the UK and will be able to claim proportionate reliefs as a non-resident if it is to his advantage.

309

If a wife accompanies her husband while he is working abroad but they have UK accommodation available, she will be treated as resident in any year when she visits the UK, however short the visit.

Earned income of visitors to the UK (TA 1970, s 181; FA 1974, Sch 2)

A visitor to the UK who does not remain long enough to be classed as resident is nonetheless liable to UK tax on UK earnings (although sometimes he may be exempt under the provisions of a double tax treaty). If the earnings are from a UK employer the tax liability arises on the whole earnings. If the visitor is not UK-domiciled and his employer is not UK-resident, he is charged to tax on only 50% of the UK earnings. Non-residents cannot normally claim UK personal allowances (except as indicated above).

If a visitor is classed as resident but not ordinarily resident he is still liable only on UK earnings (reduced by 50% if they are from a non-resident employer and he is non-UK domiciled), unless he has earnings from abroad which he remits to the UK, in which case he will be taxed as well on the full amount remitted with no percentage deduction. It is important for visitors to keep records (for example separate bank accounts for capital and for different sources of income) to enable them to demonstrate whether or not remittances out of foreign earnings have taken place.

Once a visitor has been in the UK long enough to be classed as ordinarily resident (or where he is ordinarily resident from the outset because of the length of his proposed stay) he is charged to tax in the same way as a UK citizen, except that the 50% deduction still applies to earnings from a non-resident employer if the visitor is not UK-domiciled. The 50% deduction drops to only 25% once a visitor has been resident in the UK for nine out of the previous ten tax-years.

Other income, capital gains and capital transfers of visitors to the UK who are domiciled abroad

Non-residents have no liability to UK tax on foreign income, but are fully liable to tax on income from UK sources, other than interest on various government securities that carry tax exemption if the holder is not ordinarily resident in the UK. The interest on such tax-exempt securities will be paid without deduction of tax if a claim is made to that effect (TA 1970, s 99).

If you are in the UK long enough to be classed as resident you will be liable to UK tax on foreign sources of income if you remit them to the UK. As a resident you are also liable to UK capital gains tax on chargeable gains arising in or remitted to the UK.

A gain on the disposal of your only or main residence is, subject to certain conditions, exempt from tax.

You will be liable to development land tax if you realise development value in excess of £50,000 on the sale of UK land in any tax-year (see chapter 6). Capital transfer tax will apply to gifts of UK assets (see chapter 7) but there is an annual exemption of £3,000 and the first £60,000 of chargeable transfers does not attract tax.

Social security and national insurance contributions

If you leave the UK for permanent or semi-permanent residence abroad your liability to pay national insurance contributions normally ceases when you leave, unless you work abroad for a UK employer, in which case contributions continue for the first 52 weeks. It may be to your advantage to pay voluntary contributions. Child benefit is not normally payable unless both parent and child are UK-resident, but it may be paid for up to six months in some circumstances.

Visitors and new permanent residents are normally liable to pay national insurance contributions from the date of arrival, but exemption is often given for the first twelve months. Where an employee is liable the employer will be liable to pay employer's secondary contributions unless he is not UK-resident and does not have a place of business in the UK.

The general provisions are often varied by reciprocal social security arrangements and the position can be complex. Whether you are leaving or coming to the UK it is advisable to contact the local social security office to establish your own liability to make contributions and your benefits position.

Double taxation relief for individuals (TA 1970, ss 497, 498)

The United Kingdom has entered into double tax agreements with many countries to give relief where the same income is liable to tax in both countries. The agreements exempt certain income in one country or the other, or reduce the UK tax liability by the lesser of the overseas tax liability and the UK tax liability.

Sometimes the agreements provide for a UK paying agent to adjust the UK tax he deducts to take account of the foreign tax, so that for example the deduction on a foreign dividend may be 15% overseas withholding tax and 15% UK tax, making 30% in all.

Where there is no double tax agreement you may claim unilateral relief at the lower of the UK tax and the overseas tax. If double tax relief is not claimed the income is charged to UK tax net of the overseas tax suffered, but this is clearly not so advantageous.

Double tax relief is also given in respect of overseas tax on capital gains, the credit being limited to the amount of UK capital gains tax payable.

UK companies with interests abroad (TA 1970, ss 497, 498; FA 1972, s 100)

If a UK-resident company makes investments abroad the company is liable to corporation tax on income received, before deduction of foreign taxes, the income being included either under Schedule C (interest received through paying agents), Schedule D, Case IV (foreign securities) or Case V (foreign possessions, which would include foreign branches and foreign sub-sidiaries), and also on 15/26ths of any capital gains on the disposal of foreign assets.

If a UK-resident company carries on business abroad through a branch or agency it is charged under Schedule D, Case V on all the profits of the branch or agency. Where business is carried on through a foreign subsidiary the UK company's liability would arise only on amounts received from the subsidiary by way of interest or dividends.

Double tax relief is available in respect of the foreign tax suffered on both income and gains.

Normally only direct foreign taxes are taken into account for double tax relief, but if a UK company receives dividends from a foreign company in which it owns 10% or more of the voting power, underlying taxes on the profits out of which the dividends are paid are taken into account as well. In this case the amount included in UK profits is the dividend plus both the direct and underlying foreign taxes.

Double tax relief is given either unilaterally or under the provisions of a double tax agreement.

The relief on overseas income cannot exceed the UK mainstream corpora-tion tax payable on the overseas income, after all deductions including advance corporation tax. It is, however, provided that in deciding how much corporation tax is attributable to the overseas income, charges on income may be deducted against any source of profits, including chargeable gains, in the most beneficial way, and advance corporation tax may similarly be set against any source of income so as to maximise the amount available for double tax relief, but the set-off of ACT against any source of income can never exceed the maximum, currently 30%.

Double tax relief in respect of foreign tax paid on chargeable gains is limited to the UK corporation tax payable thereon.

See example 3 generally.

Where double tax relief is restricted the unrelieved foreign tax (£10,000 in example 3) is wasted and cannot be carried forward or back.

Non-resident companies with interests in the UK (TA 1970, ss 238(2), 246)

If a non-resident company carries on business in the UK through a branch or agency it is liable to corporation tax on the trading income from the branch, income from property or rights held by the branch and capital gains on the disposal of assets situated in the UK used for the trade or by the branch or agency; the company will also be liable to income tax on other UK sources not connected with the branch or agency.

Example 3

Company's profits for year to 31 March 1983 are:	£
UK trading profits	150,000
Foreign trading profits £500,000 less overseas tax of £200,000	300,000
Chargeable gains £52,000 × 15/26ths	30,000

The company paid debenture interest of £80,000 and ACT of £100,000.

Computation of double tax relief:

	Case I	Case V	Gains	Total
Profits	150,000	500,000	30,000	680,000
Less charges—				
debenture interest	(50,000)		(30,000)	(80,000)
Profits chargeable to corporation tax	100,000	500,000	—	600,000
Corporation tax @ 52%	52,000	260,000		312,000
Less ACT:				
Against UK income (maximum)	(30,000)			(30,000)
Against foreign income (balance)		(70,000)		(70,000)
	22,000	190,000		212,000
Less double tax relief (restricted)		(190,000)		(190,000)
Final mainstream tax payable	22,000			22,000

If a non-resident company does not carry on business in the UK through a branch or agency it is not liable to corporation tax but is liable to income tax on UK sources of income, e.g. under Schedule A on rental income from UK property.

UK subsidiaries of foreign companies (FA 1972, ss 84, 86)

A UK-resident subsidiary of a foreign company is liable to corporation tax in the same way as any other resident company, and an ACT liability arises on the payment of dividends. An overseas parent is not normally entitled to a tax credit on the dividend, although some double tax treaties provide for a limited credit.

Company ceasing to be resident or transferring business to a non-resident (TA 1970, s 482)

Treasury permission must usually be obtained if a company is to become non-resident or to transfer all or part of its business to a non-resident. General permission is, however, automatically available to companies incorporated after 1 August 1951 where more than 50% of the issued share capital was then and is still owned by persons not ordinarily resident in the UK.

Transfer pricing (TA 1970, s 485)

Non-arm's length transactions between associated bodies where one is and one is not resident in the UK have to be adjusted for tax purposes to the normal arm's length price.

Tax points

- Watch the timing of overseas work periods. Thirty days straddling two tax-years will not qualify for the 25% deduction, and breaching the UK visit limits for long absences will reduce your deduction from 100% to 25%.

- If you plan to obtain the 100% deduction for employment abroad or to have a period of non-UK residence, the situation may be changed by factors outside your control. Consider taking out insurance to cover the risk of extra tax liabilities through early return.

- Try to arrange for your employer to meet the cost of overseas board and lodging, otherwise in addition to having to bear the cost yourself you will get no tax relief on it.

- If your wife accompanies you when you go to work abroad, watch the rules about her residence status, particularly if your UK home remains available for your use.

- If you are charged on the remittance basis, keep funds abroad separate where possible so that you can demonstrate for example that a remittance represents capital not income (but remember that a foreign capital gain will attract UK capital gains tax if remitted).

- If you are becoming non-resident, review your investments to make sure they are still tax effective. The notional tax credit on building society interest, for example, is not available for double tax relief. Interest on certain government securities, on the other hand, is exempt from UK tax for a non-resident.

- Where overseas tax credits will exceed the UK mainstream corporation tax payable by a company that is a member of a group, consider surrendering ACT to another group member to avoid losing the benefit of the foreign tax credits.

45
Trusts and estates

Background

A trust or settlement comes into being when someone transfers assets to trustees who hold those assets for the benefit of one or more persons who will receive income and/or capital from the trust.

A trust can be created in lifetime, or on death by a will or under the intestacy rules where a person does not leave a will (sometimes referred to as a statutory trust). Where the trust comes into being on death, the personal representatives must first complete the administration of the estate.

Administration of an estate

Personal representatives deal with the estate of a deceased either under the terms of his will or according to the rules of intestacy where there is no will. Capital transfer tax will be payable on the estate if the chargeable transfers in lifetime together with the estate at death exceed the exempt threshold (currently £60,000), but tax does not arise on property left to a surviving spouse. The way in which the tax is calculated is dealt with in chapter 7. The administration period during which the personal representatives deal with the tax liabilities and the distribution of the unsettled part of the estate may last some months or even years if the estate is complex.

Income during the administration period (TA 1970, ss 426–432)

The personal representatives are liable to income tax at the basic rate on any income arising during the administration period (but not at higher rates). They are not entitled to personal reliefs. This income will be distributed to the beneficiaries entitled to it either because they are entitled absolutely to the assets or because, while the assets remain in trust, they are entitled to the income. In the latter case, any payments on account of income during the administration period are regarded as net of basic-rate tax, the gross amount being included in the beneficiary's income of the year of receipt. When the administration period is concluded and the final amount of income due to each beneficiary ascertained, it is re-allocated over the relevant tax-years on a day-to-day basis, and the tax position of the beneficiaries for those years is adjusted accordingly.

Capital gains during the administration period (CGTA 1979, s 49 and Sch 1)

No capital gains tax arises on the transfer of assets to legatees, who are deemed to acquire them at market value at the date of death. Assets that pass to the personal representatives are also deemed to be acquired by them at market value at that date, and gains arising on any assets disposed of by the personal representatives are liable to tax. The annual exemption, currently £5,300, is available in the tax-year of death and the next two years, but not thereafter. If any losses arise they may only be set against gains. They cannot be transferred to beneficiaries.

End of administration period

The administration period will end either when the residue is finally distributed if no trust has been created, or when the residue is transferred to a trust fund. The trustees and personal representatives are usually, but not necessarily, the same persons. There is no chargeable gain on personal representatives when they transfer assets to trustees, the assets transferred to the trust being deemed to be acquired at market value at the date of death.

Tax liability on setting up a trust (TA 1970, ss 434–456; FA 1975, s 25 and Sch 5; FA 1980, s 79; FA 1981, s 78)

Where a settlement is created on death the deceased's estate will be charged to capital transfer tax on the property transferred to the trust in the usual way.

On the creation of a lifetime settlement the settlor is liable to capital transfer tax at lifetime rates on the property transferred, and the transfer has to be grossed up if the settlor also pays the tax. It is possible for the settlor to settle sums on himself or his spouse, so that any income arising is assessable as his. In that event, capital transfer tax is not payable since the settlor or his wife is still enjoying the benefit of the capital.

The transfer into trust is also deemed to be a disposal at open market value for capital gains tax, but instead of paying any tax arising at that time, the settlor may elect for the gain to be rolled over and treated as reducing the trustees' base acquisition cost.

As far as income tax is concerned, the settlor will continue to be liable for income tax on the trust income if:

(a) the period of the settlement does not exceed six years; or
(b) either the settlor or spouse has power to revoke the settlement within six years; or
(c) either the settlor or spouse retains any interest in or benefit from the income or the trust assets.

Further, where the settlor or his spouse create a settlement in favour of their own children who are under 18 years of age and unmarried, the whole of the income will be regarded as that of the settlor except in the case of accumulation and maintenance trusts (see below). The placing by the parent of any capital sum in an account in the child's name is sufficient to be regarded as a settlement.

Types of trust

There are basically three types of trust:

(a) Trusts with an interest in possession, i.e. where someone is entitled as of right to receive the income of the trust.
(b) Discretionary trusts, in which no-one is entitled as of right to the income.
(c) Accumulation and maintenance trusts, under which income is broadly accumulated for minor children until they reach a specified age.

Trusts with an interest in possession

Income Tax

Where there is an interest in possession, one or more beneficiaries is entitled as of right to the trust income.

The trustees are charged to basic-rate tax only, not to higher rates or to investment income surcharge, on income arising in the trust fund. Income is calculated in the same way as for an individual, with deductions permitted for qualifying interest paid, say on a loan to buy property for letting. Trustees are not, however, entitled to personal reliefs. There is no relief for expenses of managing the trust, which are therefore deducted from the after-tax income.

The beneficiaries entitled to the income are liable to income tax thereon at their top rate, whether they draw the income or leave it to their credit in the fund, with however a credit for the basic-rate tax paid by the trustees. If, say, the trust income is £1,000 gross, £700 net, and the trust expenses are £70, the beneficiary will receive £630, which is deemed to be gross income of £900 with a tax credit of £270. If the beneficiary's tax credit exceed his liability he may make a repayment claim.

The need to pay expenses out of the taxed income of the trust can be avoided to the extent that specific income can be mandated direct to the beneficiary, saving any administration expenses that would be incurred in passing on the income.

Capital gains tax (CGTA 1979, ss 54–56 and Sch 1)

When the trustees dispose of any chargeable assets they are liable to capital gains tax thereon, subject to an annual exemption for any tax-year (£2,650 for 1983/84). Where there are a number of settlements created by the same settlor the amount of £2,650 is divided equally between them, subject to a minimum exemption of £530 for each trust.

When a beneficiary becomes absolutely entitled to trust property following a life tenant's death, there is a deemed disposal of the relevant part of the trust property by the trustees, and the beneficiary is deemed to acquire it at its market value, but no capital gains tax liability arises, thus giving a tax-free uplift in value. A tax-free uplift also occurs on property that remains settled after a life tenant's death. When a life interest terminates other than on the death of a life tenant there is no capital gains tax effect and the property retains the value it had when it was first put into the settlement.

When a beneficiary becomes absolutely entitled to trust property other than on the death of a life tenant there is a deemed disposal at market value at that date, and tax will arise accordingly. The trustees and the beneficiary may, however, elect for the tax liability to be deferred and the gain regarded as reducing the base acquisition cost of the beneficiary.

Capital transfer tax (FA 1975, Sch 5)

Someone with a life interest in a trust, i.e. with an interest in possession, is deemed to be entitled to the underlying capital, so that he will be deemed to make a chargeable transfer thereof if he ceases to be entitled to the income either on ceasing to hold the life interest or on death. Although the tax is calculated by reference to his own cumulative transfers, the liability for payment rests with the trustees. See example 1.

Example 1

Taxpayer has made lifetime chargeable transfers of £50,000. At his death on 30 September 1983 his free estate was valued at £100,000. He was also entitled to the income from trust funds, the value of which were £50,000 and to which his daughter became absolutely entitled. He was a widower, his estate being left to his son.

The capital transfer tax payable on his death is:

		Gross	Tax
Lifetime transfers		50,000	—
Free estate at death	100,000		
Trust funds at death	50,000	150,000	56,750
		£200,000	56,750

The tax is payable as follows:

From free estate	$\dfrac{100,000}{150,000} \times$	£56,750	37,833
From trust funds	$\dfrac{50,000}{150,000} \times$	£56,750	18,917
			£56,750

319

Quick succession relief is available where there are successive charges on the trust property within five years (see chapter 7).

The inclusion of trust funds in the life tenant's estate prevents wealth being protected from capital transfer tax through the use of trusts. It does, however, have advantages, because there is no further charge when someone with a life interest receives a capital sum from the fund, since he is deemed to be entitled to the capital anyway. This means that you can transfer funds without giving the transferee absolute control over them, but with the value of the assets fixed as far as your liability is concerned at the time of the transfer. This may be better than waiting until the time when you want to give someone assets directly, because they may have increased in value in the meantime and your own wealth and cumulative transfers may also have increased so that tax would be attracted at a higher rate.

Reversion of trust funds to settlor (FA 1975 Sch 5; FA 1981, s 104)

Provision for, say, a dependent relative may take the form of a settlement of funds for the life of the relative, with the capital reverting to the settlor at the relative's death, the relative having enjoyed the income in the meantime. Example 1 above illustrates that trust funds are taken into account for capital transfer tax when the life tenant dies. The relative's capital position in these circumstances will not usually give rise to a tax liability anyway, but, even if it would, it is specifically provided that trust funds are not aggregated with the estate of the life tenant when they revert to the settlor or his spouse.

There are various anti-avoidance provisions to prevent abuse of this rule.

Discretionary trusts

Income tax and capital gains tax (FA 1973, ss 16, 17)

Where trustees have discretionary power as to the distribution of income and no-one is entitled to it as of right, then the income tax treatment is the same as that for trusts with an interest in possession, except that the trustees are liable not only at the basic rate but also at the investment income surcharge rate of 15% (with no exempt threshold available). They are, however, entitled to deduct their expenses in arriving at the amount chargeable at the additional 15% rate.

Any income paid to beneficiaries is deemed to be after deduction of 45% tax and grossed up accordingly, with the corresponding credit available to the beneficiary. Income of £110 net is thus deemed to be income of £200 from which £90 tax has been deducted.

Capital gains tax will be payable on disposals of chargeable assets by the trustees, subject to the annual exemption of £2,650 for 1983/84 (or proportionate part thereof where there are associated trusts). When a beneficiary becomes absolutely entitled to any chargeable assets of the trust, they will be deemed to be disposed of at market value at that date. Capital gains tax will be payable accordingly unless a joint election is made to defer the gain under the gifts relief provisions (see p 42).

Capital transfer tax (FA 1982, ss 101–112 and Schs 15, 17)

The capital transfer tax position of discretionary trusts is complex and is to some extent dependent upon the position of the settlor. Since there is no interest in possession, no-one is treated as entitled to the underlying capital. In order to prevent the capital transfer tax avoidance this would otherwise permit there is a charge on the trust funds every ten years. A charge also arises when funds leave the trust (called an exit charge) and when a person becomes absolutely entitled to the fund or to an interest in possession.

Accumulation and maintenance trusts

These are a special sort of discretionary trust to enable a parent to provide funds for the benefit of children without complete commitment on creation of the trust.

Income tax (TA 1970, ss 437–444)

The rule that a parent remains chargeable to income tax on income settled on his own unmarried children under age 18 does not apply where the capital and income are required to be held on accumulation and maintenance trusts for the benefit of the children, except to the extent that trust funds are used for the education and maintenance of the children.

Income accumulated within the fund is chargeable on the trustees at the basic tax rate and, since the trust is a discretionary trust, at the additional rate of 15%. When the accumulated income is transferred when the child reaches the appropriate age it does so as capital and thus does not attract tax.

The additional rate is not payable on any amounts paid out for the education or maintenance of the children. Such amounts are treated as the settlor's income, but he is entitled to recover from the trustees the tax paid by him at excess rates.

Capital gains tax

The capital gains tax position of an accumulation and maintenance trust is the same as that of any other discretionary trust (see above).

Capital transfer tax (FA 1982, s 114)

Accumulation and maintenance settlements receive favourable treatment for capital transfer tax where one or more of the beneficiaries will become entitled to the property (or an interest in possession therein) not later than age 25. To qualify for this treatment the settlement must either terminate as an accumulation and maintenance settlement not more than 25 years after its creation (or 25 years from 15 April 1976 if later) or all the beneficiaries must have a common grandparent. If such grandchildren fail to survive, their children or widows/widowers qualify. 'Children' includes step-children, adopted and illegitimate children.

The advantages of such a settlement are that there is no ten-yearly charge on the trust funds and no exit charges when a distribution is made to a beneficiary or when a beneficiary becomes absolutely entitled to the trust property or to an interest in possession. The transfer of property from the settlement to the beneficiaries is thus free of tax in these circumstances.

Position of infants

Where income is paid to beneficiaries, it is deemed to be after deduction of tax at 30%, or, for discretionary trusts, 45%. If the beneficiaries are infants a repayment of tax will often be due. The parent or guardian can make the appropriate claim, or the claim may be made by the beneficiary himself on reaching age 18, in respect of the previous six years.

Development land tax (DLTA 1976, ss 5, 9, 12 and Sch 8(54))

A liability can arise on realised development value where personal representatives sell an interest in land during the administration of an estate, or where land is disposed of by trustees of a will trust, the £50,000 exemption being available in each case.

The £50,000 exemption may not be available on a disposal by trustees where they have acquired land from a connected person within the previous six years.

Stamp Duty

There is no ad valorem duty where a trust is created by will.

A 50 pence duty will arise on a lifetime declaration of trust, but ad valorem duty will arise on the transfer of a beneficial interest.

Later transfers of property into the trust fund will depend upon what that property is and whether its transfer attracts duty.

On a transfer of trust property to a beneficiary, there is no ad valorem duty.

Tax points

- Where a person entitled to trust income has unused personal reliefs, it is better to mandate income direct to him, since in this way it will be greater than if it is first depleted by trust expenses, with a consequentially higher income tax repayment where tax has been deducted at source.

- Since capital transfer tax is reduced where the value transferred is lower, it is usually beneficial to make transfers earlier rather than later, giving the intended beneficiary an interest for the time being in the income through an appropriately drawn up trust.

The supporting capital can eventually be transferred free of capital transfer tax to the person enjoying the income, the value for capital gains tax purposes when it was originally settled also being retained.

- Where assets are put into trust, the trustees, like any other donee, may pay the capital transfer tax. If they do, and dependent upon the type of asset, the tax may be payable by instalments. The grossing-up of the gift for tax calculation purposes where the donor pays the tax is also avoided.

- A stamp duty saving will arise when making a declaration of trust where the sum originally settled is minimal, with later additions being made to the trust fund.

46
Charities and charitable trusts

Formation and legal status

Many hundreds of new charities are set up and registered each year. In order to register a charity, it is necessary to satisfy the Charity Commissioners in England and Wales, or the Inland Revenue in Scotland and Northern Ireland, that the purposes or objects of the organisation fall entirely under one or more 'heads of charity'. These are:

> The relief of poverty.
> The advancement of education.
> The advancement of religion.
> Other purposes beneficial to the community.

A charity may be a limited company with a separate legal existence independent of its members, or an unincorporated association which has no separate status so that assets must be held on its behalf by trustees.

Although charitable trusts are frequently national organisations, such as the Churches' children's organisations and bodies for medical research and care, there is nothing to prevent individuals creating and registering a charitable trust which remains under their control as trustees, so long as the 'heads of charity' are satisfied.

Tax status

Income tax and corporation tax (TA 1970, s 360)

Registered charities are exempt from tax on investment income used only for charitable purposes, including that derived from covenants. Trading profits are not automatically exempt but will be so where the trading is in the course of actually carrying out the charity's primary purpose. This includes trading that is mainly carried on by the beneficiaries of the charity.

Trading by the charity that is not within the exemption is often carried out by a separate trading organisation, which may be a conventional limited company. Although the trading organisation's profits will be liable to tax, they may be covenanted to the charity, so that the charity can reclaim the tax deducted (see below).

Capital gains tax (CGTA 1979, s 145)

A charity is not liable to capital gains tax on gains arising on the disposal of assets where the gains are applied for charitable purposes.

Development land tax (DLTA 1976, s 24)

No development land tax arises on the gift of development land to a charity, nor on the subsequent disposal or development of the land by the charity so long as the charity retains its charitable status.

Value added tax (VATA 1983, Sch 5, Group 16)

Where a charity makes taxable supplies it must register for VAT subject to the normal rules relating to exempt supplies and taxable turnover (see chapter 9). If a charity has a number of branches which are virtually autonomous, each branch having control over its own financial and other affairs, each branch will be regarded as a separate entity for VAT purposes and will be required to register only if its taxable supplies exceed £18,000.

Where a charity supplies goods or services substantially below cost (i.e. at less than 80% of cost) for the relief of distressed persons, for example meals on wheels, such supplies are not regarded as being made in the course of business and hence are not liable to VAT. Sales of donated goods at a charity shop are zero-rated provided that the charity is established for the relief of poverty or distress. Where, however, the charity sells used goods on behalf of others and charges a commission, VAT is chargeable on the commission but not on the actual sale proceeds.

Customs & Excise have produced a leaflet (701/1/81) on the subject of charities, which is available from local VAT offices.

Stamp duty (FA 1982, s 129)

No stamp duty is payable on documents transferring assets to charities (including leases).

National insurance surcharge (FA 1977, s 57)

Charities are exempt from payment of the employer's national insurance surcharge. Employer's national insurance is dealt with in chapter 14.

Rate relief

The General Rate Act 1967 provides for both mandatory and discretionary relief on premises occupied by a registered charity and used for charitable purposes. Under the Rating (Charity Shops) Act 1976 'charitable purposes' includes shops used for the sale of goods donated to the charity.

Unless expressly excluded, most charities can claim mandatory relief of up to 50% of their rates bill. Institutions which are excluded are mainly universities and colleges. Discretionary relief up to a further 50% may be extended by local authorities to all charities, including those excluded from the mandatory relief.

Giving to charity

Covenants by individuals (TA 1970, ss 434, 457; FA 1983, s 22)

The minimum period for a charity covenant is that it must be capable of exceeding three years, rather than six as with other covenants, so four years is the most popular term. Charitable covenants up to £5,000 per annum are allowable at the payer's highest rate of tax, including investment income surcharge, making this a particularly effective way of giving to a charity for higher-rate taxpayers (see page 284 for an example).

Covenants by limited companies (TA 1970, ss 177, 248, 259; FA 1972, Sch 16)

Covenanted donations to charities are treated as a charge on the profits of a company for corporation tax purposes. The after-tax cost to the company may be either 48%, 62% or $45\frac{1}{2}$% depending on whether the company is paying tax at 52%, 38% or the marginal small companies rate of $55\frac{1}{2}$%. The cost may indeed be 100% if the company has no taxable profits to cover the covenant, because no loss relief is available for charitable covenants in excess of profits (except within a group of companies by way of group relief).

Income of a close company used to pay charitable covenants may be apportioned among the members and treated as their income liable to tax at their highest rate, but only to the extent, if any, that the amount apportioned to any individual would take his charitable covenants above £5,000 per annum (see chapter 4).

Deposited covenants

Both individuals and companies can give a charity the benefit of an immediate lump sum while retaining the tax advantages of covenants by means of a 'deposited covenant'. There are in effect two transactions:

 (i) An interest-free loan repayable in four equal instalments.
(ii) A deed of covenant for four annual payments, each equal to one quarter of the loan.

The annual loan repayments are appropriated by the charity to satisfy the amount due under the covenant.

The charity benefits because it has the use of the money throughout the four years, and it can also reclaim tax on the four covenanted payments as and when they are made.

Employees seconded to charities (FA 1983, s 28)

If an employer seconds an employee to a charity but continues to pay his salary, the salary is no longer 'wholly and exclusively for the purposes of the trade' and thus is not allowable under the general expenses rule. From 1 April 1983, the salary is specifically allowable where an employee is seconded by a company (not by an individual or partnership).

Capital gains tax (CGTA 1979, s 146)

Gifts of chargeable assets to charities are exempt from capital gains tax, so neither chargeable gain nor allowable loss will arise. An asset which would produce a chargeable gain should be given direct instead of being sold first, so that no chargeable gain will arise, whereas one on which a loss will result should be sold to establish the allowable loss and the cash then given by way of deposited covenant (see above).

Capital transfer tax (FA 1975, Sch 6(10))

For transfers on or after 15 March 1983, all gifts to charity are exempt whether made in lifetime or on death. The £250,000 limit on transfers on or within 12 months before death has been removed.

Intermediary charities

Individuals and companies may want to give regularly to several charities, but may not want to commit themselves to a four-year covenant to any one of them. There are two ways of achieving this and still retaining the advantages of covenanting. The simplest way is to enter into a covenant with an intermediary organisation such as the Charities Aid Foundation. You can tell the organisation which particular charity you want to benefit. Alternatively, and especially where the size of the covenant is more significant, it is possible for individuals or companies to set up their own intermediary charity. A simple charitable trust whose objects include all the four charitable heads can be set up relatively easily. The money received by the charitable trust can be spent on any charitable purpose, and until spent it can be invested, with no tax arising on the investment income.

Tax points

- If you set up your own charitable trust, the trustees must not profit from their position or allow their duties and responsibilities to conflict with their personal interests. You can, however, appoint a professional trustee, such as a solicitor or accountant, and an appropriate charging clause in the trust deed will enable his professional fees to be paid.

- If you are considering a substantial cash gift to a charity, a deposited covenant is a very effective way of doing it, but it must be done that way at the outset—you cannot convert a donation already made into a deposited covenant.

- If you are a higher-rate taxpayer and make a deposited covenant, the relief at excess rates is not given all at once but only as each annual payment is made by taking it from the loan.

47
Subcontractors in the construction industry

The construction industry tax deduction scheme was brought in to combat the widespread evasion of tax by itinerant construction workers, which was costing the Exchequer many millions of pounds in lost revenue, but inevitably the genuinely self-employed worker has also become enmeshed in the net.

Briefly, a contractor must deduct and pay over to the Collector tax at a prescribed rate, currently 30%, from any labour payment made to a subcontractor, unless that person produces a valid 'exemption certificate', when payment can be made gross.

The rules for obtaining an 'exemption certificate' are rigorous, but basically the Inspector of Taxes to whom an application is addressed must be satisfied that an individual applicant

(a) is working in the UK in the construction industry,
(b) is trading from identifiable premises,
(c) is keeping proper records to enable accounts to be prepared,
(d) has a continuous period of working in the UK of three years in the six years immediately prior to the application (but a six-month period of unemployment within the three-year qualifying period may be ignored),
(e) has a bank account through which the business is substantially conducted, and
(f) has paid all tax and national insurance due and has kept his tax affairs satisfactorily up-to-date.

A special certificate is now available which allows payments of up to £150 per week to be made gross to individuals who may not satisfy condition (d) above because of their age, i.e. students leaving school, college or higher education, and to certain other individual applicants providing the Revenue with a guarantee.

The scheme also applies to partnerships and companies, and a 'contractor' includes any person spending substantial sums on construction—an average expenditure of £250,000 per annum over three years makes anyone a contractor.

Individuals who do not themselves satisfy the conditions cannot hide behind a limited company which has a clean taxation record. The legislation enables the Revenue to look behind the company to its shareholders and officers in determining whether a certificate should be issued.

There is a right of appeal against a Revenue refusal to issue a certificate.

Where a certificate is not forthcoming and deductions at source are made from the labour content of a payment to a subcontractor, the payer must issue a certificate of earnings and tax deducted. The earnings are brought into the self-employed accounts of the subcontractor, and the tax deducted becomes a payment on account of the tax due. The deduction of tax at source does not absolve the subcontractor from preparing accounts and submitting returns, and if his liability is greater than the tax deducted there is the possibility of interest and penalties arising if he has not complied with time limits for submission of accounts.

Tax points

- Since basic rate tax is deducted from the full labour content of a payment to a subcontractor an overpayment will normally arise because of the expenses of the trade and the personal reliefs available. This can only be obtained by the submission of accounts and returns.

- The definition of the construction industry is wide. Contractors who should have applied the scheme but have not may find themselves accountable for the tax which should have been deducted. Fringe trades should check the legislation to see if they are included.

48
Main anti-avoidance provisions

Background

The battle against tax avoidance has hotted up considerably over recent years and in addition to the wide range of specific measures in TA 1970 and later Acts the Revenue's powers have been significantly strengthened by various recent Court decisions. The full significance will not be known for some time, but it appears that artificial schemes for tax avoidance are almost certain to prove unsuccessful, and even those with bona fide commercial motives are not safe from challenge.

The legislation relating to tax avoidance, and its interpretation in the courts, are necessarily complex, and what follows is only the briefest outline. In addition to these specific provisions much recent legislation granting reliefs has anti-avoidance measures within it, e.g. demerger relief, companies purchasing their own shares and the business expansion scheme. (These reliefs are dealt with in chapter 29.) Most anti-avoidance legislation enables the Revenue to obtain information from third parties.

Stripping income from securities (TA 1970, ss 460–468)

Where in consequence of a transaction in securities a person has obtained a tax advantage, then unless he shows that the transaction was for bona fide commercial reasons or in the course of making or managing investments, and that none of the transactions had as their main object, or one of their main objects, the realising of a tax advantage, that tax advantage may be nullified.

This provision has been used particularly where elaborate schemes have been devised with the aim of extracting the undistributed profits of companies in a capital form. In view of the far reaching implications there is an appropriate clearance procedure which it is wise to follow wherever shares are being sold in close companies with significant distributable reserves.

Avoiding income on securities (TA 1970, ss 30, 469–477)

Where habitual timing of sales of securities is such that income is not received but is reflected in a capital surplus on sale, the income may be deemed to have accrued from day to day for excess liability purposes.

Change in ownership of a company (TA 1970, ss 483, 484; FA 1972, s 101)

Carry forward of trading losses and surplus ACT is prevented where within a period of three years there is both a change in ownership of a company and a major change in the nature or conduct of its trade. Reduction and resurgence of activities are sufficient to activate the legislation.

Transfer of assets abroad (TA 1970, ss 478–481; FA 1981, ss 45, 46)

The purpose of this legislation is to prevent a UK-resident individual avoiding UK tax by transferring income-producing property to trustees of a foreign settlement made by him, of which he is a beneficiary.

Sales at artificial prices (TA 1970, s 485)

Where any sales take place between persons connected with each other, including partnerships and companies, at a price other than open market value, then, if the Board of Inland Revenue so direct, the sale price of the one and purchase price of the other must be adjusted to the open market value for tax purposes. This is mainly directed at transfer pricing between the UK and overseas and does not apply where both parties are trading within the UK and the amount paid is a taxable receipt of one and allowable expense of the other. If the price is excessive, however, the payer may have difficulty proving that the expenditure is 'wholly and exclusively' for the purposes of the trade.

Transactions between associated dealing and non-dealing companies (TA 1970, s 486)

This section prevents abuse through transfer of assets by denying relief to one company where no taxable profit arises in the other.

Disguising income from personal activities as capital (TA 1970, s 487)

This prevents those with high personal earning potential, such as entertainers, contracting their services to a company in which they hold the shares and thereby turning income into capital by later selling the shares at a price reflecting the personal earnings.

Artificial transactions in land (TA 1970, ss 488–490)

The aim of this provision is 'to prevent the avoidance of tax by persons connected with land or the development of land' but it is difficult to give simple examples of when it might be applied, and in fact it is little used.

Sale and lease back of land (TA 1970, s 491; FA 1972, s 80)

Where land is sold and leased back, the deduction allowed for rent is limited to a commercial rent. A sale at an excessive price (subject to capital gains tax) cannot therefore be negated by an excessive rent payment allowable for income tax.

Further, if a short lease (less than 50 years) is sold and leased back for fifteen years or less, part of the sale price is treated as income, that part being $(16 - n)/15$ where n is the term of the new lease.

Leases other than land (TA 1970, ss 492–495)

Capital gains may in certain circumstances be treated as income, and rent payable is limited to a commercial rent.

Individuals carrying on leasing trades (FA 1976, s 41; FA 1980, s 70; FA 1982, s 70)

There are provisions to prevent first-year allowances being obtained in contrived situations, usually involving higher-rate taxpayers participating in leasing partnerships with companies.

Losses arising from first-year allowances in a leasing trade may only be set against non-leasing income if the loss arises in the course of a trade to which the individual devotes substantially the whole of his time and which has been carried on for a continuous period of six months. First-year allowances on plant and machinery bought for leasing purposes are also limited to those cases where the lessee would have qualified for first-year allowance if he had bought the machinery himself, or where the assets are let on a short lease, or where the leased assets are ships and aircraft and the lessor is primarily responsible for the navigation and running costs. Special transitional provisions apply in relation to first-year allowances on television sets and British films (see chapter 22). Where assets are leased outside the UK the writing-down allowance is reduced from the normal 25% to 10%. There are also limitations placed on the nature of the lease.

Relief for interest (TA 1970, s 496; FA 1976, s 38)

TA 1970, s 496 is aimed at preventing tax relief being obtained on interest that would not qualify for tax relief by means of various devices such as converting the interest into an annuity.

FA 1976, s 38 is almost the reverse—blocking the artificial creation of allowable interest.

Other measures

There are also measures to counter avoidance in the following circumstances:

Companies leaving a group and taking out a chargeable asset acquired intra-group within the previous six years (TA 1970, s 278)

Claiming group relief for losses when arrangements exist where a company may leave the group (FA 1973, s 29). There is also proposed legislation to prevent abuse when a company joins a group

Transfers of assets or stock between associated persons in order to obtain capital allowances or stock relief (FA 1971, Sch 8(3); FA 1981, Sch 9(22))

Losses arising from depreciatory transactions, e.g. dividend-stripping (TA 1970, ss 280, 281)

Loss relief arising from dealings in commodity futures (FA 1978, s 31)

Scrip issues of shares taken in lieu of dividends (F (No 2) A 1975, s 34)

Value passing out of shares, which could have been avoided by a controlling shareholder (CGTA 1979, s 26)

Transferring relief for partnership losses which would otherwise relate to a partner who is a company (FA 1973, s 31)

Loans to participators in close companies (see chapter 13)

Abuse of life assurance reliefs and exemptions (see chapter 43)

Transferring income from parents to minor children (see chapter 45)

Annual payments for non-taxable consideration (FA 1977, s 48)

Subject index

This index lists the main subject matter referred to in the text. It does not include matters of general application (such as payment dates or bases of assessment) for which reference should be made to the Contents list at the front of the book for the chapter on the appropriate tax.

Page numbers in **bold type** indicate a chapter, or a substantial part thereof, dealing with the subject matter in question. Again, reference may be made to the Contents list for main headings within such chapters.

Full details of all our publications
and services are in our Booklist. If
you would like a copy of this, we
would be very pleased to send you
one. Please write or telephone to:

Tolley Publishing Co Ltd,
Department BB,
Tolley House,
17 Scarbrook Road,
Croydon,
Surrey, CR0 1SQ
Tel: 01-686 0115